# ECONOMIC
# REFORM
# &
# INCOME
# DISTRIBUTION

# ECONOMIC REFORM & INCOME DISTRIBUTION

## A Case Study of Hungary and Poland

by

## HENRYK FLAKIERSKI

*M. E. Sharpe* Inc.
Armonk, New York/London

Copyright ©1986 by M. E. Sharpe, Inc.
80 Business Park Drive, Armonk, New York 10504

Available in the United Kingdom and Europe from M. E. Sharpe, Publishers, 3 Henrietta Street, London WC2E 8LU.

Published simultaneously as Vol. XXIV, No. 1-2, of *Eastern European Economics*.

**Library of Congress Cataloging in Publication Data**

Flakierski, Henryk.
  Economic reform and income distribution.

  1. Income distribution—Hungary. 2. Income distribution—Poland. 3. Hungary—Economic policy—1968–    . 4. Poland—Economic policy—1966–1980. 5. Poland—Economic policy—1981–    . I. Title.
HC300.295.I5F53    1986         339′.2′2′09438         85-26048
ISBN 0-87332-371-8

Printed in the United States of America

# Contents

# Preface

In this book the relationship between economic reforms and changes in the degree of inequality will be examined. In particular, the analysis will focus on whether or not the increased use of the market mechanism in some Eastern European countries has changed the pattern of income distribution in those countries.

It is very unfortunate that little work has been done in either the West or East in this field. No serious studies can be found on how income distribution has changed in the last 15–20 years in the East European socialist countries. Neither has there been any serious study of whether or not these changes are linked with decentralization of the economic mechanism. The aim of this study is to make a contribution to this topic.

I examine two countries, Hungary and Poland, in the period between 1965 and 1980, to illustrate the problem of income distribution and its connection with economic decentralization. Obviously the choice of these two countries requires some justification, which I will provide in full later. At this stage, however, I will simply say that the two countries represent a good test for my ideas. Hungary is the most advanced CMEA country in implementing a market mechanism, whereas Poland is a country in which the economic mechanism has not changed very much. Needless to say, my firsthand knowledge of the Polish economy and language has affected my choice to some degree.

However, I am aware that no matter how well those two countries illustrate the relationship between income distribution and economic reforms, other Eastern European countries must be taken into consideration. This is, however, difficult to do in one study. A comparison of several East European countries is very difficult because of the inadequacy of income inequality statistics in the socialist countries. For many years this area of statistics has been ''ideologically sensitive'' and deliberately neglected. Therefore I consider this study to be only a first step in the analysis of this important relationship. It is part of an ongoing research project that will be expanded in the future and will include more countries.

This book consists of five chapters. In Chapter I, the longest, the major theoretical problems of the study are presented. The chapter includes: (a) a theoretical overview of the economic reforms and their relationship to income inequalities; (b) a discussion of the rationale both for and against wage differentiation in the socialist countries; and (c) a justification for choosing Poland and Hungary, as well as a discussion of the quality of the statistical material.

In the subsequent chapters, statistical analyses of the relative dispersion of earnings and household income are presented for Hungary and Poland. The last chapter of the book contains the conclusions derived from the statistical analyses. There is also an analysis of the contribution of the independent trade union Solidarity to the question of egalitarianism and economic reform.

# List of Abbreviations

I—*In Polish*

1. R.S—*Rocznik Statystyczny* (Statistical Yearbook)
2. GUS—Główny Urząd Statystyczny (Central Statistical Office)
3. PWN—Polskie Wydawnictwo Naukowe (Polish Scholarly Publishing House)
4. PWE—Polskie Wydawnictwo Ekonomiczne (Polish Economic Publishing House)
5. KiW—Ksiązka i Więdza (Book and Knowledge Publishing House)
6. R.W.P.G—Rada Wzajemnej Pomocy Gospodarczej (Council for Mutual Economic Assistance—CMEA)

II—*In Hungarian*

1. S.E—*Statisztikai Évkönyv* (Statistical Yearbook)
2. KSH—Központi Statisztikai Hivatal (Central Statistical Office)
3. F.K.A—*Foglalkoztatottság és kereseti arányok* (Employment and Earnings Differentials)
4. A.C—*A Családi Jövedelmek Szinvonala és Szorodāsa* (The Level of Family Incomes and Their Dispersion)

# Acknowledgments

I had the privilege of staying at St. Antony's College, Oxford during the 1977/78 academic year as a senior associate member, and it was there that I started to work on the topic of income distribution in Hungary and Poland. My working papers on this subject have greatly benefited from discussions in the seminar on the Economics of Communist Countries, centered in Oxford, which was organized by W. Brus, M. Kaser, and Miss N. Watts. As a result of my research at Oxford, two papers were subsequently published in the *Cambridge Journal of Economics*. ("Economic Reform and Income Distribution in Hungary," 1979, No. 3, 15-32, and "Economic Reform and Income Distribution in Poland: the negative evidence," 1981, No. 5, 137-58.) These publications provide a foundation for further research and have assisted in the preparation of this book.

Many friends and colleagues have been kind enough to read all or parts of my manuscript in various stages of completion and to offer valuable criticism and suggestion. Among them, special thanks are due to W. Brus, M. Kaser, and P. Wiles for commenting on initial drafts of my work. I owe a debt of gratitude as well to R. McGinley for his valuable suggestions and his editorial polishing of my final manuscript. I would like as well to acknowledge my appreciation to the former director of the Oxford Institute of Economics and Statistics, Professor E. F. Jackson, and to Dr. J. Pemberton of the same Institute, for advice and help in statistical matters. And in the place of honor traditionally reserved for the end, many thanks to my wife, Judy Flakierski, for translating various Hungarian materials and for enduring my work. All of these contributions have made this endeavor possible. Needless to say, none of these people is in any way responsible for the views I have expressed or for errors my analysis may contain.

Toronto 1985

# ECONOMIC
# REFORM
# &
# INCOME
# DISTRIBUTION

CHAPTER I

# Problems and Issues

## Economic Reforms and Inequality of Earnings: A Theoretical Review

During the last two to three decades, virtually every socialist country has become aware of the need for economic reform because of marked deterioration in its economic efficiency. There have been numerous attempts, in most cases without success, to institute economic decentralization. The deteriorating economic efficiency of the socialist economies has been reflected by: (i) a decline in the rate of growth of labor productivity; (ii) an increase in the share of investment in the national product, which was halted in most countries in the '70s due to heavy indebtedness to the West[1]; (iii) a more rapid increase in fixed and circulating assets than in national output.

The deterioration of investment efficiency has been largely due to mismanagement. The fact that a given increase in the national product has required more and more units of investment is not due to any long-run change in technical conditions or in technical knowledge but rather to poorly planned and poorly implemented investment projects. This has been reflected in gestation periods for investment projects that habitually stretch much longer than originally planned, by the very low utilization rate of new factories, and by substantial waste of raw materials and fuels.

The deterioration of the efficiency of the Eastern European economies in general is deeply rooted in the highly centralized nature of their institutional framework and in the planning mechanism—which is an imitation, with certain variations, of the Soviet economic system. In this system prices essentially possess only an accounting function. Enterprises get detailed instructions from the central authorities about output targets, material inputs, employment, wages, and new investment. The main role of the managers lies in quantitatively fulfilling the plan targets to which the incentive system is subordinated.

We do not intend in this chapter to fully describe the history of economic reforms in the Eastern European countries or to give a broad analysis of the nature of the reforms and their implementation. The reforms have been exhaustively described and analyzed in both the Western and Eastern European literature.[2] But in the framework of our analysis, a brief general description of the reforms to provide better understanding of the links between them and income distribution is justified.

## The Reforms

In the second half of the '50s we observe in a number of socialist countries a wave of bold and interesting ideas and proposals concerning economic reforms. Some proponents of such ideas were E. Liberman, with his first articles in Soviet journals, F. Behrens in East Germany, and Gy. Peter in Hungary.[3] However, the views developed by Polish economists at the time stand out in terms of their consistency and theoretical rigor.

The "Polish October" in 1956 marked an important beginning for widespread discussion of economic reforms. In 1956-58, during the golden age of Poland's intellectual life in general and economic science in particular, discussion concentrated on the shortcomings of a highly centralized management model. Suggestions for a new model to be implemented were made. The general spirit at this time is best reflected in the "Thesis of the Economic Council,"[4] prepared by an advisory body composed of the most prominent Polish economists, including O. Lange, M. Kalecki, W. Brus, and others.[5] Although the proposals of the Economic Council were not favored by the government, and aside from a few minor points were never implemented, they still deserved attention because they laid the theoretical foundation for the model that emerged in the '60s of a centrally planned economy with a market-regulated mechanism[6].

This model[7] can briefly be described as follows:

1. The state decides how to divide national output between accumulation and consumption. Approximately two-thirds of the national accumulation fund should be centrally allocated, and the rest should be left to the discretion of the enterprises. The enterprise funds should be used mainly for investment in modernization so that production can be rapidly expanded in response to market demand. Decisions about major investment projects of national importance should be, as before, in the hands of the Center. Even the decentralized accumulation fund left to the discretion of the enterprises should be under some form of control of the state, subject to some limits and directives in the central plan.[8] The state also decides the structure of investment: where and how to build new capacities using the centralized accumulation fund. The state decides in what branches and sectors to invest, where to locate these investments, and the degree of technological sophistication of future capacities.

2. The state determines how wages and salaries should be distributed among major strata, groups, and sectors in society. The state maintains substantial control over major income differentials. Minimum and maximum differentials for broad categories of employment are established by the Center; more detailed pay differences are left to the discretion of the enterprises.

3. The Center decides how the income of the enterprise should be divided between centralized funds and funds for their own use.

4. The enterprise decides independently:

a) what to produce and with what inputs (these decisions being made largely on the basis of profitability);

b) from whom to buy inputs and to whom to sell their product;

c) the distribution of profit (after taxation) between personal income increases and accumulation.

5. Wage and salary increases are linked to actual performance expressed in terms of profit (or value added). In order to avoid inflation, the wage fund of the enterprises is controlled by the

mechanism of progressive taxation and other economic instruments.

6. Prices in this model are independent parameters for the enterprises (independent of their own interest), given to them as instruments to make economic choices. To ensure the parametric nature of prices, the state does not need to have control over all prices. Only where there is a danger of monopolistic practices or social preferences are at stake should the state control price formation. In cases where there is healthy competition between a sufficient number of firms and special preferences by the state are absent, price formation should be left to market forces.[9]

Considering, however, that high concentration of production in conjunction with high degrees of utilization of capacity is rather a common feature of socialist economies, the danger of monopolistic practices by the enterprises is very high.

7. Workers' councils should be freely elected in the enterprises and be given responsibility to run the enterprise in the framework of the established rules of the model.

From this brief description of the model, it is quite clear that the intention was not to abolish the centrally planned economy but rather to change the method of constructing and implementing the plan by switching from direct to indirect methods of management from the Center.[10]

The central planner in this model will help achieve a desirable size and structure of production not through orders but with economic instruments such as price policy, credit policy, taxation, interest charges, and amortization rates. In other words, the framework in which the autonomous enterprise acts on the market is determined by the central planner. It is a very special kind of market because it is shaped by the central planner's macrodecisions; the main market data (i.e., the production apparatus, its structure and total size, and the basic elements of demand structure) are given and determined by the central planner directly or through indirect economic instruments. Although it is a very specific market, it is still one in which all the rules of that ancient game are maintained. Buyers and sellers of means of production meet on the market and make decisions based on profitability calculations.[11]

The model formulated by the Polish economists was never implemented in Poland. However, a decade later the Hungarians, with some small variations, did put into operation the basic ideas of a planned economy with a regulated market.[12] The "New Economic Mechanism" established in 1968 in Hungary is to a large degree very similar to the Polish model, with one major exception—the role of workers in management. From the outset the Hungarian leadership ruled out "workers' self-management." The green light for implementing economic reforms at high speed was given by the Hungarian political leadership, provided that "one-man responsibility" for enterprise management was maintained, and the experiments in workers' self-management during the "Polish October" and the Hungarian Revolution in 1956 were not repeated or brought into the economic and political fabric of society.

In those countries where some of these economic reforms were introduced, enterprises did gain some control over their wage fund and, with it, some discretion over how to distribute earnings among employees. Investigating whether a gradual increase in the role of the market mechanism linked with the economic reforms affected the degree of earnings inequality will shed some light, therefore, on the relationship between reforms and income distribution.

To put the investigation into proper perspective, before presenting the statistical evidence, it is worthwhile to set out some existing theoretical views about the relations between recent reforms in the Soviet-type system and changes in income distribution.

*The theoretical background*

The issues have recently been succinctly posed by Wiles. He discounts any incentive effect of inequality between "noncompeting groups" (e.g., between academics and manual workers), for "it is only within a competing group that factor rewards are rigorously determined by supply and demand." Claiming that managers tend to believe that their hierarchical superiority should be buttressed with monetary rewards, he judges the post-1965 East European reforms as "objectively anti-proletarian," in that the manager has taken advantage of the fact that "he may hire and fire more freely than of old and is freer to strike a wage bargain."[13] The same view—that differentials have widened since the accordance of greater importance to incentive schemes under the economic devolutions of the past decade—had been previously held by economists such as Sweezy and Ellman and by sociologists such as Parkin and Lane.[14] Like Wiles, they drew attention to the high degree of inequality in Yugoslavia. But others, notably Brus,[15] suggest that the introduction of a socialist market, more regulated than the Yugoslav, need *not* involve socially undesirable changes in the distribution pattern. Such was certainly the claim of the theoreticians behind the "New Economic Mechanism" as it was applied from 1968 in Hungary: they stated that an increase in dispersion would take place only if the Center wanted it.[16] The proponents of a decentralized model with a controlled or regulated market mechanism maintain that the basic framework of distribution is controlled (the ratio of consumption to accumulation, etc.), as before, by the state, although Brus accepts that some aspects of distribution are left to market forces. The latter point is quite important.

The theoretical proponents of the decentralized model with a regulated market mechanism, especially Brus, stress that in the socialist countries there is no direct and simple relationship between economic decentralization and increasing income disparities. A strong case can be made, according to Brus, that the economic reforms do not represent an introduction of material incentives (which have always been in existence and were even pronounced at the peak of the Stalinist period) but rather an alteration of their nature in order to ensure a proper link between individual and social interests. Since the aim of the reforms is not to increase differentials, it is unwarranted to equate strong incentives with increasing differentials. The objectives of the reformed material-incentive system, according to Brus, are to create proper bonds between the actual performance of the enterprise and its earnings and to create initiative in the subsystems for innovation.[17]

An echo of some of Brus's ideas about the nature of the new incentives system in the economic reforms can be found in the "new sociological school" in Hungary, concentrated around Hegedus, Heller, Markus, and others. Their point is that the old material-incentive system is not actually linked to labor contribution but to political privilege and patronage. The neo-Lukács school calls this "nonwage hierarchical differentiation," which has a tendency to increase.[18] Such privileges include better housing, higher subsidies for housing than low-income groups, special holidays, access to kindergartens and nurseries, etc.

Professor Brus has a point when he argues that there is no simple link between decentralization and income inequality in the socialist countries. In the framework of his controlled market model, however, he is aware of the fact that there is some contradiction between linking enterprises' earnings with their performance and maintaining equal pay for equal work. He stresses even more strongly that this contradiction will tend to deepen as the reforms progress. He is optimistic, however, about the possibilities of cushioning this contradiction with the overall increase in the efficiency of the economy that the reforms will bring about. He believes, to put it figuratively, that a larger loaf will be easier to distribute than a smaller one. I find this optimism slightly overstated. The experience of all capitalist and socialist countries has proven that a bigger loaf is not always divided more equally, and that the connection between higher efficiency and economic justice is very complicated.

The decentralized model, even with a regulated market mechanism, is by no means neutral as far as distribution is concerned; the claim of its proponents that the model does not predetermine the contents of distribution policy is not entirely convincing. A decentralized market economy incorporates a certain intrinsic pattern of distribution. Although the economic policy of the socialist state can counteract this distribution—examples are numerous—such an intervention negates the groundrules established by the reforms and hence adversely affects the achievements of its objectives. The change in income distribution depends on how far the market is allowed free rein and how far the consequences of this freedom are compatible with what the state desires the dispersion of income to be.

In analyzing changes in the dispersion of incomes over time, we will distinguish between those that result from: (a) government action in the form of specific policy toward incomes,[19] and (b) the spontaneous working of the market mechanism. In Hungary these two aspects of change are strongly interrelated because the state has, so to speak, provided the first push for the functioning of the market mechanism by implementing the reforms with a set of guidelines and decrees governing the working of the market mechanism in the framework of the established model. At the same time, however, having implemented the reforms, the state then put into operation specific individualized economic rules for some enterprises, such as subsidies and other forms of help to struggling units, high tax rates on profits for very profitable units, and differential rules for receiving credit and other financial assistance. These individualized economic rules no doubt counteract the logic of the regulated market. In these circumstances it is not easy to separate the "pure" effect of the market mechanism on income disparities from other factors. However, we should not overestimate the difficulties in this matter. Once the reforms are put in motion by the state, we can then recognize which changes are a result of the rules of the game of the reform and which are a result of government policies aimed at cushioning some enterprises and groups of employees from the harsh rules of the market. We will try, whenever possible, to differentiate sources of changes in income disparities.

In spite of these difficulties, the question of whether the "New Economic Mechanism" has promoted income inequality remains a valid one. It cannot be denied that the state has maintained a substantial degree of control over income differentials. The lowest and the highest income scales for all enterprises in the socialized sector are established centrally. However, some freedom to change income disparities has emerged.

The basic principle of the reform is to link increases in wages and salaries directly to productivity increases in each enterprise, a principle which by its very nature is a factor leading to an increase in dispersion of earnings.[20] Since the scope for technical improvement, market conditions, etc., will differ, enterprises in the same industry will not be able to pay their employees the same increase in earnings for the same job. This will lead, *ceteris paribus*, to an increase in relative dispersion of earnings across the country as a whole. Moreover, enterprises have been given some discretion in setting rates of pay for various skills, within the limits laid down by the state. This discretion could, in certain circumstances, increase the dispersion of wages and salaries if enterprises were able to compress pay scales for lower-skill grades and, at the same time, widen those for higher grades. By so doing, the enterprise would be able to pay a few highly skilled employees considerably higher wages and salaries than before, without exceeding the ceiling imposed on average increases.

Of course, turning this possibility into reality is not easy. The differentiation between rates of pay for various skills and the number of workers employed on each pay scale is not entirely under the control of the enterprise, which has to negotiate with trade unions on labor market conditions. When there are labor shortages, it is not easy to recruit unskilled workers by offering them the lowest possible rates. However, the reforms may have increased pressure to pay higher earnings to the more skilled as a means of improving performance.

Abstractly speaking, we can envisage a situation where linking wages with the perfomance of the enterprise, as a major principle of economic reform, can lead to a reduction of wage differentiation between enterprises. This will happen when less efficient enterprises make better use of the opportunities created by market forces. It can be argued that the possibilities for rapid improvement in the utilization of resources in less technologically advanced firms with higher costs are larger than in more advanced ones. The potential for an increase in so-called X-efficiency[21] is larger in enterprises with higher cost and lower labor productivity. It stands to reason that in this type of firm, the pace of work is slower, and more raw materials are wasted. If market conditions allow an increase in sales by those firms, they will be better suited to reduce costs and increase profits and wages faster than advanced firms. As a result, their relative wage situation will improve vis-à-vis the more advanced firms. Of course, the greater potential for improvement in less advanced firms does not in itself turn it into a reality. But we can assume, at least theoretically, that in those enterprises there will be more pressure than in good ones to make use of existing "reserves." Against this approach it could be argued that better use of labor time and of raw materials and equipment is a one-shot improvement. Once those reserves are used, this source of improvement ends, and only expansion of resources can improve efficiency. This argument is by and large correct. But there is no reason, at least formally, to preclude that under favorable market conditions, such firms will not be able to use modernization investment as a new potential source of improvement in X-efficiency.

Although we do not exclude the possibility that less advanced enterprises may take advantage of market forces and reduce cost relatively faster than more advanced ones, the likelihood of this happening in practice is not very high. Poor management is in most cases an intrinsic feature of less advanced firms, which reduces the ability of these firms to tap their unused resources and improve X-efficiency. In practice, more advanced firms will be better prepared to take advantage of favorable market conditions than less advanced ones.

In a social environment where the state maintains a substantial degree of control over the means of production, and where the major parameters of social stratification are in the hands of the state (as is the case in all socialist countries, including Hungary), the state can, within certain limits, change inequality in the distribution of earnings by using the power of the Center directly, or by using the market mechanism, or by a combination of both. Although government policy cannot in any management system change the differentiation of earnings at will, the ability to change the distribution pattern is not the same in different management systems. The point can be made that a centralized management system has a higher degree of freedom in changing the relative dispersion of earnings than does a more decentralized, market-oriented economy.

To analyze this problem further, let us distinguish between horizontal and vertical differentiation. The first establishes differences in pay within the same category of workers employed in different enterprises. The second shows differences in pay between major social strata, occupational groups, trades, and professions in every branch and sector of the socialized economy. Needless to say, vertical differentials are the more decisive factor in establishing the stratification pattern of society. They include the average differences in earnings between white- and blue-collar workers, differences between workers and managers, between skilled and unskilled manual workers. Horizontal differentials affect only differences in pay for the same job in different enterprises.

In Hungary, as in the highly centralized management systems of the Soviet type, vertical differentials are established by the Center. Differentials between various occupations and between trades and professions, both inside and between branches and industries, are deteremined by the central authorities.[22]

However, these two management systems differ in the way horizontal differentials are established. In a highly centralized management system, as in Poland or the Soviet Union, the Center determines both the vertical and horizontal differentials, whereas in the Hungarian type of economy the Center usually leaves horizontal differentials to market forces. This manifests itself mainly in the fact that employees of the same category, occupation, and trade in a particular branch can earn more in one enterprise than another because of differing performances as measured by market criteria.

In Hungary a "division of labor" takes place between the

Center and the regulated market mechanism in establishing disparities of wages and salaries. One is, so to speak, responsible for the vertical and the other for the horizontal differentials. From our discussion it follows that these two management systems have a different degree of freedom to change the overall relative dispersion of earnings. This fact is especially apparent when the objective of the state is to reduce *overall* relative disparities in pay. Reducing horizontal differentiation in the Hungarian type of market economy requires the state to intervene in the working of the market mechanism, with all the consequences of this interference for the coherence and effectiveness of the reform. The state is able to reduce overall dispersion, without abolishing the rules of the game of the reform, only by substantially reducing vertical differentials to offset growing inequalities in horizontal differentiation brought about by the functioning of the market mechanism. A sharp change in vertical differentiation can, however, be difficult to achieve. In a more centralized management system, such difficulties are not encountered to the same degree. It is enough for the state, given the "neutrality" of horizontal differentials, merely to reduce vertical differentials by a certain magnitude in order to achieve a reduction in the overall relative dispersion of earnings of the same magnitude. There is no need in the highly centralized management system to reduce vertical differentials sharply in order to offset the increase in the horizontal ones, as in the Hungarian system.[23]

Claiming that the more centralized management systems have a higher degree of freedom to change differentials than the more market-oriented systems does not mean, as P. Wiles has suggested, that in the highly centralized Soviet-type economies the leadership has full freedom to establish whatever differentials it finds suitable. Such a suggestion grossly departs from reality. First, it should not be overlooked that in the centralized Soviet-type economies, the state does not fully control the supply side of the labor market, especially in the short run. Differentials that have been established in an arbitrary manner create shortages in some categories of labor, high rates of turnover in certain industries and occupations, falling participation rates, etc. There is also a built-in rigidity of existing differentials that cannot easily be changed due to opposition from different forces whose interests are at stake. It is not by accident that, for example, the ordering of industries and sectors in terms of average earnings has not changed in many socialist countries for the last twenty years. The wage leaders and laggards are always more or less the same.

Second, the Center's control over all elements of earnings is far from complete. Even in highly centralized management systems, the Center has full control only over wage rates and basic salary rates. Other elements of earnings, like payment for over-fulfillment of norms in piecework and a multitude of bonuses and premiums, are only partially controlled. The crux of the matter is to control the average wages of piecework employees, who even now account for a large part of the work force. (In the USSR, for example, in 1972, 56.8% of manual employees were paid according to piecework, whereas in 1965 this figure was 77.6%.)[24] But having such control is not an easy matter. The Center would need at least complete control of work norms. But determining the so-called technically warranted production norms is very time consuming; hence the Center is forced to cede most norm setting to the enterprises. Unfortunately, norms established by the enterprise are very often slack. Production norms meant to be an incentive to increase output become instead a tool to increase wages in the enterprise to a desirable level. Large overfulfillment of norms has become common practice in many industries in the socialist countries. In an environment where wage rates are inflexible and supposed to be stable for a long time, the only way to increase wages is to adapt norms to a "decent level" of wages. Similarly in case of time work, bonuses and premiums are a tool to guarantee workers "proper" pay. Although bonuses are somewhat regulated directly or indirectly by establishing general principles for distributing them, the enterprise is left with some discretion in dividing them.

It cannot be denied that the state, by controlling the increase in the wage fund or in the average wage in the enterprise, and by controlling the basic principles of allocating bonuses, reduces the enterprises' discretion over the distribution of pay.[25] The distribution of some earnings in the enterprises in accordance with their own independent preferences creates an opportunity for actual overall earnings differentiation to be not what the government wants.

Third, certain changes in the distributional pattern of income are exogenous to government policy—changes in the differentiation pattern will sometimes take place independently of any action or lack of action by the government. Such changes might be the result of a shift in the supply of labor, changes in the age composition of the population, demographic and stratification changes, accidental factors, etc.[26]

In view of the above we must clearly distinguish between changes in differentials that are a result of deliberate government policies and changes that are the result of other factors.

Obviously, the greater potential to reduce inequalities of pay in a more centralized management system than in a less centralized one is not automatically realized. Highly centralized systems have experienced increases in inequalities, often more rapid and more pronounced increases than in market-oriented economies. What is more, a lack of reforms can, in itself, lead to an increase in dispersion that has nothing to do with any deliberate policy of the Center. Indeed, an increase in dispersion of earnings can emerge precisely because reforms are absent. The acute shortages and imbalances that the centralized model inherently creates and the neglect of services that is a trademark of this mode of management are bound to create a wild and uncontrolled "second economy." The redistributive effect of the second economy is bound to be stronger in a centralistic model than in a Hungarian-type model, because in the latter type of economy supply is better adapted to the needs of the consumers and producers, and thus a substantial part of the second economy is legalized and partially controlled, whereas in the centralized economies this sector is the domain of shady deals and the black market. The Polish experience is a good case in point because it demonstrates how the complete disorganization of nearly all markets, generated by the rigid Polish management system itself, leads to a second economy of an enormous scale and, as a consequence, a change in the distribution pattern unfavorable to the weak and the poor segments of urban society. Apart from the extreme Polish case, it is well known that in the Soviet-type economies, the second economy is not a marginal phenomenon.[27] Although it is difficult to quantify the sector's weight, it is obvious that it tends to grow and thus change the official distributional pattern. It is an irony of history that the system whose objective is to gradually overcome market relations as a sign of maturity of socialist relations of production is creating the worst kind of parasitic, uncontrolled black markets.

From the fact that decentralized management systems may have greater difficulties in reducing inequalities of pay we should not infer, as Sweezy and other left-wing economists do,[28] that any effort by the state to reduce inequalities is doomed to failure in every market-oriented economy. According to these writers, in a market-oriented economy one can "drive" only in one direction: one can increase pay inequalities but never reduce them. This kind of reasoning has some validity only if we deal with the market in general, especially in its capitalist framework, without specifying what kind of market we have in mind. But to analyze the influence of the market on wage differentiation, especially in a socialist context, we must ask to what degree the state controls the framework of the market, and to what degree important decisions in the field of distribution are taken out of the "hands" of the market. As we have mentioned before, both the Hungarian model and the highly centralized model of management leave the major differentials between trades, professions, branches, and strata under the control of the central authorities. In the Hungarian model only horizontal differentials are left to market forces. The control of the state over pay differentials is still much stronger in Hungary than in any capitalist market economy (even the most egalitarian) with the highest degree of state intervention. This powerful tool to control pay differentials in the socialist countries gives the state a degree of freedom, unknown in the capitalist world, to intervene in the distributional pattern.

As practice shows, this ability to intervene in pay differentials is in most cases effective, although not without cost. The Hungarian state has already, in the fourteen years of the existence of the reform, intervened in both directions in the distributional pay pattern. It has vacillated between increasing and decreasing both vertical and horizontal pay differentials. In Hungary, for example, initially the reform was consciously aimed at increasing earning differentials in the socialist sector. R. Nyers, the party Politburo member responsible for the reform, made it clear in a speech at the Party School in Budapest in 1970[29] that he thought that differentials between trades and occupations were too narrow and that they must be increased. At no time, however, has the leadership pursued a deliberate policy of increasing the dispersion of per capita household incomes. On the contrary, the aim has been to maintain or even level off this dispersion, while increasing the dispersion of wages and salaries, which it was thought would result in an increase in productivity.

The fathers of the Hungarian reform have tried quite consciously to reallocate rewards among different social groups (managerial strata and manual workers, skilled and unskilled workers, etc.). It is no accident that one of their first steps was to sharply differentiate (percentage wise) the increase in bonuses paid out of profits between management and workers. But strong differentiation of bonuses expressed as a percentage of the basic wage or salary was abolished after a year due to strong pressure by the workers.

In 1970-71 the Hungarian government implemented a modification of wage tariffs aimed at increasing differentials in branches and enterprises. As a result of this policy, we observe an increase in relative dispersion of earnings in 1970-74. Under pressure from workers at weaker enterprises, which could not pay the same pay increases as the strong ones, the state decided to partially reverse the tendency to increase wage differentials. In 1976 the direct link between remuneration and enterprise performance was weakened.[30] This commitment by the leadership to reduce relative dispersion of earnings did not, however, last very long. The worsening general economic situation, especially in foreign trade in 1978 and 1979, was a prelude to strong decentralized measures. At the end of 1979, in order to improve the efficiency of the economy, the leadership decided to grant enterprises more freedom of action and to increase the role of the market in allocation of resources.[31] As a part of the package, anti-egalitarian measures were also taken. A deliberate policy of increases in wage differentials was implemented in 1980. The old 1976 ceiling of 6% increases in earnings was abolished. Since 1980 the increases in earnings linked to enterprise performance have fluctuated between 2 and 9% per annum and, not as before, between 2 and 6%. Preferential treatment in earning increases was granted to enterprises that not only have good profit records but also show an absolute reduction in employment.

This vacillation between an increase and a decrease in the role of the market in shaping the distributional pattern is not accidental. It reflects the objective of the state in the field of pay and income distribution. This objective, as we will see later, is not without ambiguity.

To conclude this part of our analyses, the relationship between economic reforms and changes in the inequality of earnings is not a simple one; moreover, it cannot be explained only on the basis of the logic of the economic system. The economic policy of the state and its limitations are also important factors in understanding this relationship.

## Wage Differentials in the Socialist Economy

*Theories*

What is the theoretical basis for differentiating earnings in the socialist countries? What do these countries expect to achieve through unequal pay, and is this always a stimulus to greater efficiency?

In the socialist countries the Marxian distribution principle "from each according to his ability, to each according to his labor" is the theoretical base for differentiation of earnings. But the measurement of individual labor was never satisfactorily explained in Marx's and Engels's writings. The concept of social necessary labor as a standard of measurement in a socialist society has never been unambiguously explained. This lack of clarity is especially evident in their writings about complex and simple labor as a basis of differentiation of earnings under socialism. How should one deal with complex labor? Should a skilled worker receive a multiple of the wage of an unskilled one; and if so, how should this multiple be determined? The answers to these questions are not clear, and yet they are essential if labor is to provide a basis for the differentiation of earnings in socialism.

We find in Marx's writings about this issue two different lines of thought. In the *Critique of the Gotha Program* we find the following statement:

> Every worker will receive a wage proportional to the amount of labor performed, measured in terms of socially necessary labor. Complex labor will be paid as a multiple of simple labor.[32]

On the other hand, we can find pronouncements which suggest that only differences in duration or intensity of labor should be recognized. In *The Civil War in France*, for example, Marx stated, "From the members of the Commune downwards, the public service had to be done at workmen's wages. The vested interest and the representation allowances of the high dignitaries of State disappeared along with the high dignitaries themselves."[33] This passage has become the ideological basis for the famous provision of the so-called Party Maximum, according to which in the Soviet Union just after the revolution no party members could earn more than a skilled worker. Engels, in *Anti-*

*Dühring*, even more categorically denied the right of highly skilled and educated people to receive higher pay:

> In a society of private producers, private individuals or their families pay the cost of training the qualified worker; hence the higher price paid for qualified labour power accrues first of all to private individuals. . . . In a socialistically organized society these costs are borne by society and to it therefore belong the fruits of the greater values produced by complex labour. The worker himself has no claim to extra pay.[34]

But the theoretical ambiguity in Marx's writing does not negate the very clear egalitarian ethos that he sees in socialist society. Marx perceived future socialist society not only as more egalitarian than capitalist society but, of even greater importance, as a society that will gradually and persistently reduce inequalities to the lowest possible level. From the logic of Marx's ideas it follows that the spread of earnings in socialism cannot be substantial if the differentiation of earnings is based on labor contribution. This approach is reinforced when differences in the contribution of complex and simple labor are not fully recognized as a justification for differentiation of earnings. In other words, if we exclude interoccupational differentials, differences in wages can be linked only with the duration and intensity of work in every kind of job. But those differences by their very nature cannot be very large. One would expect as well that according to Marx, the role of nonpecuniary rewards should be larger in socialism than in capitalism: "Power, prestige and social obligation . . . are motives which will play a great role in socialism, hence a possibility will emerge to reduce pecuniary differentials."[35]

But the distributional pattern in Marx's ideas cannot be reduced solely to the principle of differentiation of earnings or that of distribution of individual consumption. An important role is played by the distribution of public consumption. Here his egalitarian approach is very visible.

In the *Critique of the Gotha Program* he emphasized that public consumption (education, culture, pensions, child care, sport, and recreation) should increase faster than the national output and the individual consumption fund. For Marx this is a social imperative for the gradual building of a new communist society, for the gradual achievement of the goal to provide to everyone in accordance with their needs.

Living socialism of today does not in any meaningful way conform to Marx's vision of a socialist society. Nevertheless, certain elements of Marx's arguments have some validity for today's socialist countries. Namely, the smaller earnings differentials in the socialist countries than in the capitalist ones are mainly a result of elimination of earnings from property.[36] The increase in the share of public consumption in national output and as a ratio to individual consumption has continued for a long time in the socialist countries. This tendency, given the relative dispersion of incomes from employment, is an equalizing factor of income distribution, although, as we will see later, the role of public consumption in this matter is not without its pitfalls and contradictions, especially as far as common access to goods and services of public consumption is concerned. However, we should not overlook the fact that an increase in the share of public consumption in national output is not typical solely of socialist countries. In many welfare states in the West we can observe, for at least a few decades, the same trend. True, this tendency is narrower in scope (only for some countries) and of shorter duration than in the socialist countries.[37]

Economists in the socialist countries have tried to interpret Marx's principle "to each according to his work." But as A. Nove emphasized, "to each according to his work" is nothing more than words.[38] To translate these words into a set of concrete differentials for a multitude of functions, occupations, trades, and skills appears to be an insurmountable task.

Soviet economists and sociologists by and large do agree that differences in pay are justified by differences in contribution to societies' economic and cultural life. But how we should measure these differences in contribution is a matter of dispute between economists in the Soviet Union and other Eastern European countries. Two major theoretical points of view, and many variations, have emerged in the Soviet Union on this matter.

The first point of view can be labeled the "workers equivalent concept." It is expressed clearly by two leading Soviet labor economists in the following way: "Given the wage fund, the shares of individual producers are determined by the law of distribution according to labor and only by that law."[39] In this view the pay differentials should reflect differences between complex and simple labor. But how do they propose to reduce complex labor to simple? Their answer is: the magnitude of earnings (not only wage rate pay), which has emerged as a sort of average in the framework of a given occupation, trade, etc., should be the basis for reducing complex to simple labor. Needless to say, this is a sham solution because it is a "vicious circle." The reduction of labor is based on earnings, which in turn should be based on the reduction of labor. This proposal simple means that whatever earning differentials exist reflect the law of distribution in accordance with the quantity and quality of labor. This does not take us very far.

The second point of view stresses as a criterion for pay differentiation the value of the reproduction of labor power. V. F. Maier[40] claimed that the law of distribution according to labor manifests itself in socialism as the law of reproduction of labor power. The higher the cost of reproducing the labor power, the higher should be the remuneration of a particular category of labor. Moreover, in accordance with Marx's ideas, this law requires that even the lowest pay must be sufficient to cover the cost of production and reproduction of labor power. This requires a minimum compensation for all employees independent of their contribution in terms of labor. But how should the reproduction of labor be measured? Most economists in this stream are inclined to measure it by the cost of training and educating the particular labor categories. In conformity with this point of view, some economists of this persuasion have interpreted the principle of remuneration for complex labor more in the vein of Engels than

Marx, namely, that in a socialist environment complex labor deserves higher remuneration only to the extent that the cost of its training and education is effectively borne by the worker or by his family in the form of foregone remuneration.[41] But this is rather a minority point of view among Soviet economists. As can be expected, the proponents of strict adherence to the principle of distribution according to labor have attacked the advocates of reproduction of labor power as a base for pay differentiation, using the old orthodox scare that such approach is tantamount to perceiving labor power in socialism as a commodity whose value is determined, as for all other commodities, by its labor cost of production and reproduction.[42]

As usual, behind the theoretical smokescreen of debate, there is a hidden problem which has to do more with differences in practical policies than with differences in theory. The first group of economists suspects that the beliefs of the others logically lead to a reduction in pay differentials, especially via substantial increases in minimum wages. Their suspicion is not without some foundation. Some economists in the "labor power reproduction camp" advocate an increase in the minimum wage and a reduction in pay differentials.[43] They justify this demand on the basis that the earnings of the lowest paid group have long been inadequate to cover the normal cost of production and reproduction of labor power. Sharp increases in the minimum wages in the '60s, according to them, can hardly be explained by the principle that pay is in accordance with contribution to the quantity and quality of work performed. Moreover, some have gone even further, linking the objective need to reduce pay differentiation for higher qualification to changes in the nature of work. The greater the intellectual and creative content of work (and this increases with the level of education and standard of life), the less important becomes the incentive effect of differential pay. Opportunities for promotion to jobs intellectually more rewarding may be, according to them, as effective as an increase in pay.[44] Wage increases become rather important as an incentive for those who are forced to stay in manual, arduous, low-skilled, and uninteresting occupations. Wage increases become a sort of compensation for the disadvantage of holding such jobs.

*Flaws in the theories*

Our short review of the main theoretical views about the base of pay differentiation reveals a few fundamental shortcomings common to both views.

The majority of Soviet economists and sociologists, with some exceptions, formulate the principles of distribution as socioeconomic laws independent of the will of the state. What all such theories ignore is the role of political power in shaping the distributional structure of pay. The way state agencies establish the "contribution" of different occupations and strata reflects economic and political priorities. Hence the issue of power is of paramount importance.[45] Economic policy, as we have argued, is not omnipotent; it must take into consideration many factors over which it has little or limited influence; however, its influence on shaping pay differentiation is still considerable. The state has many times violated the "objective laws"[46] in pursuit of such goals as mitigating poverty, some equity in pay differentiation patterns, etc.

The criteria for measurement in both concepts lacks a real quantitative dimension. Is it the concept of labor contribution or labor power? No satisfactory way to measure these categories has been devised. Both concepts are based on the Marxian labor theory of value, which irrespective of its theoretical merit or demerit, is not and cannot be a practical yardstick to compare different kinds of labor[47] and on this basis establish an objective set of relative differentials in a socialist economy.

In spite of the lip service paid by those in power in the socialist countries to the Marxian principle of distribution under the so-called first phase of communism, most economists have given up the idea of finding a single precise yardstick that would reduce complex to simple labor. The experiment with labor money undertaken by the Bolsheviks in 1920 has been judged totally unsuc-

cessful and unpromising.[48] Instead economists in the socialist
countries have attempted to describe in practical terms the com-
plexities of different kinds of labor. The Soviet theory of occupational differentials—shared by most socialist countries—specifies
the numerous criteria for distinguishing the various types of labor. According to this theory the quality of labor, or its complexity, is determined by five dimensions: (a) the conditions under
which the labor is performed; (b) the skill involved; (c) the role of
the branch in the national economy; (d) the regional location; and
(e) the type of enterprise in which the work takes place. The
utmost attention is paid by labor theorists to the skill component.
This component takes into consideration the length of time necessary to acquire the skills and the person's work experience (some
economists also consider the length of time the worker remains in
employment). This skill component is sort of a crude version of
the human capital theory. In reality we do not know exactly on
what basis the skill component is established.[49] However, one
thing is clear—the existing practice of wage differentials has very
little theory behind it.

Yet "who gets what" in the socialist countries is not entirely
arbitrary. The distributional pattern in these countries is linked to
some degree to the economic objectives of the state. The prevailing view in the socialist countries is that the distributional pattern
of earnings must serve the state's two major objectives: (a) to
achieve a just distribution of income in general, and (b) to promote efficiency, understood in most cases as encouragement of
more effort, better work, and the acquisition of new, desirable
skills. The incentive effect of wage differentials on allocation of
labor between industries is less emphasized, although in practice
no less important than the above objective.[50]

In actuality the two major objectives are not clear. For the first
objective to be clear, the state would need either an unambiguous
scale by which to judge what a just distribution of income is or a
clearly expressed social consensus concerning this matter. We
must also assume that the efficiency requirement is very clearly
formulated and its link with the distribution problem unambi-

guously established. This expectation is far from realistic. Whatever the ambiguities in this matter, the state in a socialist country
must reconcile the need for economic efficiency with ethical
considerations of social justice in the field of distribution. This
reconciliation of productivity and egalitarianism is obviously not
an easy matter. It is a contradictory process and to a large degree,
as mentioned before, explains the fluctuations in distribution
policy in the socialist countries. Increases and decreases in wage
differentiation reflect a real contradiction that the leadership in
all socialist countries must face. They would like to achieve
higher efficiency, but at the same time they do not wish to pay too
large a price in terms of increasing inequality.

This tension between efficiency and egalitarianism or, more
accurately, perhaps between stimulation and equality, has haunted
the socialist countries from their inception. The elite in power and
some of the higher-paid working class have always perceived that
stimulation of good work and proper performance cannot easily
be reconciled with small differentials. However, because it is
committed to some degree of egalitarianism and at the same time
to rapid increases in productivity, the ruling elite tries to find a
compromise between these two elements, attempting to hold the
two sides in balance, bending now in one direction, now in
another, moving a step forward and then retreating. This movement is a reflection of tension and ambivalence, which constitute
a systemic problem.

Of course, although economic efficiency requires some differentials in pay, it does not follow that the existing differentials are
either just or necessary. No reason has been advanced to establish
that the set of existing differentials in the socialist countries is
either fair or conducive to economic efficiency.[51] The justification for occupational and other differentials usually advanced in
the socialist countries is, interestingly enough, not very different
from the Western sociological functional theory of stratification
formulated by Davis and Moore.[52] The gist of the functional
theory of distribution can be briefly described: Certain positions
in any society are functionally more important than others. They

are the jobs which require skills, responsibility, etc. Adequate performance in these positions requires appropriate talent and training. But talent and resources for training are scarce commodities in any society. It is therefore necessary to motivate the talented to undergo sacrifices for appropriate training and education, to attract them to functionally important positions, and to motivate them to perform adequately in those positions. The motivating force to achieve these objectives is differential material incentives. These differentials constitute social inequality, which insures that the most talented individuals occupy and properly perform in functionally important positions. Income and social inequality is therefore a universal law for any society with a developed division of labor and specialization irrespective of the ownership structure.

The functional theory of stratification has many flaws.[53] To mention only a few that are especially relevant in the socialist context:

1. The definition of an important position in society depends on the social values of a given society or the objective requirements of the system. In a socialist society a coal miner has more prestige and income than an average manager,[54] whereas in a capitalist society it is the other way around.

2. The concept of training for important positions as a sacrifice is exaggerated in a society where the cost of education and training is to a large degree covered by the state. Only a part of income, under these circumstances, can be considered foregone by being at school instead of on the assembly line, not to mention the fact of the more pleasant environment of learning in comparison with factory work.

3. A major exaggeration is that the only way to mobilize talent and specific skills for specific jobs is via unequal rewards. This disregards the intrinsic benefits of different positions which are of a nonmonetary nature (more interesting jobs, the possibility to set your pace of work in some professions, a more interesting environment, etc.). It leaves out of the picture a person's love of a certain profession. (A potential surgeon will be attracted to the job without special pay.) It fails to mention job satisfaction, the

desire for knowledge, skill, authority, and the ethos of social and public service.

4. Even if a certain validity remains in the functional theory—the fact that to fill some jobs you must differentiate earnings—the theory has never addressed one question: What are the income differences *required* to allocate properly the labor force between different positions? Virtually any pattern of income discrepancies can be justified in the framework of functional theory. Precisely this "virtue" of the theory makes it popular with the bureaucratic elite in the socialist countries, because it fits into their voluntaristic decision process as far as a change in the distribution pattern is concerned.[55] Moreover, the lip service which the elite in power pays to the Marxian principle of distribution under the first phase of communism—to each according to his work—in practice does not contradict the functional theory. This version of the socialist distributional credo emphasizes such different factors as the level of education, the role of the branch in the national economy, territorial location, the degree of responsibility, unpleasantness and arduousness of work, etc.[56] As we can see, these differentiating factors are very similar to those in the functional theory; what is more, no specific objective yardstick exists to measure any aspects of quality of work except the priority established by the political leadership regarding which functions are more important or responsible, complex, etc.

Unfortunately the sociological concept of a simple relationship between inequality and efficiency, propagated by the functional theory of stratification, is widely shared both in the West and in the East. There is assumed to be a sort of natural trade-off between high efficiency and higher inequality of pay: if you want more productivity, you need higher differential pay.[57]

It is difficult to deny that some links between productivity and differential pay exist; however, these links are usually expressed in general terms. Differentials are frequently justified as a means to achieve higher productivity. But the question remains: Are all differentials and incentives conducive to higher productivity, or are only some of them?

Our knowledge of the relationship between income differentials and incentives to good work is hardly reliable. No empirical studies exist that analyze the effects of differentials on work incentives; we do not know quantitatively the adverse effects in comparison with the positive ones. Many experiments describe quite well how particular sampled individuals react to changes in differential rewards, but we do not know how representative these findings are. It is therefore questionable to claim that smaller differentials always reduce incentives, whereas larger ones stimulate them.[58]

Many misconceptions exist in both the literature and social practice. Money rewards are often confused with differential money rewards. In some cases money rewards may be necessary as an incentive, whereas differential money rewards are not. For example, a substantial increase in money for all employees on an equal percentage basis (or even a differentiated one that is slightly in favor of the low earner) can be conducive to better work. A reduction in differentials in order to raise money for low-wage groups may increase their incentive to work. This point is very strongly emphasized by R. A. Dahl and C. E. Lindblom: "From the scanty evidence available in the literature . . . it is quite as difficult to show that smaller differentials threaten incentive as to show that they would stimulate incentive."[59]

But even in those cases in which differential rewards are needed for incentives, it is not altogether obvious which is more effective, one's rank on the income ladder or the size of the differentials. If one is at the top of the wage bracket, one has high prestige even when the pay differential is relatively small. As long as there are initial differences in income, increases in money wages, even when they are relatively undifferentiated, will probably create incentives. The prestige of winning higher wages or salaries is sufficient to create incentives. It is not necessary in all cases to pay different relative incrementals (a different percentage increase) to different employees to promote good work because prestige and satisfaction are very often linked with the absolute size of the salary rather than with the size of its incremental.

Many supporters of increased inequality still repeat the nineteenth-century psychological concept that high and differentiated incomes induce individuals to work instead of be idle. This concept has some validity at a low level of development, where wages merely provide a basic subsistence level of existence. But in societies where wages are above the minimum needs of survival—and in most socialist countries in Eastern Europe this is now the case—it can be argued that higher incomes will dispose individuals to leisure. Although high incomes make work more attractive, leisure also becomes more attractive. The choice between extra work and leisure is on the margin, as Dahl and Lindblom[60] rightly emphasized; but we do not know much about these marginal preferences, and they are probably different for different income groups and strata. It is my view that only some differentials and material incentives promote better work, whereas others have a neutral or even negative effect on performance at the workplace. It is therefore the objective of a material-incentive system to implement those differentials that will have a beneficial effect on productivity and to avoid differentiating pay when it does not positively influence good work. Wholesale increases in differentials will not achieve this objective. In spite of our limited knowledge of how various wage differentials affect performance, let us try to shed some light on this problem.

## Differentials and performance

In all Western and Eastern European countries there has been a decline in some occupational wage differentials. This trend, linked with the democratization of the education and training system, is even more pronounced in the socialist countries, where the cost of education and training is borne to a large extent by social funds. In such a social environment the fruit of this education and training cannot be claimed by the individual alone. Although by and large education and training are financed to a larger degree from social funds in the socialist countries than in the Western ones, there are exceptions. Some Western European welfare states are more generous in funding education than any Eastern European socialist countries. For example, the system of scholarships for university students, free books, and other facilities in primary and secondary education is more universal in Sweden than in the Soviet Union, which has the best record in this respect in the socialist countries.[61]

In spite of major achievements in the Soviet Union and other socialist countries in financing education from social funds, the costs borne by the students and their families are still far from negligible. To the degree that the financial burden of education is carried by the students and their families, differential pay as compensation for costs borne and income foregone is justified. However, the claim that a substantial amount of income is foregone by being at school instead of on the assembly line should not be exaggerated. There is no reason to believe that without strong differential reward, people will not become educated. Higher rewards for skill and education are only one, although an important, incentive for improving one's expertise and qualifications. There are intrinsic rewards in education, independent of money, such as a more interesting job, a better social and cultural environment, the opportunity to set your own pace of work, etc. Though extramaterial reward is not the only stimulus for education and training, we should not infer that differential pay is not of some importance for proper performance. Although reduced wage differentials for education and training will probably not reduce the number of prospective candidates for training in the professions and skilled occupations,[62] it will, however, create a real danger of negative selection. Relatively low-paid occupations have a tendency to attract less talented, less ambitious, and less hard-working people, thereby negatively affecting the performance of a given profession or trade as a whole.

Somewhat more complicated is the link between strength, talent, etc., and higher pay. A genius in mathematics is going to be a mathematician, irrespective of monetary rewards. The supply of talent is not very sensitive to material incentives. However, the allocation of natural abilities to the right employment is not

entirely independent of material rewards. Jobs that require phys-
ically strong workers will not attract strong men if they are not
well paid. The strong man, if not rewarded, would rather choose
an occupation that does not require special strength. It stands to
reason that a person with natural endowments should be given
some differential reward in order to ensure employment in occupations where this talent can be best utilized. It is interesting to
note that in all socialist countries the relative pay for dirty and
tough jobs has increased, owing to an acute shortage of people to
do such work. This is partly because little progress has been made
in mechanizing jobs requiring special physical strength or jobs in
an unpleasant environment. The shortages in these kinds of work
obviously cannot be eliminated by high wage differentials alone.

Now we will turn our attention to differentials within each
occupation and trade. In all socialist countries, in any workplace,
the differences in earning between workers who accomplish a
great deal and those who perform poorly are very small. In
Hungary the dispersion of earnings in identical jobs was not more
than 30-35% of the average earnings; even this small dispersion
is not always linked to actual performance but rather to seniority
and other factors very loosely connected to better work.[63] The
difficulty in linking better and more work to higher pay does not
lie only in the egalitarian ethos which prevails in the socialist
countries; it has partially to do with the difficultires of measuring
performance in the same job in an unambiguous manner. In those
cases where workers do not depend on each other in the production process and in which performance can be ascribed to a
particular worker, piece rates can be a good measure for wage
differentiation. In other cases measurement of performance is
more difficult and must be left to the judgment of foremen and
production engineers on the shop floor.

In all socialist countries the common complaint is that wage
payment is overcentralized, that foremen, section heads, and
shop-floor engineers usually have no say in fixing workers' wage
rates. Top management's lack of knowledge concerning the experience and strong and weak points of particular workers very

often makes wage rates completely unconnected with the real performance of the workers. For technological reasons the performance of a worker is strongly dependent on the collective efficiency of the integrated team, which makes a separate evaluation of his performance difficult or even impossible. It is no accident that individual piecework and other quantity-determined wage systems have a tendency to decline in all industrial countries. Although piecework is much more prevalent in socialist countries than in the West, the percentage of workers to which this method is applied is declining.[64] Moreover, the possibilities of paying higher wages even on piecework for better performance are not sufficiently progressive. The need of the Center to control inflation forces it to restrict the ability of enterprises to increase their average wages. This restriction occurs through different means, including, as in Hungary, the tax system. Small increases in the average wage of the enterprise do not allow a sufficient progressive remuneration for good performance; hence the incentive system has limited results.

In the seventies two Soviet bloc countries—Hungary and Poland—abolished direct personal income taxes for employees in the socialized sector.[65] Excessive demand was checked and macroeconomic equilibrium on the consumer market achieved by taxing the increase in the wage fund and profit of an enterprise progressively, provided the increases were above a certain ceiling. The state had also given up personal income tax as a tool to redistribute earnings in the socialized sector; this function was left to the taxation of the enterprise wage fund. Taxes on personal income were left only in the private and cooperative sectors. In the socialized sector personal income tax had become completely marginal and applied only to very high earnings as a sort of enrichment tax.

Those who wished to abolish comprehensive personal income tax falsely assumed that in a social environment, where the main differentials were established by the state and the state controlled the wage fund through taxing the enterprise wage increases, there was no need for a system of personal income tax. Moreover, it was assumed that personal income tax was a disincentive to more and better work, and replacing it by taxing the enterprise wage fund would eliminate this disincentive. However, experience has shown that this is not the case. Both countries, by taxing the wage fund of the enterprise, have not avoided serious disproportions in earnings between sectors and between different groups of employees, disproportions undesirable from a macro point of view. In Poland, especially, we observe an increase in differentials within the same categories of workers employed in different enterprises, which are not, by any means, a result of differences in labor productivity or more difficult work conditions. Needless to say, these differentials are not an incentive to a more efficient performance. In both countries, although not to the same degree, the actual differentials very often differ from those planned. The reasons for this are various: The planned differentials do not fit the balance of supply and demand for particular categories of labor, and there are specific pressures in the enterprise to "overpay" some workers; these pressures stem from production needs as well as the lobbying abilities of some ministries, enterprises, and employees.

A lack of discipline in differentiating wages is only one aspect of a general lack of discipline in wage expenditures—which is a characteristic of an economy working under a soft budget constraint. The reinstatement of income tax is desirable as far as the proper allocation and use of qualified labor is concerned. The existing practice in most socialist countries, preoccupied with distributional justice, is to centrally establish relatively low pay for highly skilled and educated manpower, which does not reflect the degree of its scarcity, thus distorting the enterprise's cost calculations. Because the social cost of training and education is not included in the wages and salaries of skilled manpower, the enterprise, so to speak, receives a free gift from society that convinces it that skilled manpower is cheap and there is no need to economize on it by using it properly. To avoid this misallocation of scarce skilled manpower on the enterprise level, wages should be relatively high; but the tax system should make sure that through personal income tax this group loses a part of its income, if the state decides that it does not deserve it, because it has not paid for its education and training. The tax mechanism thus makes it possible to reconcile the efficiency requirement with the just distribution principle.

The mechanism of direct income tax also adds an additional dimension of control over both the actually achieved and initially planned differentials. When the authorities find out *ex post facto* that the actual differentiation of earnings does not conform to the planned one or that the planned differentials were set wrong and do not conform to a desirable distributional pattern from a socio-political point of view, the state, using the personal income tax mechanism, can correct in time the undesirable events.

The existing personal tax system, levied only on excessive earnings, is not able to reduce these kinds of unjustified differentials because it has a marginal character. Only a comprehensive, direct personal income tax gives the state an instrument to correct unjustified differences in earnings.[66] Besides, a tax system can also be instrumental in shaping individual consumption patterns using a preferential tax for incomes which are channeled into purchasing specific consumption items, such as, for example, housing and furnishings.

The egalitarian ethos in Poland has brought to the fore demands for taxing not the individual employee's income but the household's per capita income. The higher the household per capita income, the higher the tax rate. Obviously such a tax system would not be an incentive to more and better work and would sever the link between net earnings of an employee and his effort at work, instead connecting his earnings with his family situation.

All available information indicates that both Poland and Hungary are moving toward reinstating a comprehensive personal tax system where the basis for taxation will be the employee's income rather than the per capita income of the household.

## Why Hungary and Poland?

The reader is justified in asking why have we chosen Poland and Hungary to investigate the relationship between economic reform and income inequality.

To analyze the relationship between economic reforms and inequality over time, one must observe a country in which a decentralized model with a regulated market has been introduced consistently and implemented over a considerable length of time. There is only one country in Eastern Europe where these conditions exist—Hungary. In all other socialist countries the economic reform has fallen short of implementing the decentralized market model, and the new measures have in most instances been quickly withdrawn and followed by a retreat to the old ways. In Poland, for example, the Gierek reforms of 1973 were abandoned even before the mechanism and its new rules could start to work on a full scale, and before its economic consequences could be observed. In Hungary, however, the new economic mechanism is already seventeen years old; and although certain changes and corrections have taken place, by and large the basic core of the model has been maintained. In 1980 a further decentralization of the economy was affected, whereby market pressures would increase on the firms and "harden," as Kornai expressed it, the budget constraint.[67]

The reader is also justified in asking why we consider Hungary and not Yugoslavia, where marketization of the economy has been most advanced. There are several reasons why the author would like to stick to the decentralized model with a regulated market of the Hungarian type. First, it is our firm belief that the Hungarian model has much more potential to be emulated in other socialized countries than does the Yugoslav, because the macroeconomic consequences of a full marketization of the economic mechanism (as in Yugoslavia) are profoundly feared in those countries. As we will argue later, the serious danger of unemployment, open inflation, and a sharp increase in inequality of income, which an unregulated market creates, will not be acceptable to the people. The latest events in Poland show the egalitarian ethos to be very strong in the working class in the East European countries. The outburst of discontent in the "hot" summer of 1980 was partially linked with the excessive privileges and income inequalities the Gierek regime had created. Solidarity has made it clear that they expect a sharp reduction in earned-income differences and a more equal distribution of social benefits, both in kind and in cash.[68] It is true that this egalitarian ethos in Solidarity has gone hand in hand with a populistic belief that far-reaching decentralization of economic life is a panacea for all economic ills. These contradictory elements of their philosophy are a result of: (1) the collapse of the old centralistic model in Poland, and (2) a desire to break the bureaucratic power structure of the party and the state by depoliticization of the economic sphere. Whatever the historical fate and impact of Solidarity, the egalitarian demands of the workers will not be overlooked by the rulers in all socialist countries.[69]

Second, we can observe a tendency in Yugoslavia for more central control over the economy in general, and over income distribution in particular. It is well known in Yugoslavia that central direction of the economy was abandoned consistently only after 1965, when macroeconomic investment planning was abolished, foreign and domestic markets liberalized, and more freedom to differentiate earnings was granted to the enterprises.[70] But this "honeymoon" was over in 1975. The Yugoslav leadership blamed the lack of ex ante coordination for such serious structural flaws as duplication of production, increases in the disparity of development between regions, excessive differentiation of earnings and incomes, difficulties in foreign trade, etc. A firm decision has been made to reestablish some form of central planning, as expressed in a new legislative document, "The Law of Social Planning" (February 1976). The national plan is to be based on plans originated from below by the self-managing organizations. The plans of the enterprises worked out on the basis of a common methodology, common assumptions, and common length of planning period are aggregated and reconciled with the national plan in terms of intersectorial and macroeconomic consistency and then returned to the self-managing unit for approval. The signature of approval by the enterprise to a part of the plan is a commitment to a certain investment policy, to a certain price and personal income level, and to a certain distribution pattern. It is, as the Yugoslavs put it, a "social contract" between the state and the self-governing unit. The objective of the "social contract" is to reduce the uncertainty that was present in the market mechanism. Although the new planning principles do not represent a return to Soviet-style central planning, they are closer to this type of planning than the previous practice of indicative planning. It is in one form or another an ex ante coordination of social goals. For example, the social contract contains guidelines for minimum and maximum differentials between and within occupations. These guidelines, though formally voluntary, in reality are a recurrence of central control over earnings;[71] in this respect the Yugoslav reality is now more similar to the Hungarian than before. It is therefore reasonable to conclude that Hungary is a good test ground for the relationship between decentralization reforms and the pattern of income distribution.

For our analysis we also need a country with a highly centralized model of management in which the market plays no role in determining the distributional pattern of earnings, and in which changes in inequality are only a result of state incomes policy. In other words, we need a country where it is difficult to link changes in income disparities with market-oriented reforms. We have therefore chosen Poland for a comparative analysis with Hungary.

Some elements of the Polish economic reforms that were implemented in 1973 were similar to the Hungarian ones—particularly the material-incentive aspect of these reforms in which increased wages were linked with actual increased output. However, their scope and duration were too insignificant to affect the distributional pattern. It was, rather, the centrally guided en masse increase in wages that was ordered by the new Gierek regime in 1972 for nearly all employees of the socialized sector, and implemented in 1972-75, which has had a much more pronounced influence on the distribution pattern than the new incentive system, aborted in 1975, of the short-lived eighteen-month economic reform.[72]

Although the Polish experience does not allow us, as in Hungary, to link relative disparities of wages with economic reforms, it does allow us to see how the distribution pattern compares with that of Hungary. Are there some common trends irrespective of the differences in management systems?

The analysis of the relative distribution of wages and incomes in Poland is, so to speak, a part of the negative evidence concerning the link between inequality and decentralized market-oriented reforms. The choice of Poland for comparison with Hungary is justified by certain important similarities of both countries. For example:

1. *Socioeconomic structures before the war.* In both countries the industrial sector in terms of both employment and output was relatively small. Agriculture, which relied on peasant farming, was the predominant sector of the economy. Nearly 40% of the output of the two nations was produced in agriculture, and over 60% of the gainfully occupied population was working in agriculture, whereas in industry the figure was only about 12-15%. In both countries agriculture has also suffered from certain remnants of the old agrarian structure, although these problems have occurred to a greater extent in Hungary than in Poland.

2. *Achieved stage of development in terms of per capita income and other indicators.* According to calculations by the World Bank and the CMEA, the differences in per capita income are approximately 10% in favor of Hungary. In 1980 both countries surpassed $3,800 in per capita income.[73]

3. *The density of population and other such indicators.* The population per square kilometer in both countries is nearly identical. The level in 1982 in Hungary was 115, and 116 in Poland. The ratio of urban to rural population is also very similar in both

countries, as are other indicators of urbanization.[74]

These similarities are quite important as a requirement for valid comparison of different countries.[75]

A clear knowledge of how the relative disparity of incomes has changed in the two countries is of value in itself; but this analysis may also shed some light on a broader socioeconomic problem, namely, the limitations of and perspectives for reform in the socialist countries.

## The Statistical Material and Its Quality

We begin our investigation of the income distribution pattern of Hungary and Poland with an empirical analysis of the relative dispersion of wages and salaries in the socialized economy in general and in some sectors in particular. After analyzing the relative dispersion of earnings, we concentrate on the distribution of household per capita income of the total population in general, of major strata, and of specific groups. The analysis must nevertheless be prefaced by a few words about the quality of the statistical material in this field. The statistics on income distribution in Hungary and Poland, as in all other countries, suffer shortcomings:

1. Earnings of employees in the socialized sector of Poland, Hungary, and in other socialist countries are divided into manual and nonmanual categories. This classification has a long history in the official statistics. The major criterion for such a classification was the nature of the job: Does it require mostly physical or mental effort? Technological progress and automation have made such a distinction more difficult and very often impossible or irrelevant. In spite of strong criticism[76] from many quarters, the manual-nonmanual classification has been maintained, and the labor laws existing in Poland and Hungary entail separate rules for manual and nonmanual employees. Although many such differences in the labor law have disappeared, different regulations still exist for manual and nonmanual employees in the case of, for example, paid holidays, sick-leave payment, principles of pay-

ment (weekly or monthly), and the amount of hours on the job. Irrespective of formal regulations in the labor laws (e.g., longer paid holidays for nonmanual than for manual workers in some socialist countries), enduring socioeconomic differences have not, as we will argue later, been overcome between manual and nonmanual employees. In some socialist countries, mostly in Hungary, the division of manual and nonmanual employees' earnings and incomes is further differentiated into the following categories:

manual workers' earnings and incomes of:
- skilled workers
- semiskilled workers
- unskilled workers

nonmanual employees' earnings and incomes of:
- top official and high-level professionals
- medium-level managers and professionals
- clerical employees

However, data concerning these occupational categories are not systematically published, especially in the case of per capita household income. In most cases these data appear occasionally in specialized statistical bulletins. In addition, all socialist countries divide all nonmanual employees' earnings into: (a) earnings of technical-engineering personnel, and (b) earnings of administrative personnel. The traditional white-collar employees belong to the administrative category. Here again data over time are not systematic or consistent. In some years data are given for one category but are absent for the others, or the categories are slightly changed and are thus not comparable over time.

2. Although the household statistics in Hungary are among the best in the world (111,000 people were sampled), they are not published in a systematic way in the annual yearbook but only every five years; special reports about the stratification of incomes are published in separate abstracts. Unfortunately not all the material is available in the West.[77]

3. It is impossible to get data outside Hungary about intra- and interbranch differentials and about differentials between

different occupations and trades.

The statistics on income distribution in Poland are much inferior to the Hungarian statistics in several respects:

a) Official statistics in Poland have never regularly included the decile distribution of per capita household income;

b) There have been changes over time in the coverage of the statistics. Before 1972 data for the socialized sector were divided into manual and nonmanual per capita income. In 1973 for the first time not only households of employees of the socialized sector but households of pensioners and mixed households of workers and peasants[78] were also covered.

c) The number of income brackets for reporting purposes is smaller than in Hungary, and the intervals change frequently.

d) Until 1970 the distribution of wages and salaries was recorded before taxation; afterwards, net of taxes. To make the data comparable over time, it is necessary to deduct taxes from gross earnings in the pre-1970 period;

e) The classification of different sectors (especially sectors of the nonproductive sphere)[79] has changed frequently, for example, from "education and schooling" to "education, science, and culture." This makes analysis of the nonproductive sectors impossible.

f) Data in open-ended brackets of earnings are very seldom available for the extreme 1% of the lowest or highest incomes.

A few well-known statistical measures of inequality are used in this work:

1. A set of ratios of incomes at selected percentiles to the median:[80]

$$Pi = \frac{Yi}{Y_{50}}$$

where $Yi$ is income at the ith cumulative percentile of recipients from low to high, calculating the following percentiles:

$$Y_1, \ Y_2, \ Y_5, \ Y_{10}, \ Y_{15}, \ Y_{25} \text{ in the lower tail and}$$

$Y_{25}$, $Y_{85}$, $Y_{90}$, $Y_{95}$, $Y_{98}$, $Y_{99}$ in the upper tail.

2. The ratio of the upper quartile to the lower quartile $(Y_{25}/Y_{75})$
and the interquartile range expressed in terms of the median $(Y_{25}-Y_{75})/Y_{50}$.[81]

3. The ratio of the average earnings and incomes of those in the top and bottom decile groups.

4. The quotient.[82]

5. The equalization parameter $(E)$ determines the percentage of wages or income which should be transferred from decile groups receiving above 10% to groups receiving below 10% of the total wage (or income) in order to achieve a fully equal distribution. This parameter is more frequently used in Poland than in Hungary.

We are using many indicators and measures of inequality because no single measure alone can fully reflect the dispersion of earnings and incomes. They all suffer from some deficiencies; some of them work well in some cases, but in general, they are all too primitive to capture all the complicated nuances of income inequality.[83]

CHAPTER II

# Distribution of Wages and Salaries in Hungary and Poland

## Hungary

Table 1 shows that we can distinguish, as far as relative dispersion of wages is concerned, two subperiods: (a) 1966-74, when the relative dispersion of wages increased, and (b) 1974-80, when a decline of relative dispersion took place.[1] Let us now analyze these two periods in more detail.

In all the analyzed state sectors apart from agriculture, the relative dispersion of earnings was more pronounced in 1974 than the prereform year of 1966, whatever statistical measure of inequality is used.[2]

The increase of inequality in all analyzed sectors (except in the "nonmaterial production sector" and construction) is more pronounced in the upper tail of the distribution than in the lower one. Moreover, the relative dispersion of earnings changed faster in the extreme part of the distribution, measured by the ratios $P_{99}/P_1$, $P_{98}/P_2$, $P_{95}/P_5$, than in the middle part, expressed by the ratio $Q_3/Q_1$.

The increase in the relative degree of inequality was faster in construction and transport than anywhere else, whatever statistical measures are used. The median earning in construction also grew faster than in any other sector, including agriculture, in 1966-74. By 1974 the level of the median was the highest of any sector.

This more rapid increase in relative degree of inequality in construction and transport than elsewhere was not the result solely of spontaneous forces. In 1970, when a nationwide review of pay scales was undertaken, many differentials within and between sectors were changed. The government made a deliberate decision to increase differentials in these two sectors more than elsewhere.

Unfortunately, as is usually the case, the rationale for such an incomes policy has never been publicly explained by the state. We can only surmise that specific labor shortages and the strategic importance of housing and transport put those sectors on the priority list in this matter.

Agriculture is the only sector of the economy with not only a decline in relative dispersion but a very dynamic increase in earnings. As can be seen from Table 1, earnings in agriculture in 1974, expressed by the size of the median, were only marginally lower than in industry, whereas in 1966 they were substantially so. It is no exaggeration to claim that agriculture has received very favorable treatment compared with the rest of the Hungarian economy in the period under consideration.

Women's earnings measured by the median over the whole period were less than men's by approximately 40-50% (see Appendix Table A).[3] In all sectors of the economy except construction, the relative dispersion of women's earnings increased much faster than men's at the extreme part of distribution, measured by the ratio $P_{95}/P_5$. For example, in 1966-74 this ratio increased by 5% for men in industry and by 20% for women. Some sectors showed even larger differences.

However, in the middle of the distribution, measured by $Q_3/Q_1$, the opposite trend is apparent; the relative dispersion of women's earnings declined slightly, whereas that of men's slightly increased. This makes it difficult on the basis of available statistics to compare changes over time in the overall distribution of earnings of women and men. Even if we take account of the compensating effect of favorable changes in the middle of the distribution of women's earnings, it still remains a fact of some importance that women's relative dispersion at the extreme poles not only increased but increased much faster than men's. This could hardly be considered a success in reducing inequalities between the sexes.[4]

The fact that on average lower wages are paid to women than to men is the result of many factors, not the least important of which is simple discrimination. One of the most commonly stressed factors in explaining women's economic disadvantage is the inferior level of their education.[5]

Although in the last 30 years the educational gap between sexes has been considerably reduced, still the university-educated proportion of the age group 25 years and older[6] is more than twice as high for men as for women.

What is more, women with higher education tend to be overrepresented in institutions of lower academic prestige and underrepresented in branches that prepare for higher-level administrative and managerial decision-making jobs.[7]

Unfortunately it is not possible to say whether the overall increase in dispersion of total earnings is a result of changes in differentials within branches, changes in differentials between branches, or a combination of the two. The data required are still not available, though Levcik believes that countervailing forces have been at work to neutralize changes in the inequality of earnings.[8] It is quite possible, according to him, that occupational wage differentials—i.e., those within branches—have widened, while interbranch differentials have narrowed.

Michal argues in an interesting paper of 1972[9] without strong proof that equalization of earnings in the socialist sector should be linked to a sharp decline of interoccupational, interage, and interregional differentials, whereas in fact differences in earnings between industries and by sex are still substantial. But these valuable thoughts are still only based on inference and not on empirical data.

The increase in the dispersion of earnings in 1966-74 shown above can in some sense be attributed to the New Economic Mechanism. Logically it may be claimed that there is a strong positive correlation between effective functioning of the regulated market mechanism and a state policy of nonegalitarian income distribution because a so-called take-off period for successfully implementing the new mechanism depended on a deliberate wid-

Table 1

## Distribution of Full-Time Earnings in the State Sector in Hungary

| | Industry | | | | | | Agriculture and forestry | | | | | |
|---|---|---|---|---|---|---|---|---|---|---|---|---|
| | 1966 | 1968 | 1974 | 1976 | 1978 | 1980 | 1966 | 1968 | 1974 | 1976 | 1978 | 1980 |
| $P_1$ | 0.47 | — | 0.40 | 0.41 | 0.45 | 0.46 | — | — | 0.37 | 0.37 | 0.44 | 0.44 |
| $P_2$ | 0.51 | — | 0.46 | 0.49 | 0.50 | 0.51 | — | — | 0.41 | 0.48 | 0.50 | 0.51 |
| $P_5$ | 0.58 | 0.57 | 0.57 | 0.58 | 0.57 | 0.58 | 0.51 | 0.49 | 0.54 | 0.55 | 0.57 | 0.58 |
| $P_{10}$ | 0.63 | 0.62 | 0.64 | 0.64 | 0.65 | 0.65 | 0.58 | 0.57 | 0.63 | 0.63 | 0.65 | 0.66 |
| $P_{15}$ | 0.68 | 0.68 | 0.69 | 0.69 | 0.70 | 0.70 | 0.65 | 0.62 | 0.69 | 0.69 | 0.71 | 0.72 |
| $P_{25}$ | 0.78 | 0.78 | 0.78 | 0.78 | 0.79 | 0.79 | 0.75 | 0.72 | 0.79 | 0.79 | 0.81 | 0.82 |
| $P_{75}$ | 1.27 | 1.28 | 1.30 | 1.28 | 1.27 | 1.26 | 1.25 | 1.19 | 1.25 | 1.23 | 1.20 | 1.20 |
| $P_{85}$ | 1.42 | 1.46 | 1.49 | 1.46 | 1.45 | 1.44 | 1.44 | 1.35 | 1.41 | 1.37 | 1.32 | 1.32 |
| $P_{90}$ | 1.59 | 1.60 | 1.64 | 1.60 | 1.59 | 1.58 | 1.55 | 1.46 | 1.53 | 1.48 | 1.41 | 1.41 |
| $P_{95}$ | 1.83 | — | 1.93 | 1.87 | 1.85 | 1.83 | 1.79 | 1.67 | 1.76 | 1.68 | 1.59 | 1.59 |
| $P_{98}$ | 2.15 | — | 2.34 | 2.26 | 2.29 | 2.24 | — | — | 2.06 | 1.92 | 1.87 | 1.85 |
| $P_{99}$ | 2.63 | — | 2.72 | 2.52 | 2.58 | — | — | — | 2.33 | 2.15 | 2.08 | 2.06 |
| Median estimated in forints | | | | | | | | | | | | |
| (M) | 1,783 | 1,834 | 2,775 | 3,176 | 3,741 | 4,112 | 1,589 | 1,787 | 2,697 | 3,159 | 3,598 | 3,971 |
| $P_{99}{:}P_1$ | 5.60 | — | 6.80 | 6.15 | 5.73 | — | — | — | 6.30 | 5.81 | 4.73 | 4.68 |
| $P_{98}{:}P_2$ | 4.22 | — | 5.09 | 4.61 | 4.58 | 4.39 | — | — | 5.02 | 4.00 | 3.74 | 3.63 |
| $P_{95}{:}P_5$ | 3.15 | — | 3.38 | 3.22 | 3.24 | 3.16 | 3.51 | 3.41 | 3.26 | 3.05 | 2.79 | 2.74 |
| $P_{90}{:}P_{10}$ | 2.52 | 2.58 | 2.56 | 2.50 | 2.45 | 2.43 | 2.67 | 2.56 | 2.43 | 2.35 | 2.17 | 2.14 |
| $Q_3 - Q_1/M$ | 0.49 | 0.50 | 0.52 | 0.50 | 0.48 | 0.47 | 0.50 | 0.47 | 0.46 | 0.43 | 0.39 | 0.38 |
| $Q_3{:}Q_1$ | 1.63 | 1.63 | 1.67 | 1.64 | 1.61 | 1.59 | 1.66 | 1.65 | 1.59 | 1.56 | 1.48 | 1.46 |

Table 1 (continued)

|  | Construction | | | | | | Transport and communications | | | | | |
|---|---|---|---|---|---|---|---|---|---|---|---|---|
|  | 1966 | 1968 | 1974 | 1976 | 1978 | 1980 | 1966 | 1968 | 1974 | 1976 | 1978 | 1980 |
| $P_1$ | 0.43 | — | 0.39 | 0.43 | 0.45 | 0.45 | 0.53 | — | 0.31 | — | 0.41 | 0.47 |
| $P_2$ | 0.46 | — | 0.47 | 0.48 | 0.49 | 0.49 | 0.57 | — | 0.39 | 0.37 | 0.48 | 0.50 |
| $P_5$ | 0.63 | 0.53 | 0.54 | 0.55 | 0.56 | 0.57 | 0.60 | 0.57 | 0.55 | 0.53 | 0.57 | 0.58 |
| $P_{10}$ | 0.61 | 0.62 | 0.62 | 0.63 | 0.64 | 0.65 | 0.66 | 0.64 | 0.64 | 0.63 | 0.65 | 0.64 |
| $P_{15}$ | 0.69 | 0.71 | 0.67 | 0.69 | 0.70 | 0.71 | 0.71 | 0.70 | 0.70 | 0.69 | 0.70 | 0.70 |
| $P_{25}$ | 0.81 | 0.80 | 0.79 | 0.80 | 0.80 | 0.81 | 0.82 | 0.82 | 0.79 | 0.78 | 0.80 | 0.79 |
| $P_{75}$ | 1.25 | 1.22 | 1.27 | 1.25 | 1.24 | 1.23 | 1.22 | 1.24 | 1.26 | 1.25 | 1.23 | 1.25 |
| $P_{65}$ | 1.41 | 1.39 | 1.45 | 1.42 | 1.42 | 1.38 | 1.35 | 1.35 | 1.42 | 1.40 | 1.38 | 1.39 |
| $P_{90}$ | 1.55 | — | 1.60 | 1.56 | 1.58 | 1.51 | 1.42 | 1.49 | 1.55 | 1.52 | 1.49 | 1.50 |
| $P_{95}$ | 1.79 | — | 1.87 | 1.83 | 1.83 | 1.70 | 1.60 | 1.62 | 1.75 | 1.71 | 1.72 | 1.68 |
| $P_{98}$ | 2.12 | — | 2.33 | 2.17 | 2.24 | 2.06 | 1.79 | — | 2.06 | 1.98 | 2.02 | 1.92 |
| $P_{99}$ | 2.50 | — | 2.77 | 2.56 | 2.42 | — | 1.92 | — | 2.36 | 2.19 | 2.34 | 2.09 |
| Median estimated in forints | | | | | | | | | | | | |
| (M) | 1,885 | 2,035 | 3,243 | 3,680 | 4,130 | 4,666 | 1,780 | 1,845 | 2,749 | 3,170 | 3,851 | 4,310 |
| $P_{99}:P_1$ | 5.81 | — | 7.10 | 5.95 | 5.38 | — | 3.62 | — | 7.61 | — | 5.71 | 4.45 |
| $P_{98}:P_2$ | 4.61 | — | 4.96 | 4.52 | 4.57 | 4.20 | 3.14 | — | 5.28 | 5.35 | 4.21 | 3.84 |
| $P_{95}:P_5$ | 2.84 | — | 3.46 | 3.33 | 3.27 | 2.98 | 2.66 | 2.84 | 3.18 | 3.22 | 3.02 | 2.90 |
| $P_{90}:P_{10}$ | 2.54 | — | 2.58 | 2.48 | 2.47 | 2.32 | 2.15 | 2.33 | 2.42 | 2.41 | 2.29 | 2.34 |
| $Q_3 - Q_1/M$ | 0.43 | 0.41 | 0.48 | 0.45 | 0.44 | 0.42 | 0.40 | 0.41 | 0.47 | 0.47 | 0.43 | 0.46 |
| $Q_3:Q_1$ | 1.53 | 1.51 | 1.61 | 1.56 | 1.55 | 1.52 | 1.48 | 1.50 | 1.59 | 1.60 | 1.54 | 1.58 |

Table 1 (continued)

| | Trade | | | | | | Material production sector total | | | | | |
|---|---|---|---|---|---|---|---|---|---|---|---|---|
| | 1966 | 1968 | 1974 | 1976 | 1978 | 1980 | 1966 | 1968 | 1974 | 1976 | 1978 | 1980 |
| $P_1$ | — | — | 0.42 | 0.39 | 0.46 | 0.47 | — | — | 0.38 | 0.38 | 0.43 | 0.45 |
| $P_2$ | — | — | 0.46 | 0.45 | 0.51 | 0.53 | 0.48 | — | 0.44 | 0.48 | 0.49 | 0.50 |
| $P_5$ | 0.54 | 0.52 | 0.57 | 0.56 | 0.59 | 0.58 | 0.57 | 0.56 | 0.56 | 0.57 | 0.56 | 0.57 |
| $P_{10}$ | 0.64 | 0.62 | 0.65 | 0.64 | 0.65 | 0.65 | 0.62 | 0.61 | 0.63 | 0.63 | 0.64 | 0.64 |
| $P_{15}$ | 0.68 | 0.66 | 0.71 | 0.70 | 0.71 | 0.71 | 0.67 | 0.67 | 0.69 | 0.69 | 0.69 | 0.70 |
| $P_{25}$ | 0.77 | 0.76 | 0.79 | 0.78 | 0.79 | 0.79 | 0.77 | 0.78 | 0.78 | 0.79 | 0.79 | 0.79 |
| $P_{75}$ | 1.26 | 1.29 | 1.30 | 1.28 | 1.27 | 1.26 | 1.26 | 1.27 | 1.29 | 1.27 | 1.26 | 1.26 |
| $P_{65}$ | 1.47 | 1.46 | 1.51 | 1.48 | 1.46 | 1.45 | 1.41 | 1.44 | 1.47 | 1.45 | 1.43 | 1.42 |
| $P_{90}$ | 1.57 | 1.63 | 1.67 | 1.62 | 1.61 | 1.60 | 1.56 | 1.58 | 1.62 | 1.58 | 1.57 | 1.55 |
| $P_{95}$ | 1.83 | — | 1.97 | 1.90 | 1.89 | 1.87 | 1.79 | — | 1.90 | 1.84 | 1.83 | 1.79 |
| $P_{98}$ | — | — | 2.39 | 2.30 | 2.30 | 2.25 | 2.13 | — | 2.29 | 2.19 | 2.21 | 2.14 |
| $P_{99}$ | — | — | 2.75 | 2.57 | 2.65 | 2.53 | — | — | 2.63 | 2.48 | 2.54 | 2.42 |
| Median estimated in forints | | | | | | | | | | | | |
| (M) | 1,586 | 1,671 | 2,469 | 2,834 | 3,248 | 3,638 | 1,746 | 1,812 | 2,777 | 3,195 | 3,735 | 4,138 |
| $P_{99}:P_1$ | — | — | 6.55 | 6.59 | 5.76 | 5.38 | — | — | 6.92 | 6.53 | 5.91 | 5.38 |
| $P_{98}:P_2$ | — | — | 5.20 | 5.11 | 4.51 | 4.25 | 4.44 | — | 5.20 | 4.56 | 4.51 | 4.28 |
| $P_{95}:P_5$ | 3.39 | — | 3.46 | 3.39 | 3.20 | 3.22 | 3.14 | — | 3.39 | 3.23 | 3.27 | 3.14 |
| $P_{90}:P_{10}$ | 2.45 | 2.63 | 2.57 | 2.53 | 2.48 | 2.46 | 2.52 | 2.59 | 2.61 | 2.51 | 2.45 | 2.42 |
| $Q_3 - Q_1/M$ | 0.49 | 0.53 | 0.51 | 0.50 | 0.48 | 0.47 | 0.49 | 0.49 | 0.51 | 0.49 | 0.47 | 0.47 |
| $Q_3:Q_1$ | 1.64 | 1.70 | 1.64 | 1.64 | 1.61 | 1.59 | 1.63 | 1.63 | 1.65 | 1.63 | 1.59 | 1.59 |

Table 1 (continued)

| | Nonmaterial production sector | | | | | | State sector total | | | | | | |
|---|---|---|---|---|---|---|---|---|---|---|---|---|---|
| | 1966 | 1968 | 1974 | 1976 | 1978 | 1980 | 1966 | 1968 | 1974 | 1976 | 1978 | 1980 | 1982 |
| $P_1$ | — | — | 0.35 | — | — | 0.41 | — | — | 0.37 | — | 0.34 | 0.41 | — |
| $P_2$ | — | — | 0.42 | — | 0.31 | 0.44 | 0.47 | — | 0.41 | 0.40 | 0.44 | 0.49 | 0.46 |
| $P_5$ | 0.51 | 0.50 | 0.48 | 0.46 | 0.49 | 0.53 | 0.54 | 0.54 | 0.53 | 0.52 | 0.54 | 0.54 | 0.53 |
| $P_{10}$ | 0.57 | 0.57 | 0.58 | 0.57 | 0.58 | 0.59 | 0.61 | 0.61 | 0.61 | 0.61 | 0.62 | 0.63 | 0.62 |
| $P_{15}$ | 0.63 | 0.63 | 0.66 | 0.63 | 0.63 | 0.65 | 0.66 | 0.66 | 0.68 | 0.67 | 0.68 | 0.68 | 0.67 |
| $P_{25}$ | 0.73 | 0.73 | 0.76 | 0.72 | 0.73 | 0.74 | 0.76 | 0.77 | 0.77 | 0.77 | 0.77 | 0.78 | 0.76 |
| $P_{75}$ | 1.33 | 1.30 | 1.35 | 1.35 | 1.33 | 1.31 | 1.27 | 1.28 | 1.29 | 1.28 | 1.27 | 1.27 | 1.28 |
| $P_{65}$ | 1.51 | 1.55 | 1.56 | 1.57 | 1.54 | 1.52 | 1.42 | 1.45 | 1.49 | 1.47 | 1.45 | 1.44 | 1.47 |
| $P_{90}$ | 1.71 | 1.74 | 1.74 | 1.75 | 1.71 | 1.69 | 1.58 | 1.61 | 1.64 | 1.61 | 1.59 | 1.58 | 1.62 |
| $P_{95}$ | 2.00 | — | 2.07 | 2.06 | 2.03 | 2.01 | 1.74 | — | 1.93 | 1.88 | 1.86 | 1.84 | 1.88 |
| $P_{98}$ | — | — | 2.53 | 2.48 | 2.49 | 2.51 | 2.15 | — | 2.35 | 2.25 | 2.26 | 2.20 | 2.25 |
| $P_{99}$ | — | — | 2.85 | 2.82 | 2.86 | — | — | — | 2.70 | 2.55 | 2.60 | 2.49 | 2.55 |
| Median estimated in forints | | | | | | | | | | | | | |
| (M) | 1,648 | 1,690 | 2,459 | 2,761 | 3,368 | 3,767 | 1,731 | 1,793 | 2,707 | 3,098 | 3,657 | 4,054 | 4,550 |
| $P_{99}{:}P_1$ | — | — | 8.14 | — | — | — | — | — | 7.30 | — | 7.65 | 5.93 | — |
| $P_{98}{:}P_2$ | — | — | 6.02 | — | 8.03 | 5.70 | 4.57 | — | 5.73 | 5.62 | 5.14 | 4.49 | 4.89 |
| $P_{95}{:}P_5$ | 3.92 | — | 4.31 | 4.48 | 4.14 | 3.79 | 3.22 | — | 3.64 | 3.61 | 3.44 | 3.41 | 3.55 |
| $P_{90}{:}P_{10}$ | 3.00 | 3.05 | 3.00 | 3.07 | 2.95 | 2.86 | 2.59 | 2.64 | 2.69 | 2.64 | 2.56 | 2.51 | 2.61 |
| $Q_3 - Q_1/M$ | 0.60 | 0.57 | 0.58 | 0.63 | 0.60 | 0.57 | 0.50 | 0.51 | 0.52 | 0.51 | 0.50 | 0.49 | 0.52 |
| $Q_3{:}Q_1$ | 1.82 | 1.78 | 1.76 | 1.87 | 1.82 | 1.77 | 1.66 | 1.67 | 1.68 | 1.66 | 1.65 | 1.63 | 1.68 |

ening of wage differentials by the state. It is therefore not as much the spontaneous forces of the market that can be "blamed" for increased inequalities of pay so much as the state's deliberate policy of creating preconditions for effective operation of the market mechanism in general and incentives in particular. In this sense, at least, the reform can be judged responsible for an increase in inequality in distribution of wages and salaries between 1966 and 1974.

This inegalitarian trend was sharply reversed in 1974–80 in all sectors of the socialized economy except the nonmaterial production sphere, where the relative dispersion of wages was basically the same in 1978 as it was in the prereform year of 1966 in the middle of the distribution, while it shows an increase in inequality only in the extreme part ($P_{98}/P_2$, $P_{95}/P_5$). Moreover, as can be seen from Table 1, the nonmaterial production sector has the highest level of inequality, which reflects on the one hand the special privileges the upper echelons of the army, the policy, administration, and the top party apparatus enjoy in the socialist countries and on the other hand the very low wages paid to clerical and medical personnel. In no other sector of the socialized economy did the lowest 2% and 5% of earners receive so small a part of the median as in the nonmaterial sphere, whereas

Notes to Table 1

---

*Source*: *S.E. 1966* (Budapest: KSH, 1967), Table 16, 60; ibid., *1968* (1969), Table 16, 84; *F.K.A. 1974* (Budapest: KSH, 1976), Table 9, 136–7; ibid., *1976* (1978), Table 23, 98–9; ibid., *1978* (1980), Table 20A, 164–5; ibid., *1980* (1981), Table 33A, 232–3; Statistical Pocket Book of Hungary 1983 (Budapest, KSH, 1984) Table 4, 34.

*Notes*: The figures relate to September of each year and cover both male and female employees. Separate details for males and females. See Table A in appendix.

$P_5$, $P_{25}$, etc., refer to the 5th, 25th, etc., percentiles of earnings expressed as a ratio of the median, ordering wage and salary earners from low incomes to high incomes; e.g., $P_5$ refers to the bottom 5% of earners and $P_{95}$ to the top 5%).

$Q_1$ is the lower quartile.
$Q_3$ is the upper quartile.
M is the median.

The percentage distribution of the total gainfully employed workforce of 5.07 million in 1974 was: industry 35.8%; agriculture and forestry 20.0%; construction 8.2:; transport 7.6%; trade 8.7%; nonmaterial production 16.4%. In 1980 it was, respectively 34%, 20.5%, 8%, 9.6%, 19%.

Table 2

## Measures of Inequality in the Socialized Sector

| Year | Share of total earnings received by: bottom 20% of earners | top 20% of earners | Ratio of average earnings of top and bottom deciles | Quotient |
|---|---|---|---|---|
| 1966 | 12.1 | 31.9 | 3.37 | 1.79 |
| 1968 | 12.1 | 32.2 | 3.29 | 1.83 |
| 1970 | 10.7 | 33.4 | 4.04 | 1.88 |
| 1972 | 10.8 | 32.8 | 4.15 | 1.91 |
| 1974 | 10.8 | 32.8 | 4.06 | 1.90 |
| 1978 | 11.2 | 32.2 | 3.85 | 1.85 |
| 1980 | 11.4 | 32.0 | 3.68 | 1.82 |

*Sources: F.K.A. 1977* (Budapest, KSH, 1979), 12; ibid., *1978* (1980), 15; ibid., *1980* (1981), 20; *Eletszinvonal 1960-1980* [The Standard of Living in 1960–80] (Budapest: KSH, 1981).

Table 3

| | Quotient | | | | | |
|---|---|---|---|---|---|---|
| | 1970 | 1972 | 1974 | 1976 | 1978 | 1980 |
| Industry | 1.87 | 1.89 | 1.88 | 1.83 | 1.81 | 1.79 |
| Construction | 1.87 | 1.82 | 1.81 | 1.76 | 1.74 | 1.70 |
| Agriculture and forestry | 1.77 | 1.74 | 1.76 | 1.72 | 1.63 | 1.60 |
| Transport and communications | 1.71 | 1.75 | 1.76 | 1.75 | 1.70 | 1.69 |
| Trade | 1.95 | 1.92 | 1.88 | 1.85 | 1.87 | 1.78 |

*Source*: See Table 2.

at the same time, the top 1%, 2%, and 5% of earners received a higher proportion of wages *expressed as a part* of the median than any other sector of the economy.[10]

A decline in relative dispersion of earnings in the socialized sector in the period 1974-1980 is shown in Table 2.

This egalitarian tendency is even more obvious for some major sectors of the socialized economy (see Table 3).

Table 4

## Average Monthly Wages and Earnings* in Hungarian Socialized Industry (Manual Workers' Earnings = 100)

| Year | Technical personnel | | Administrative personnel | | Nonmanual workers | |
|---|---|---|---|---|---|---|
| | wages | earnings | wages | earnings | wages | earnings |
| 1955 | 174.8 | | 104.8 | | | |
| 1960 | 156.2 | | 94.4 | | | |
| 1965 | 155.1 | | 96.3 | | | |
| 1968 | 153.8 | | 98.5 | | | |
| 1969 | 153.6 | 163.5 | 98.7 | 101.7 | | |
| 1970 | 152.2 | 160.8 | 98.0 | 100.1 | | |
| 1972 | 150.4 | 159.6 | 98.7 | 101.6 | | |
| 1973 | 144.8 | 154.1 | 94.3 | 97.2 | | |
| 1974 | 143.6 | 154.9 | 93.5 | 98.2 | | |
| 1975** | 140.4 | 149.8 | — | | 117.5 | 124.7 |
| 1976 | 138.7 | 147.1 | — | | 117.5 | 124.0 |
| 1977 | 136.4 | 142.7 | — | | 116.7 | 121.6 |
| 1978 | 135.1 | 140.8 | — | | 115.5 | 120.0 |
| 1979 | 135.8 | 140.3 | — | | 116.3 | 119.8 |
| 1980 | 137.5 | 141.5 | — | | 117.5 | 120.6 |
| 1981 | 138.1 | 142.3 | — | | 118.0 | 121.5 |
| 1982 | 138.0 | 142.7 | — | — | 117.7 | 121.6 |

*Sources*: Calculated on the basis of: *S.E. 1976* (Budapest: KSH, 1977), table 23, 143; ibid., *1978* (1979), table 24, 183; ibid., *1980* (1981), table 24, 189; ibid, *1981* (1982), table 9.27, 132; ibid *1982* (1983), table 9.29, 125; *Statistical Yearbook* (English version) for years from 1959 to 1975 (Budapest: Central Statistical Office), tables 14 and 17 for industry. Source for 1955 is from *O. Kishāzi Bērrendszerünk* [Our Wage System] (Budapest: Kossuth, 1958), p. 66.

*In Hungary starting in 1969 a new classification for incomes from employment in the socialized sector was introduced: Wages [Berek] and Earnings [Kereset]. Wages are only those items of pay included as an element of production cost. Wages supplemented by bonuses financed from the sharing fund fed by profit together constitute earnings (kereset). Prior to 1969 Hungarian statistics used the term wages [bér] for incomes from employment in the socialized sector, which included all kinds of bonuses as well, whereas after 1968 figures for wages [berek] do not include bonuses. Considering that the figures given for wages [berek] are not fully comparable for the pre- and post-reform years, we have calculated both wages [berek] and earnings [kereset] for 1969-1983.

**After 1975 a new classification was used. Wages [Berek] and earnings [kereset] were divided into manual and nonmanual wages and earnings, with nonmanual including only technical personnel wages and earnings. No data for administrative personnel are available.

Although in this book we analyze only differentiation of earnings that can be linked to economic reforms, a statistical analysis of pay differentiation between strata and occupational groups can shed some light on whether the economic reform in Hungary has influenced this process, and whether the trend here differs from that in Poland, where there was no economic reform.

In Hungary as in Poland, there are no data about differences in average earnings between major strata employed in the socialized sector as a whole. We must therefore be content, as in the Polish case, with data only on differences in average wages between main strata in industry. This we present in Tables 4 and 5.

A glance at Tables 4 and 5 shows that the earnings of two groups of nonmanual workers—technical and administrative personnel—did not grow as fast as workers' earnings. The relative position of these groups markedly deteriorated after 1972. Hence Hungarian manual workers are not doing badly in relative terms. They reduced the distance between them and highly skilled personnel and have overtaken white-collar workers in average wages. For example, the earnings of an engineer barely exceed the earnings of a skilled worker.[11]

Moreover, the trend toward equalizing earnings between major occupational groups did not halt after the implementation of the economic reform in Hungary and continued unabated in the '70s. What are the reasons for so strong a tendency to level off differences in earnings between manual and nonmanual employees, between workers and professional groups? There are many, but we will mention only a few.

1. The elites in all Eastern European countries fear workers, especially industrial workers, much more than they do the intelligentsia. Alienating workers is politically more dangerous than alienating the nonmanual strata. The policy of preferential treatment for workers is also an instrument used to divide the workers from the intelligentsia, especially in times of crisis. The old game of divide and rule has been well mastered by the establishment in the socialist countries.

2. The official ideology claims that the countries are workers'

Table 5

**Average Earnings of Various Groups of Enterprise Executives as a Ratio to the Average Earnings of Manual Workers**

|  | 1975 | 1976 | 1977 | 1978 |
|---|---|---|---|---|
| 1. Directors and their deputies | 2.98 | 2.98 | 2.53 | 2.49 |
| 2. Heads of departments and their deputies | 2.46 | 2.37 | 2.12 | 2.12 |
| 3. Heads of sections and their deputies | 1.98 | 1.93 | 1.72 | 1.72 |

Source: Calculated on the basis of K.S. Falus, "Wage Differentials, in Hungary," *Acta Oeconomica*, (Vol. 25, 1–2, 1980), table 4, 169.

states; hence it is "natural" to care most about workers, especially low-paid workers.

3. A factor that does not entirely depend on the deliberate policy of the state is the "proletarization," as M. Yanowitch calls it, of the lower strata of technical and administrative employees and changes in the composition of young manual workers.[12] A large increase in the supply of graduates from engineering and technical schools has made it possible to moderate increases in pay for those groups. At the same time, the composition of young people taking manual jobs has changed in the process of industrialization. They are no longer predominately rural in origin, ready to accept any nonagricultural job. More and more young people come from cities and are reluctant to accept low-skilled jobs; hence a need has arisen to pay them better in order to retain their services.

4. Priorities given to heavy industry were also a factor conducive to reducing pay differences between social strata in the socialized sector. A special "workers' aristocracy" was created in some leading industries (e.g., mining, oil, steel, etc.) whose average pay was often higher than nonmanual specialists in nonpriority industries. It must be stressed, however, that this phenomenon is more pronounced in the highly centralized economies than in Hungary; nevertheless it was not entirely eliminated from Hungarian life after the reforms.

5. Some factors conducive to levelling earnings are partially spontaneous and "technical" in nature. They spring from imperfections in planning and control. Thus it is much easier to control the earnings of nonmanual employees than manual ones, especially those who do piecework.[13] As a result the earnings of manual workers have a tendency to exceed expected levels more than those of the nonmanual ones.

The deterioration in the relative pay position of nonmanual employees has had serious negative consequences, including:

a) Managers, planners, and other specialists are not stimulated materially to improve their specialized knowledge or to keep up with the latest achievements in their field.

b) The existing differentials do not encourage enough people to work hard to get into responsible positions where their abilities could be utilized.

c) The economic degradation of nonmanual employees, as well as of the professions, has led to a major decline in managerial authority and, linked with it, poor labor discipline in the enterprises.

d) The economic degradation of professions has also led to the demoralization of some of them, most vividly in the case of physicians. Some of them expect to be tipped for their services, with the quality of service very often dependent on the size of the tip.[14]

## Poland

Tables 6 and 7 show that in 1965–78,[15] the relative dispersion of earnings in the Polish socialized sector increased. Taking the percentile ratios ($P_{95}:P_5$, $P_{90}:P_{10}$), Table 6 shows that for all employees, inequality declined from 1967 to 1972 and then increased, returning in 1978 to approximately the 1967 level. Taking the quartile ratio ($Q_3:Q_1$) inequality increased between 1967 and 1972 and then declined, but was still greater in 1978 than in 1967.[16] Increasing inequality is especially visible in the extreme tail of the distribution. Both manual and nonmanual earnings in

Table 6

**Distribution of Full-Time Earnings in the Socialized Sector in Poland. Net Monthly Wages and Salaries**

| | 1965 | | | 1967 | | | 1970 | | | 1972 | | | 1973 |
| | Total | Manual | Non-manual | Total | Manual | Non-manual | Total | Manual | Non-manual | Total | Manual | Non-manual | Total |
|---|---|---|---|---|---|---|---|---|---|---|---|---|---|
| $P_1$ | — | — | — | — | — | 0.47 | — | — | — | — | — | — | — |
| $P_2$ | — | — | — | — | — | 0.50 | — | — | 0.49 | — | — | 0.51 | — |
| $P_5$ | — | — | 0.55 | 0.51 | 0.49 | 0.57 | 0.50 | — | 0.57 | 0.51 | — | 0.58 | 0.53 |
| $P_{10}$ | 0.59 | 0.55 | 0.63 | 0.59 | 0.56 | 0.64 | 0.58 | 0.55 | 0.64 | 0.60 | 0.59 | 0.63 | 0.59 |
| $P_{15}$ | 0.65 | 0.62 | 0.68 | 0.66 | 0.63 | 0.70 | 0.65 | 0.62 | 0.68 | 0.65 | 0.64 | 0.68 | 0.66 |
| $P_{25}$ | 0.76 | 0.75 | 0.78 | 0.77 | 0.75 | 0.79 | 0.75 | 0.74 | 0.77 | 0.71 | 0.74 | 0.78 | 0.77 |
| $P_{75}$ | 1.30 | 1.28 | 1.32 | 1.31 | 1.31 | 1.32 | 1.31 | 1.28 | 1.36 | 1.31 | 1.29 | 1.34 | 1.34 |
| $P_{65}$ | 1.48 | 1.46 | 1.60 | 1.59 | 1.54 | 1.68 | 1.53 | 1.62 | 1.68 | 1.56 | 1.55 | 1.56 | 1.54 |
| $P_{90}$ | 1.79 | 1.69 | 1.90 | 1.85 | 1.81 | 1.89 | 1.73 | 1.82 | 1.91 | 1.70 | 1.69 | 1.75 | 1.74 |
| $P_{95}$ | 2.15 | 2.09 | 2.20 | 2.11 | 2.11 | 2.12 | 2.00 | 2.01 | 2.10 | 2.04 | 2.02 | 2.06 | 2.15 |
| $P_{98}$ | 2.38 | 2.34 | — | — | 2.29 | — | 2.48 | — | — | 2.64 | 2.54 | 2.60 | 2.53 |
| $P_{99}$ | — | 2.42 | — | — | — | — | 2.99 | — | — | 2.90 | 2.84 | 3.04 | 3.05 |

| | 1,772 | 1,754 | 1,824 | 1,892 | 1,847 | 1,963 | 2,098 | 2,044 | 2,141 | 2,373 | 2,310 | 2,465 | 2,713 |
|---|---|---|---|---|---|---|---|---|---|---|---|---|---|
| Median estimates in zlotys (M) | | | | | | | | | | | | | |
| Average wage | 1,868 | | | 2,025 | | | 2,232 | | | 2,511 | | | 2,798 |
| Minimum wage as a percentage of average wage | 0.40 | | | 0.42 | | | 0.40 | | | | | | |
| $P_{99}:P_1$ | — | — | — | — | — | — | — | — | — | — | — | — | — |
| $P_{98}:P_2$ | — | — | — | — | — | — | — | — | — | — | — | 5.10 | — |
| $P_{95}:P_5$ | — | — | 4.00 | 4.14 | 4.31 | 3.72 | 4.00 | — | 3.68 | 4.00 | — | 3.55 | 4.06 |
| $P_{90}:P_{10}$ | 3.03 | 3.07 | 3.02 | 3.14 | 3.23 | 3.12 | 2.98 | 3.31 | 2.98 | 2.83 | 2.86 | 2.78 | 2.95 |
| $Q_3 - Q_1/M$ | 0.54 | 0.53 | 0.54 | 0.54 | 0.56 | 0.53 | 0.56 | 0.54 | 0.59 | 0.60 | 0.55 | 0.56 | 0.57 |
| $Q_3:Q_1$ | 1.71 | 1.71 | 1.69 | 1.70 | 1.75 | 1.67 | 1.75 | 1.73 | 1.77 | 1.84 | 1.74 | 1.72 | 1.70 |

Table 6 (continued)

| | 1976 | | | 1978 | | | 1980 | | | 1982 | | |
|---|---|---|---|---|---|---|---|---|---|---|---|---|
| | Total | Manual | Non-manual | Total | Manual | Non-manual | Total | Manual | Non-manual | Total | Manual | Non-manual |
| $P_1$ | — | — | — | — | — | — | — | — | — | — | — | — |
| $P_2$ | 0.41 | — | — | — | — | 0.46 | — | — | — | — | — | 0.55 |
| $P_5$ | 0.48 | 0.56 | 0.54 | 0.48 | 0.48 | 0.50 | 0.51 | 0.48 | 0.55 | 0.58 | 0.57 | 0.61 |
| $P_{10}$ | 0.57 | 0.62 | 0.60 | 0.56 | 0.54 | 0.59 | 0.59 | 0.56 | 0.62 | 0.64 | 0.63 | 0.66 |
| $P_{15}$ | 0.63 | 0.73 | 0.66 | 0.63 | 0.61 | 0.67 | 0.64 | 0.63 | 0.67 | 0.70 | 0.69 | 0.72 |
| $P_{25}$ | 0.74 | — | 0.77 | 0.75 | 0.74 | 0.76 | 0.76 | 0.75 | 0.78 | 0.80 | 0.80 | 0.82 |
| $P_{50}$ | 1.33 | 1.33 | 1.32 | 1.33 | 1.33 | 1.32 | 1.34 | 1.33 | 1.35 | 1.25 | 1.26 | 1.24 |
| $P_{75}$ | 1.57 | 1.58 | 1.56 | 1.56 | 1.56 | 1.55 | 1.53 | 1.53 | 1.54 | 1.42 | 1.44 | 1.38 |
| $P_{90}$ | 1.77 | 1.76 | 1.75 | 1.75 | 1.74 | 1.73 | 1.73 | 1.71 | 1.76 | 1.55 | 1.62 | 1.51 |
| $P_{95}$ | 2.10 | 2.10 | 2.08 | 2.12 | 2.11 | 2.10 | 2.04 | 2.01 | 2.07 | 1.88 | 1.95 | 1.77 |
| $P_{98}$ | 2.60 | 2.58 | 2.59 | 2.58 | 2.53 | 2.57 | 2.44 | 2.38 | 2.54 | — | — | 2.10 |
| $P_{99}$ | 2.92 | 2.79 | 2.99 | — | 2.77 | — | 2.72 | 2.65 | 2.89 | — | — | — |

Median estimated in zlotys

| | | | | | | | | | | | | |
|---|---|---|---|---|---|---|---|---|---|---|---|---|
| (M) | 3,651 | 3,582 | 3,772 | 4,386 | 4,331 | 4,474 | 5,418 | 5,562 | 5,147 | 10,349 | 10,451 | 10,159 |
| Average wage Minimum wage | 3,971 | — | — | 4,686 | — | — | 5,789 | — | — | 11,631 | | |
| as a percentage of average wage | 0.33 | | | 0.34 | | | 0.41 | | | | | |
| P$_{99}$:P$_1$ | — | — | — | — | — | — | — | — | — | — | — | — |
| P$_{98}$:P$_2$ | 6.34 | — | — | — | — | 5.59 | — | — | — | — | — | 3.82 |
| P$_{95}$:P$_5$ | 4.37 | — | — | 4.42 | 4.40 | 4.20 | 4.00 | 4.19 | 3.76 | 3.24 | 3.42 | 2.90 |
| P$_{90}$:P$_{10}$ | 3.11 | 3.14 | 2.97 | 3.13 | 3.22 | 2.93 | 2.93 | 3.05 | 2.84 | 2.42 | 2.60 | 2.29 |
| Q$_3$ – Q$_1$/M | 0.59 | 0.60 | 0.55 | 0.58 | 0.59 | 0.56 | 0.58 | 0.58 | 0.57 | 0.45 | 0.46 | 0.36 |
| Q$_3$:Q$_1$ | 1.80 | 1.82 | 1.71 | 1.77 | 1.80 | 1.74 | 1.76 | 1.77 | 1.73 | 1.56 | 1.58 | 1.51 |

*Source: R.S.*, 1967, 1968, 1970, 1971, 1972, 1973, 1974, 1975, 1976, 1977, 1978, 1981, 1983 (Warsaw: GUS): *Tendencje Rozwoju Spolecznego* [Tendencies in Social Development] (Warsaw: GUS 1979), table 51, 98.

*Note*: See Table 1 for definitions of percentiles.

Table 7

## Distribution of Full-Time Earnings in the Socialized Sectors in Poland. Net Monthly Wages and Salaries

| | Industry | | | | | | | | Construction | | | | | | | |
|---|---|---|---|---|---|---|---|---|---|---|---|---|---|---|---|---|
| | 1965 | 1967 | 1970 | 1972 | 1973 | 1976 | 1978 | 1980 | 1965 | 1967 | 1970 | 1972 | 1973 | 1976 | 1978 | 1980 |
| $P_1$ | — | — | — | — | — | 0.39 | — | 0.42 | — | — | — | — | — | — | — | 0.42 |
| $P_2$ | — | 0.45 | — | 0.48 | 0.47 | 0.43 | 0.43 | 0.46 | — | — | — | — | 0.39 | 0.36 | — | — |
| $P_5$ | 0.53 | 0.54 | 0.54 | 0.56 | 0.53 | 0.52 | 0.49 | 0.54 | 0.49 | 0.47 | 0.57 | 0.49 | 0.46 | 0.46 | 0.45 | 0.50 |
| $P_{10}$ | 0.63 | 0.63 | 0.62 | 0.62 | 0.62 | 0.60 | 0.59 | 0.62 | 0.58 | 0.57 | 0.63 | 0.57 | 0.56 | 0.55 | 0.56 | 0.58 |
| $P_{15}$ | 0.70 | 0.69 | 0.67 | 0.68 | 0.70 | 0.67 | 0.66 | 0.68 | 0.66 | 0.64 | 0.75 | 0.64 | 0.63 | 0.62 | 0.63 | 0.65 |
| $P_{25}$ | 0.78 | 0.78 | 0.77 | 0.80 | 0.79 | 0.77 | 0.76 | 0.78 | 0.74 | 0.75 | — | 0.76 | 0.74 | 0.74 | 0.75 | 0.76 |
| $P_{75}$ | 1.27 | 1.26 | 1.27 | 1.32 | 1.31 | 1.34 | 1.33 | 1.30 | 1.27 | 1.38 | 1.34 | 1.27 | 1.34 | 1.40 | 1.32 | 1.27 |
| $P_{65}$ | 1.53 | 1.59 | 1.51 | 1.52 | 1.51 | 1.62 | 1.56 | 1.52 | 1.63 | 1.65 | 1.56 | 1.60 | 1.60 | 1.60 | 1.53 | 1.49 |
| $P_{90}$ | 1.78 | 1.78 | 1.66 | 1.70 | 1.68 | 1.76 | 1.76 | 1.71 | 1.82 | 1.79 | 1.77 | 1.76 | 1.84 | 1.83 | 1.73 | 1.61 |
| $P_{95}$ | 2.02 | 1.96 | 1.96 | 2.02 | 2.07 | 2.20 | 2.09 | 2.02 | 2.03 | — | 2.20 | 2.26 | 2.11 | 2.19 | 1.99 | 1.89 |
| $P_{98}$ | — | — | 2.46 | 2.55 | 2.40 | 2.52 | 2.51 | 2.41 | — | — | 2.71 | 2.85 | 2.74 | 2.84 | 2.36 | 2.22 |
| $P_{99}$ | — | — | 2.81 | 2.73 | 2.83 | 3.18 | — | 2.65 | — | — | 3.22 | 3.27 | 2.95 | 3.30 | — | 2.46 |

Median estimated in zlotys

| (M) | 1,972 | 2,097 | 2,291 | 2,545 | 2,857 | 3,923 | 4,745 | 6,042 | 2,082 | 2,261 | 2,504 | 2,839 | 3,388 | 4,301 | 5,058 | 6,204 |
|---|---|---|---|---|---|---|---|---|---|---|---|---|---|---|---|---|
| Average wage | 2,027 | 2,152 | 2,394 | 2,634 | 2,873 | 4,234 | 4,942 | 6,181 | 2,178 | 2,385 | 2,675 | 2,992 | 3,471 | 4,633 | 5,298 | 6,369 |
| $P_{99}:P_1$ | — | — | — | — | — | 8.15 | — | 6.31 | — | — | — | — | — | — | — | — |
| $P_{98}:P_2$ | — | — | — | 5.31 | 5.10 | 5.86 | 5.84 | 5.24 | — | — | — | — | 7.02 | 7.89 | — | 5.29 |
| $P_{95}:P_5$ | 3.81 | 3.63 | 3.63 | 3.61 | 3.91 | 4.23 | 4.26 | 3.74 | 4.14 | — | — | 4.61 | 4.59 | 4.76 | 4.42 | 3.78 |
| $P_{90}:P_{10}$ | 2.83 | 2.82 | 2.68 | 2.74 | 2.71 | 2.93 | 2.98 | 2.76 | 3.14 | 3.14 | 3.11 | 3.09 | 3.29 | 3.33 | 3.09 | 2.78 |
| $Q_3 - Q_1/M$ | 0.49 | 0.48 | 0.50 | 0.52 | 0.52 | 0.57 | 0.57 | 0.52 | 0.53 | 0.63 | 0.59 | 0.51 | 0.60 | 0.66 | 0.57 | 0.51 |
| $Q_3:Q_1$ | 1.63 | 1.62 | 1.65 | 1.65 | 1.66 | 1.74 | 1.75 | 1.67 | 1.72 | 1.84 | 1.79 | 1.67 | 1.81 | 1.89 | 1.76 | 1.67 |

64

Table 7 (continued)

| | Transport and communications | | | | | | | | Trade | | | | | | | |
|---|---|---|---|---|---|---|---|---|---|---|---|---|---|---|---|---|
| | 1965 | 1967 | 1970 | 1972 | 1973 | 1976 | 1978 | 1980 | 1965 | 1967 | 1970 | 1972 | 1973 | 1976 | 1978 | 1980 |
| $P_1$ | — | 0.50 | — | — | 0.44 | 0.41 | — | 0.43 | — | — | — | — | — | — | — | — |
| $P_2$ | — | 0.54 | — | 0.50 | 0.50 | 0.45 | 0.45 | 0.47 | — | — | — | — | — | 0.50 | — | — |
| $P_5$ | 0.60 | 0.60 | 0.56 | 0.58 | 0.56 | 0.54 | 0.51 | 0.54 | — | 0.57 | — | — | 0.59 | 0.56 | 0.57 | 0.59 |
| $P_{10}$ | 0.68 | 0.67 | 0.63 | 0.64 | 0.65 | 0.61 | 0.60 | 0.62 | 0.63 | 0.64 | 0.69 | 0.67 | 0.66 | 0.65 | 0.62 | 0.67 |
| $P_{15}$ | 0.73 | 0.72 | 0.68 | 0.69 | 0.73 | 0.67 | 0.67 | 0.69 | 0.65 | 0.70 | 0.78 | 0.73 | 0.70 | 0.70 | 0.67 | 0.71 |
| $P_{25}$ | 0.81 | 0.80 | 0.77 | 0.79 | 0.80 | 0.77 | 0.77 | 0.78 | 0.78 | 0.79 | 0.78 | 0.81 | 0.79 | 0.78 | 0.77 | 0.79 |
| $P_{75}$ | 1.25 | 1.29 | 1.27 | 1.28 | 1.30 | 1.17 | 1.31 | 1.30 | 1.24 | 1.27 | 1.28 | 1.26 | 1.26 | 1.30 | 1.30 | 1.27 |
| $P_{85}$ | 1.44 | 1.51 | 1.45 | 1.51 | 1.48 | 1.59 | 1.52 | 1.50 | 1.43 | 1.44 | 1.44 | 1.45 | 1.45 | 1.53 | 1.51 | 1.50 |
| $P_{90}$ | 1.65 | 1.79 | 1.64 | 1.63 | 1.65 | 1.75 | 1.69 | 1.64 | 1.58 | 1.57 | 1.59 | 1.60 | 1.63 | 1.63 | 1.65 | 1.65 |
| $P_{95}$ | 2.06 | 2.08 | 1.84 | 1.91 | 1.97 | 2.06 | 1.99 | 1.58 | 1.90 | 2.03 | 1.87 | 1.89 | 1.82 | 2.07 | 1.92 | 1.87 |
| $P_{98}$ | 2.32 | 2.26 | 2.21 | 2.31 | 2.35 | 2.49 | 2.30 | 2.16 | 2.43 | 2.38 | 2.19 | 2.22 | 2.21 | 2.46 | 2.35 | 2.20 |
| $P_{99}$ | 2.40 | — | 2.49 | 2.66 | 2.48 | 2.63 | 2.58 | 2.36 | 2.62 | 2.49 | 2.49 | 2.47 | 2.64 | 2.98 | 2.64 | 2.50 |

Median estimated in zlotys

| $(M)$ | 1,770 | 1,861 | 2,152 | 2,417 | 2,813 | 3,765 | 4,557 | 5,878 | 1,546 | 1,668 | 1,786 | 1,984 | 2,188 | 3,040 | 3,670 | 4,472 |
|---|---|---|---|---|---|---|---|---|---|---|---|---|---|---|---|---|
| Average wage | 1,889 | 2,005 | 2,281 | 2,573 | 2,933 | 4,105 | 4,837 | 6,123 | 1,624 | 1,787 | 1,939 | 2,156 | 2,321 | 3,349 | 3,851 | 4,717 |
| $P_{99}:P_1$ | — | — | — | — | 5.64 | 6.41 | — | 5.49 | — | — | — | — | — | — | — | — |
| $P_{98}:P_2$ | — | 4.18 | — | 4.62 | 4.70 | 5.53 | 5.11 | 4.60 | — | — | — | — | — | 4.92 | — | — |
| $P_{95}:P_5$ | 3.43 | 3.47 | 3.29 | 3.29 | 3.52 | 3.81 | 3.90 | 3.48 | — | 3.56 | — | — | 3.08 | 3.70 | 3.37 | 3.17 |
| $P_{90}:P_{10}$ | 2.43 | 2.67 | 2.60 | 2.55 | 2.54 | 2.87 | 2.82 | 2.65 | 2.51 | 2.45 | — | 2.39 | 2.47 | 2.49 | 2.66 | 2.46 |
| $Q_3 - Q_1/M$ | 0.44 | 0.49 | 0.50 | 0.49 | 0.50 | 0.40 | 0.54 | 0.52 | 0.46 | 0.48 | 0.50 | 0.45 | 0.47 | 0.52 | 0.53 | 0.48 |
| $Q_3:Q_1$ | 1.54 | 1.61 | 1.65 | 1.62 | 1.62 | 1.52 | 1.70 | 1.67 | 1.59 | 1.61 | 1.64 | 1.56 | 1.59 | 1.67 | 1.69 | 1.61 |

Table 7 (continued)

| | Housing | | | | | | | | Health, welfare, sport and recreation | | | | | | | |
|---|---|---|---|---|---|---|---|---|---|---|---|---|---|---|---|---|
| | 1965 | 1967 | 1970 | 1972 | 1973 | 1976 | 1978 | 1980 | 1965 | 1967 | 1970 | 1972 | 1973 | 1976 | 1978 | 1980 |
| $P_1$ | — | — | — | — | — | — | — | 0.48 | — | — | — | — | 0.54 | — | — | — |
| $P_2$ | — | — | — | — | 0.46 | 0.42 | — | 0.54 | — | — | — | — | 0.57 | — | — | — |
| $P_5$ | 0.52 | 0.54 | 0.51 | 0.53 | 0.52 | 0.52 | 0.50 | 0.54 | — | — | — | — | 0.62 | 0.58 | — | — |
| $P_{10}$ | 0.60 | 0.61 | 0.60 | 0.61 | 0.59 | 0.60 | 0.58 | 0.61 | — | — | — | — | 0.66 | 0.64 | 0.68 | 0.69 |
| $P_{15}$ | 0.67 | 0.66 | 0.66 | 0.66 | 0.65 | 0.67 | 0.66 | 0.67 | — | — | 0.67 | — | 0.71 | 0.69 | 0.72 | 0.73 |
| $P_{25}$ | 0.78 | 0.76 | 0.76 | 0.77 | 0.77 | 0.77 | 0.76 | 0.77 | 0.75 | 0.75 | 0.74 | 0.77 | 0.79 | 0.79 | 0.83 | 0.82 |
| $P_{75}$ | 1.24 | 1.29 | 1.29 | 1.29 | 1.33 | 1.30 | 1.30 | 1.34 | 1.36 | 1.29 | 1.29 | 1.30 | 1.28 | 1.36 | 1.34 | 1.28 |
| $P_{65}$ | 1.40 | 1.48 | 1.47 | 1.53 | 1.50 | 1.58 | 1.52 | 1.55 | 1.53 | 1.54 | 1.55 | 1.55 | 1.58 | 1.62 | 1.62 | 1.52 |
| $P_{90}$ | 1.50 | 1.76 | 1.68 | 1.65 | 1.69 | 1.73 | 1.69 | 1.73 | 1.74 | 1.75 | 1.76 | 1.78 | 1.75 | 1.83 | 1.86 | 1.78 |
| $P_{95}$ | 1.90 | 2.04 | 1.88 | 1.93 | 1.95 | 2.03 | 2.02 | 2.04 | 2.05 | 2.29 | 2.14 | 2.25 | 2.21 | 2.36 | 2.27 | 2.12 |
| $P_{98}$ | 2.24 | 2.22 | 2.26 | 2.29 | 2.45 | 2.45 | 2.37 | 2.41 | 2.81 | 2.75 | 2.53 | 2.76 | 2.86 | 3.02 | 2.80 | 2.55 |
| $P_{99}$ | 2.36 | 2.28 | 2.55 | 2.65 | 2.62 | 2.58 | 2.62 | 2.65 | 3.15 | 2.91 | 2.90 | 2.98 | 3.07 | 3.43 | 3.19 | 2.89 |

Median estimated in zlotys

| | | | | | | | | | | | | | | | | |
|---|---|---|---|---|---|---|---|---|---|---|---|---|---|---|---|---|
| (M) | 1,746 | 1,884 | 2,094 | 2,376 | 2,637 | 3,831 | 4,455 | 5,533 | 1,256 | 1,454 | 1,550 | 1,689 | 2,279 | 2,725 | 2,984 | 3,861 |
| Average wage | 1,711 | 1,890 | 2,148 | 2,400 | 2,596 | 4,014 | 4,711 | 5,912 | 1,472 | 1,622 | 1,738 | 1,981 | 2,433 | 3,360 | 3,588 | 4,718 |
| $P_{99}{:}P_1$ | — | — | — | — | — | 5.83 | — | 5.02 | — | — | — | — | 5.69 | — | — | — |
| $P_{98}{:}P_2$ | — | — | — | — | 5.33 | 3.90 | 4.04 | 3.78 | — | — | — | — | 5.02 | — | — | — |
| $P_{95}{:}P_5$ | 3.65 | 3.78 | 3.69 | 3.64 | 3.75 | 2.88 | 2.91 | 2.84 | — | — | — | — | 3.56 | 4.07 | — | — |
| $P_{90}{:}P_{10}$ | 2.50 | 2.88 | 2.80 | 2.70 | 2.86 | — | — | — | — | — | — | — | 2.65 | 2.86 | 2.73 | 2.58 |
| $Q_3 - Q_1/M$ | 0.46 | 0.53 | 0.53 | 0.52 | 0.56 | 0.53 | 0.54 | 0.57 | 0.61 | 0.54 | 0.55 | 0.53 | 0.49 | 0.57 | 0.51 | 0.46 |
| $Q_3{:}Q_1$ | 1.59 | 1.70 | 1.70 | 1.68 | 1.73 | 1.69 | 1.71 | 1.74 | 1.81 | 1.72 | 1.74 | 1.69 | 1.62 | 1.72 | 1.61 | 1.56 |

Table 7 (continued)

| | Education and training | | | | | Science | | | |
|---|---|---|---|---|---|---|---|---|---|
| | 1970 | 1972 | 1973 | 1976 | 1978 | 1970 | 1972 | 1978 | 1980 |
| $P_1$ | — | — | — | — | — | — | — | 0.40 | 0.44 |
| $P_2$ | — | — | — | — | — | — | 0.42 | 0.42 | 0.47 |
| $P_5$ | — | — | — | — | — | 0.46 | 0.50 | 0.49 | 0.54 |
| $P_{10}$ | — | — | 0.52 | 0.50 | 0.54 | 0.55 | 0.58 | 0.60 | 0.61 |
| $P_{15}$ | — | — | 0.58 | 0.57 | 0.61 | 0.62 | 0.65 | 0.65 | 0.68 |
| $P_{25}$ | 0.73 | 0.66 | 0.73 | 0.72 | 0.73 | 0.75 | 0.76 | 0.77 | 0.78 |
| $P_{75}$ | 1.29 | 1.29 | 1.29 | 1.28 | 1.29 | 1.37 | 1.31 | 1.30 | 1.31 |
| $P_{65}$ | 1.46 | 1.53 | 1.53 | 1.48 | 1.47 | 1.52 | 1.54 | 1.51 | 1.50 |
| $P_{95}$ | 1.63 | 1.68 | 1.65 | 1.60 | 1.59 | 1.60 | 1.69 | 1.71 | 1.66 |
| $P_{98}$ | 1.96 | 1.96 | 1.98 | 1.98 | 1.82 | — | — | 1.98 | 1.92 |
| $P_{99}$ | 2.30 | 2.34 | 2.50 | 2.26 | 2.11 | — | — | 2.34 | 2.25 |
| $P_{90}$ | 2.75 | 2.78 | 2.78 | 2.74 | 2.44 | — | — | — | 2.44 |

Median estimated in zlotys

| | | | | | | | | | |
|---|---|---|---|---|---|---|---|---|---|
| (M) | 1,722 | 2,270 | 2,396 | 3,065 | 3,743 | 2,612 | 2,900 | 5,062 | 5,729 |
| Average wage | 1,933 | 2,321 | 2,566 | 3,309 | 3,885 | 2,718 | 3,174 | 5,384 | 6,185 |
| $P_{99}:P_1$ | — | — | — | — | — | — | — | — | 5.55 |
| $P_{98}:P_2$ | — | — | — | — | — | — | — | 5.57 | 4.79 |
| $P_{95}:P_5$ | — | — | — | — | — | — | — | 4.04 | 3.56 |
| $P_{90}:P_{10}$ | — | — | 3.17 | 3.20 | 2.94 | 2.91 | 2.91 | 2.85 | 2.72 |
| $Q_3 - Q_1/M$ | 0.56 | 0.63 | 0.56 | 0.56 | 0.56 | 0.62 | 0.55 | 0.53 | 0.53 |
| $Q_3:Q_1$ | 1.77 | 1.95 | 1.77 | 1.78 | 1.77 | 1.83 | 1.72 | 1.69 | 1.65 |

*Source*: See Table 6.

Table 8

## Percent of Total Earnings Accruing to Earners in Successive Decile Groups

| Decile groups | 1970 | 1972 | 1976 | 1978 | 1980 | January 1981 | 1981 | 1982 |
|---|---|---|---|---|---|---|---|---|
| I | 4.5 | 4.6 | 4.4 | 4.4 | 4.6 | 5.3 | — | — |
| II | 5.9 | 6.0 | 5.8 | 5.7 | 6.0 | 6.6 | — | — |
| III | 7.0 | 7.0 | 6.8 | 6.8 | 6.9 | 7.5 | — | — |
| IV | 7.9 | 7.8 | 7.7 | 7.7 | 7.8 | 8.3 | — | — |
| V | 8.7 | 8.7 | 8.5 | 8.6 | 8.7 | 9.0 | — | — |
| VI | 9.7 | 9.5 | 9.5 | 9.5 | 9.6 | 9.8 | — | — |
| VII | 10.7 | 10.6 | 10.6 | 10.7 | 10.7 | 10.7 | — | — |
| VIII | 12.0 | 11.9 | 12.0 | 12.0 | 12.0 | 11.9 | — | — |
| IX | 13.9 | 13.9 | 14.3 | 14.3 | 14.0 | 13.5 | — | — |
| X | 19.7 | 20.0 | 20.4 | 20.4 | 19.7 | 17.4 | — | — |
| Ratio of average earnings of top and bottom decile groups | 4.38 | 4.35 | 4.64 | 4.64 | 4.28 | 3.28 | — | — |
| Coefficient of maximum equalization (E) | 16.5 | — | 17.5 | 17.5 | 16.6 | 13.5 | 15.2 | 14.2 |
| Decile ratio* | 2.84 | 2.82 | 3.05 | 3.05 | 2.88 | 2.36 | 2.53 | 2.35 |

*Sources: R.S. 1975,* (Warsaw: GUS), table 6(158), 118; ibid., *1977,* table 7(150), 167; ibid., *1981,* table 9(184), 167, and table 10(188), 169; ibid., *1983,* table 10(210), 146; data for January 1981, Jan Kordos "Szacunek rozkładu zatrudnionych w gospodarce uspołecznionej według wysokości płac za styczeń 1981" [An estimation of dispersion of wages of the employees in the socialized sector as of January 1981], in *Wiadomości statystyczne,* 1981, No. 6, part 3.

*The decile ratio is the ratio of the highest earnings in the bottom 90% of earnings to the highest earnings in the bottom 10% of earnings. The decile ratio can also be expressed as the ratio of the highest earnings in the ninth decile group to the highest earnings in the first decile group. In short, it is the ratio of the ninth to the first decile ($D_9/D_1$).

the socialized sectors exhibit the same trend, but the earnings of manual workers are more unequally distributed, at least on the extreme tail of the distribution (see $P_{95}/P_5$, $P_{90}/P_{10}$).

Data in Tables 6 and 7 show that the relative dispersion measured by all indicators of inequality used in this book in the main sectors of the socialized economy increased from 1972 to 1978 much more than in the socialized sector as a whole. Three major productive sectors, construction, industry, and transport, which together comprise about 50% of all employees in the socialized sector, led in changes in relative dispersion of earnings.[17]

More rapid changes in relative dispersion in some specific sectors than the socialized sector as a whole can be partly explained by the remarkable decline in wage differentials between sectors. As can be seen from the data in Table 7, the differences in the median of the highest- and the lowest-paid sectors in 1970–78 substantially declined. The reduction of intersectoral differentials is noticeable as well if measured by differences in average money wages. Official spokesmen have promised further reductions in intersectoral differentials in years to come.[18]

Despite a decline in wage differentials between sectors, the leading sectors and those that trail behind are always the same. Those sectors that thirteen years ago had earnings either below or above the national average were in 1980 still in exactly the same situation.

Although the changes in relative dispersion of earnings were rather modest, although not negligible, the absolute changes in dispersion were very substantial, especially in 1972–74, due to the much more rapid increase in wages and salaries that took place after the downfall of Gomulka at the end of 1970. The new Gierek regime immediately granted very substantial increases in wages in 1971. This abrupt spurt of wage increases was unprecedented in previous decades.

Although the decile distribution of wages for the socialized sector in Poland is not available for all years analyzed here, the available data in Table 8 establish without doubt that there was a major increase in dispersion of wages in Gierek's Poland in

1972–78. This process changed abruptly in the summer of 1980 with the ascendence of the Solidarity movement, whose demands, expressed in the Gdansk Accord, for a more egalitarian income distribution[19] were partially implemented between 1980 and 1982. Although there is no doubt that even the partial implementation of Solidarity's wage and incomes policy has reduced inequalities, the spectacular drop in relative dispersion of earnings between 1980 and 1982 claimed by the official statistics is probably exaggerated, because the official statistical data in this period of turmoil are particularly unreliable.

As can be seen from Table 8, although the extreme differences are substantial, at the same time we observe a very high concentration of wages. For 80% of employees (measured by the ratio of the ninth to the first decile) the differences are not larger than 3 times, and for 90% of the employees (measured by the ratio of the ninth decile to the minimum wage) not more than 3-4.5 times.

For the overwhelming majority of employees in all sectors, differences in wages are small; only for the lowest and highest 10% of wage earners are wage differences relatively high.[20] The pressure of Solidarity for a more egalitarian distribution of wages has further deepened the process of concentration of wages, reducing even more sharply differences in wages between 80 and 90% of all employees. Lidia Beskid[21] called such a distribution pattern egalitarian-elitarian.

Time series data for most nonmaterial sectors are incomplete and defective, so no full analysis of changes in relative dispersion is possible. However, these data do support the conclusion that the relative dispersion of distribution has narrowed (see the health sector and education and training) and is not significantly different from the major productive sectors, with the exception of construction, and is rather higher than in such material production sectors as housing and trade.

The relatively high degree of dispersion of earnings in health and education as compared, for example, with housing and trade relates to the relatively low pay received in this sector by employees at the lower end of the distribution; whereas in the upper end

Table 9

## Average Pay by Occupational Category in State Industry (Manual Workers = 100)

| | 1965 | 1970 | 1972 | 1973 | 1974 | 1975 | 1977 | 1978 | 1979 | 1980 | 1981 | 1982 |
|---|---|---|---|---|---|---|---|---|---|---|---|---|
| 1. Technical-engineering personnel | 161 | 150 | 146 | 144 | 141 | 138 | 132 | 132 | 131 | 125 | 120 | 120 |
| 2. Administrative and clerical personnel | 108 | 103 | 101 | 100 | 97 | 94 | 88 | 88 | 87 | 85 | 86 | 87 |

*Source:* Calculated from *R.S 1976* (Warsaw: GUS), table 28(231); ibid., *1979*, table 12(195); ibid., 1981, table 7(185), 164; ibid., *1982*, table 7(163), 125; ibid., *1983*, table 7(207), 142; *Mały Rocznik Statystyczny 1980* (Warsaw: GUS), table 15(99), 107.

of the distribution, especially in the top wage brackets, earnings are comparable or at least are not much lower than in other sectors.[22]

Referring back to Table 6, differences in earnings measured by a comparison of the median manual and the median nonmanual wage are very low indeed and have a tendency over time to become even more marginal. For example, in 1967 nonmanual earnings measured by the median were 6% higher than manual earnings, whereas in 1978 they were only 3% higher. Of course, these comparisons between the earnings of these two strata reflect broad averages. Differences between high-ranking officials and skilled and unskilled workers are still substantial although difficult to document for the socialized sector as a whole.[23] Some available evidence on wage differences between major occupational groups in socialized industry is summarized in Table 9.

Table 9 suggests that:

a)  Differences in earnings among strata have declined—a tendency discernible in other socialist countries.[24]

b)  The pay of highly educated employees (technical-engineering personnel) is still substantially higher, and they constitute the most privileged group in terms of wages.

c)  The biggest losers are routine white-collar workers, whose relative position is visibly deteriorating.

d)  The manual workers are not doing badly. They have overtaken the routine white-collar workers and have reduced the distance between them and top personnel.

Are the official figures in Table 9 sufficient to justify the claims of socialist authorities that they have overcome the manual and nonmanual dichotomy? That egalitarianism, the great promise of a classless society, has indeed been achieved? Such an optimistic view is far from reality. The nonmanual/manual stratification dichotomy is still very much alive.

There are several important factors that make the official data on wage differences between manual and nonmanual inadequate as an accurate indicator of differences in well-being between these two strata.

First, conditions of work are less favorable for manual than nonmanual employees. For example:

a) Manual workers are more exposed to the health hazards of noise, toxic substances, high temperature, accidents, and injuries.

b) Manual workers are subjected to tighter work discipline than nonmanual employees. Manual workers are not only subject to their superiors but are also controlled by machines and production quotas. Very often work is performed in tiring positions.

c) A manual worker's earnings are less stable and to a larger degree depend on the supply of new materials, the quality of tools and equipment, stoppages, and other factors over which he has no control, especially in an environment where his participation in management is very limited or nonexistent.

Second, official distribution statistics suffer a number of important limitations, one of which is that they do not encompass all incomes from work by particular groups. Opportunities for performing extra work and therefore obtaining extra pay are not uniformly available. A sociological study of Lodz (the second largest city in Poland) showed that 25% of the intelligentsia but only 6.3% of the skilled and 3.3% of the unskilled manual workers had additional jobs.[25]

Third, the housing conditions of nonmanual workers are substantially better than those of manual workers. A study by the Polish Institute of Housing[26] shows vividly that:

a) Nonmanual families have substantially more space per person on the average than manual families.

b) A much larger proportion of nonmanual families have more modern facilities in their homes. For example, central heating has been installed in only 24.1% of the flats of manual employees but in 54.2% of the flats of nonmanual employees, and bathrooms are even more unevenly divided between the housing of the two groups.[27]

c) The percentage of nonmanual households that have received new and better flats is larger than the percentage of manual households. This is true both of flats allocated free by state enterprises and of those allocated through different cooperative forms. These privileges are usually explained by the greater influence and "connections" of nonmanual employees in the enterprises and social institutions that make the allocation decisions. Not without importance in achieving those privileges is the "strength and vitality" of this social stratum in pursuing its interests. Superior lobbying ability due to better knowledge, education, and social prestige help the nonmanual stratum get many legal and semilegal privileges.

Although discrepancies between nonmanual and manual earnings have declined in Poland, as in other socialist countries, in comparison with the prewar period and are smaller than in the Western countries,[28] differences in terms of earnings from a second job, access to superior housing, and working conditions are still substantial, as are differences in education and lifestyle. Manual workers, particularly the unskilled and semiskilled, are the underdogs in these societies despite any rhetoric about the privileged position of the working class. Even the skilled workers, if we take into consideration special benefits and other incomes not reported in the official statistics, are still worse off than white-collar clerical personnel.

I do not share the view of some Western sociologists that the "big gap" between manual and nonmanual exists only in capitalist and not socialist countries. Parkin and Lane[29] have argued that in many Eastern European countries, highly skilled manual workers enjoy a higher position in the scale of material and status rewards and promotion prospects than lower nonmanual employees. Therefore they suggest that the major stratification break lies between the skilled and unskilled categories, irrespective of whether they are manual or nonmanual employees. Although there is some validity to their observations, they are quite exaggerated. They do not take into consideration the factors mentioned above, which go beyond mere differences in official wages and salaries: certainly the assertation of skilled workers having greater prospects for promotion is more wishful thinking than reality. The chances for social and professional advancement for people working as manual workers are quite limited. Studies done by the Polish sociologist H. Najduchowska,[30] have shown that it is quite rare for someone to advance from a manual worker position directly to a director's job without going through the lengthy process of obtaining formal education in evening colleges and universities in order to be eligible for these responsible jobs. Moreover, relatively speaking, not many manual workers participate in this kind of schooling. There is instead a tendency for manual workers to upgrade their qualifications as skilled manual workers. Thus the division along manual/nonmanual lines still better reflects the real stratification process than the division of all employees into skilled and unskilled.[31] Thus the socialist countries have not as yet done away with the major socioeconomic differences between the categories of manual and nonmanual employees.[32]

If concern is focused on the lower end of income distribution, other negative aspects of the Polish experience become apparent. For example, the Polish authorities were not very successful in bringing the lowest wages nearer the average level. Although the minimum wage has frequently been increased, the gap between it and the average wage has not changed over time. In 1970 the minimum wage was 40% of the average wage; in 1976, 1978, and 1980 this ratio was, respectively, 33, 34, and 41, according to the data in Table 6.[33]

A decline over time in the share of the lowest 2, 5, and 10 percentiles of earners ($P_2$, $P_5$, $P_{10}$) in industry is another indication that the distance between low-wage earners and the average wage level has increased. Although as time goes by the proportion of the labor force in the lowest income brackets has declined, still the proportion of all employees who received less than the average wage in 1978 actually did not change.[34] In this respect there has been no tangible progress in the '70s compared to the '60s. Another indicator of inequality, the ratio of the highest to the lowest wage, has also deteriorated. In 1978 the ratio of the highest to the lowest wage was 11:1 (17,600 Zl/1,600 Zl), whereas in the '60s this ratio was smaller.[35]

As suggested above, wage disparities captured by our statistical analysis, although important, are not sufficient to measure actual earning differences. The differentiation of legal and semi-legal privileges substantially affects the purchasing power of earned money wages. The importance of wage differentials is declining because there exist ways to spend wages differently. There are, as A. Tymowski excellently put it, "zloties which are heavy and zloties which are light."[36] The dispersion of actual earnings is determined not only and not mainly by money wages but, in addition to the "moonlighting" already mentioned, also by special benefits deriving from the state and the ability to obtain scarce goods and services due to "connections" and position.[37] Although obviously there are no published data, it is possible to infer the main beneficiaries of these privileges by noting who has attractive vacation houses in the country and abroad, foreign currency to travel, subsidies for cars,[38] subsidies for relatively large flats, etc. All these privileges can increase relative dispersion of real earnings, especially between the extreme percentiles of the distribution. The official statistical ratio of 11:1 for the highest to the lowest level of earnings in 1978 thus may well be greatly underestimated.[39]

Such abnormalities in distribution spurred a lively discussion in *Polityka* and other journals between the egalitarianists (for example, A. Tymowski) and the nonegalitarianists on the eve of the Eighth Party Congress in 1980. The proponents of egalitarianism proposed: (a) a maximum wage ceiling linked to the increase in the lowest wage; (b) a more rapid increase in minimum than in maximum wages; (c) expansion of services and consumer goods for the lower- and middle-income groups before catering to the demands of the more affluent; (d) an end to the augmentation of high incomes through the granting of special privileges. Other authors, for example, E. Skalski and K. Daszkiewicz,[40] supporting by and large A. Tymowski's point of view, went further and proposed that all benefits in kind should gradually be converted to cash payments and included in the maximum wage ceiling. As a result, all incomes of the privileged would be accounted for.

Many authors deny that maximum or minimum wage ceilings will reduce relative dispersion of earnings as long as the actual relative dispersion continues to be affected by the receipt of illegal and semilegal and unrecorded incomes in the form of bribes, tips, gifts, moonlighting, etc., characteristic of the so-called second economy. These sources of incomes have increased in the last ten years and, according to some authors, have become, together with nonmoney privileges granted by the state, the main source of increased inequality.[41]

This position is not shared by all economists in the socialist countries. Some high-ranking economic functionaries in Hungary firmly believe that, for example, moonlighting as a part of the "second economy" actually equalizes incomes because, according to their estimates, while 30% of the lowest wage bracket moonlight, only 2% of the highest wage bracket do so. The majority of middle-income earners are not involved in the "gray" income sphere.[42] Moreover, according to the proponents of this point of view, in the first lowest quartile (Q) the "gray" income represents approximately one-third of normal (white) income, whereas in the top brackets, "gray" income represents a smaller part of total earnings.[43] It is thus difficult to judge whether earnings derived from the "second economy" increase or decrease the relative dispersion of all real earnings. Different components of the "second economy" may have different effects. What is apparent, however, is that the actual distribution differs from the recorded statistical picture. In the presence of a substantial "second economy" it is very difficult to establish with any certainty who gets what.

Whatever the origins of the second economy in socialist countries, its development is closely linked with the existence of shortages. A "good market" is a good antidote for the second economy. Although all socialist countries are encountering some disequilibria in the consumer market, Poland's shortages in the last couple of years provide an extreme case of disequilibrium with grave social and political consequences. An analysis of such imbalance is beyond the scope of this work, but one point is worth stressing: Poland cannot overcome its serious economic crises without major socioeconomic reforms that eliminate the reasons for disequilibrium and accompanying social tension, as the events in Poland since the summer of 1980 have made clear.

With the help of Table 1, which provides comparable information for Hungary to that provided by Table 6 and 7 for Poland, the following summary comparison of distribution in Poland and Hungary can be made.

1. Relative dispersion of wages in the '60s and '70s in the whole socialized sector, as in most of its segments, is substantially higher in Poland than in Hungary. In 1982 the situation was reversed, and relative dispersion of earnings, according to official statistics, was in the socialized sector slightly higher in Hungary than in Poland.

2. Changes in relative dispersion of earnings are going in the same direction in these two countries. In Hungary, for the whole period 1966-78, despite the decline in the relative dispersion of wages in the period 1974-78, the inequality of distribution in the socialized sector has increased. The same trend is visible in Poland for the whole period of 1965 to 1978. However, there are some differences between these two countries in the direction of changes in the subperiods under investigation. In Hungary from 1966 to 1974 we have a clear increase in relative dispersion of earnings, and only in the last four years do we observe a decline in it that partially balances the previous inegalitarian trend; whereas in Poland in 1965–72, changes are marginal, and only in 1972–78 does relative dispersion increase substantially.

3. In Hungary both inter- and intrasectoral differences in dispersion of wages increased (see Appendix Table B),[44] whereas in Poland only intrasectoral differences widened. A decline in intersectoral differentials in Poland worked against the increase in intrasectoral differences in wages. As a result of changes in different directions in the intra- and intersectoral differentials, the relative dispersion of wages in the socialized sector as a whole increased much less than its major segments.

4. Differences in average wages and median earnings between

sectors of the socialized economy from 1968 to 1978 declined in
Poland, while they increased in Hungary. However, differences
in Hungarian average wages between sectors are still much smaller than in Poland.

5. In both countries the differences between manual and nonmanual earnings are very small, and in both countries the discrepancies between earnings of nonmanual and manual employees have declined. However, in Poland, the relative gains of the
manual workers in this respect are more strongly pronounced than
in Hungary.[45]

# CHAPTER III

# The Distribution of per Capita Household Income in Hungary

To find a framework to analyze how different variables affect the distribution of per capita household income,[1] the Hungarian Statistical Office has proposed an identity equation which we will use for our analysis of both Hungary and Poland. The formula is:

$$\frac{Y}{N} = B_1 \cdot \frac{W/K}{B_1} \cdot \frac{K}{N} \cdot \frac{Y}{W},$$

where

$Y =$ total income of the household,

$N =$ number of persons in the household,

$B_1 =$ average earnings of the head of household,

$W =$ wages and salaries of the household,

$K =$ number of active earners in the household,

$W/K/B_1 =$ the ratio of average earnings to those of the head of the household,

$B_1 \cdot W/K/B_1 = W/K =$ average earnings per earner in the household,

$K/N =$ the proportion of active earners in the total household, or its rate of activity,

$Y/W =$ an index showing the proportion of total income exceeding wages and salaries (this reflects social benefits).

From the formula the average per capita household income depends on:

a) average earnings per active member of the household $(W/K)$;

b) the rate of activity of the household $(K/N)$;

c) the proportion of total income to wages and salaries combined $(Y/W)$.

The relative dispersion of per capita household income depends respectively on:

a) the relative dispersion of earnings per active household member;

b) the relative dispersion of the households' activity rates;

c) the relative dispersion of the ratio $Y/W$.

To explain the variables that dynamically affect the distribution of per capita income in terms of the formula, it would be necessary to establish the contribution of each factor to changes in relative dispersion of per capita household income $(Y/N)$ in quantitative terms. To do so we would need to compute the variance of $Y/N$ in terms of the variances of the elements of the right-hand side of the equation $(W/K \cdot K/N \cdot Y/W)$ and the covariances between those elements. However, we do not have statistical data for such computation, specially data about the relative dispersion of household activity rates and social benefits in total through time. We can therefore use this formula only as a framework for a priori reasoning.

Statistical analysis has shown that differences in per capita household income between social strata and occupational groups reflect primarily differences in earnings of the head of the household (there is a linear relationship between the two).[2] Demographic factors—the average size of households and the ratio of wage earners to dependents $(K/N)$—are more or less the same on average across all groups of activities,[3] and therefore explain only a small part of differences in per capita household income between strata. By contrast, so far as differences in household income per capita within social and occupational groups are concerned, the only influences of any importance are the size and the earner-dependent ratio of the household $(K/N)$. This is evident from the fact that the per capita income levels of large households are much lower than those of small or single-person households. The difference between per capita incomes of one- and six-member households, for example, is 2:1 (in Poland in 1978 this ratio was 2.7:1). There is therefore no strong relationship between the standard of living (measured by per capita income) of the household and its average earnings. A highly skilled worker can belong to the highest wage bracket, but his household can belong to the lowest per capita income bracket if he has many children, and if his household is therefore characterized by an unfavorable earner-dependent ratio.

By and large in the total worker-employee population, two factors combined determine differences in per capita household incomes:[4]

a) The place of the active members of the household in the social division of labor (whether manual or nonmanual workers, skilled or unskilled, managers, clerks, etc.). Their place in a particular group of activity will affect their average earnings.

b) The composition of the households. This determines to a large degree the differences in per capita household income within every strata and group.

Together these two factors account for more than 60% of the overall differences in per capita household incomes.[5]

Some Hungarian economists[6] firmly believe that wages have a weak stimulative effect in large households with unfavorable earner-dependent ratios. On the other hand, one questions whether wage incentives are in fact heavily reduced because of the composition of the household.

The incentive role of wages in large households with an unfavorable ratio of earners to dependents is a complex problem not very well researched in economic literature. However, a few general points can be made that rather stress the incentive role of wages, despite the unfavorable composition of the households.

1. Earnings are rightly perceived in the first place as payments to the individual for work and not as a remuneration to the household. Peer pressures on the shop floor create an atmosphere

Table 10

**Dispersion of Household Income Per Capita in Hungary, 1962, 1967, 1972, and 1977**

|  | 1962 | 1967 | 1972 | 1977 |
|---|---|---|---|---|
| Share of total per capita income received by: |  |  |  |  |
| Bottom decile group | 3.6 | 4.1 | 4.0 | 4.5 |
| Top decile group | 20.7 | 18.9 | 19.9 | 18.6 |
| Ratio of average per capita income in top and bottom decile groups | 5.8 | 4.6 | 5.0 | 4.1 |
| Monthly household income per capita in forints received by: |  |  |  |  |
| Average per capita income of bottom decile group | 334 | 494 | 676 | — |
| Average per capita income of top decile group | 1,920 | 2.275 | 3,366 | — |
| Difference | 1,586 | 1,781 | 2,690 | — |

Source: For 1962, Z. Mihály, "Alakosság jövedelme és fogyasztásá alakulásának tendenciái" [Changes in the income and consumption of the population], *Statisztikai Szemle*, table 14, 1204, December 1977; for 1967, 1972, and 1977, see *A. C 1972* (Budapest: KSH, 1975), 65; *A.C 1977* (1980), 107.

of "competition" and drive to achieve the highest possible earnings as a part of one's self-worth.

2. Earnings comprise even more than half of the total income (including all benefits) of most low per capita income households with an unfavorable earner-dependent ratio. Only in extreme cases, when there is only one breadwinner with low skills and a lot of children to maintain, will earnings represent less than half of the total income of the household.

3. The marginal utility of money wages of the poor households, which are mostly large, is higher than of well-to-do households, which are usually smaller.

Hungary began its economic reform after a long period during which the relative dispersion of per capita household income had been declining. Table 10 shows that in 1962, the top 10% of the population received nearly six times more per capita household income than the lowest 10% of the population, and that by 1967, this had declined to only 4.6 times.[7]

Table 11

## Per Capita Household Income of Main Strata of the Population Relative to Manual Workers Per Capita Household Income in Hungary, 1965 to 1977*

| Years | Peasants | Double-income group** | Nonmanual workers | Pensioners, etc., | Total |
|---|---|---|---|---|---|
| | | | (Manual Workers = 100) | | |
| 1965 | 93 | 98 | 133 | 79 | 103 |
| 1966 | 94 | 100 | 132 | 80 | 103 |
| 1967 | 98 | 101 | 133 | 79 | 104 |
| 1968 | 102 | 105 | 132 | 78 | 106 |
| 1969 | 102 | 106 | 133 | 76 | 107 |
| 1970 | 104 | 111 | 134 | 75 | 108 |
| 1971 | 106 | 111 | 137 | 77 | 109 |
| 1972 | 106 | 112 | 137 | 77 | 109 |
| 1973 | 107 | 114 | 134 | 80 | 109 |
| 1974 | 105 | 113 | 130 | 80 | 108 |
| 1975 | 103-4 | 112 | 129 | 80 | 107 |
| 1977 | — | 114 | 127 | 84 | 105 |

*Source*: J. Bálint, "Társadalmunk rétegeződése és a jövdelemarányok a statisztika tükrében" [Societies' stratification and distribution of income in statistical terms], *Társadalmi Szemle*, April 1976, 44; for 1977: *A.C 1977* (Budapest: KSH, 1980), 33.

 *Including social benefits in cash but not in kind.

**Double-income groups are households that derive their incomes from both agriculture and other sectors.

It must be stressed, however, that the decline in overall inequality of per capita income dispersion was not the result of any levelling of wages and salaries but rather of a more rapid increase in the incomes of peasants than of other social groups, brought about by a deliberate state policy. This enabled them to catch up and even overtake the workers in per capita household income (see Table 11).

Another factor that contributed to a decline in the relative dispersion of per capita household income, in both the pre- and post-reform periods, was, *ceteris paribus*, a very rapid increase in social benefits,[8] which grew much faster than earned income

Table 12

**Per Capita Monthly Income in the Households of Different Types of Occupation**

| In households where the head is: | Unskilled workers = 100 | | | |
|---|---|---|---|---|
| | 1962 | 1967 | 1972 | 1977 |
| Leading officials and high level professionals | 186.6 | 166.0 | 171.1 | 171.9 |
| Medium-level professionals | 154.9 | 144.0 | 145.9 | 132.7 |
| Clerical employees | 145.0 | 131.0 | 125.9 | 117.6 |
| Skilled workers | 132.6 | 122.0 | 116.3 | 115.7 |
| Semiskilled workers | 114.7 | 108.0 | 104.0 | 108.0 |
| Agricultural manual workers | 106.0 | 116.0 | 122.5 | 121.7 |
| Pensioners or nonearners | 101.6 | 94.0 | 96.1 | 106.0 |
| Total | 121.4 | 117.0 | 116.2 | 116.6 |

*Source*: For 1962: *Social Stratification in Hungary* (Budapest: Central Statistical Office, 1967), 19, 38; for 1967: *A Lakosság jövedelme és fogyasztása 1968–1969* (Budapest, KSH, 1970), 30-32; for 1972 and 1977: *A.C 1972* (Budapest, KSH, 1975), 33: ibid., *1977* (1980), 33.

and represented 1/3 of all incomes in 1982 and 1983, whereas this figure was only 18.7% in 1960 (see Appendix C). Especially rapid growth occurred in social benefits, paid in cash. From 1960 to 1979 social benefit in cash increased (in money terms) 8.5 times, whereas social benefit in kind rose only 4.5 times.[9]

In the prereform period differences in average per capita household income between strata had become very moderate (see Table 11 and 12). Nonmanual employees had, on the average, a per capita income no more than 32% higher than manual workers. The leading officials' household per capita income in comparison with the unskilled workers' household declined from 186.6 in 1972 to a modest 166% in 1967.

However, the proportion of households with high and low per capita income varies considerably between different social strata and occupational groups. For example, in 1967 there were 9–10 times more leading professional households with 2,000 forints per capita incomes per month than was the case with unskilled workers, while only 2.9% of leading professional households had a per capita income below 800 forints, compared with 31%[10] for unskilled workers. Differences between the lowest and highest per capita incomes of the population are therefore quite substantial.

In the first five years of the reform, changes in the relative dispersion of per capita household income were less favorable to lower-income groups than before the reform. Table 11 shows that between 1967 and 1972, workers lost slightly to all social strata except pensioners.[11] At its November plenum of 1972, the Party Central Committee made a dramatic decision to reverse this trend. In 1973 a one-time 8% increase in manual workers wages and other social policies partially restored the 1970 relative position of the peasants and nonmanual workers; since 1973 the relative position of the nonmanual employees has obviously deteriorated compared to that before the reform.

Certain inegalitarian tendencies are evident as well if the relative per capita position of different groups is compared by type of activity (see Table 12). In 1972 there was, in comparison to 1967, an increase in disparities between leading officials and professionals and the unskilled workers. However, if we take into consideration the whole period from 1962 to 1977, we see a decline in the relative position of the privileged group. For example, households of leading officials and professionals received 1.72 times the per capita income of unskilled workers in 1977, whereas in 1962 they received 1.87 times.[12]

By and large, changes in dispersion of per capita income between social strata in the postreform period have not been substantial. Household per capita incomes for all major social strata have grown more or less at the same rate. However, as mentioned above, differences in average per capita household incomes between major strata and occupational groups conceal greater differences within each stratum and occupational group. In 1967, 1972, and 1977, the disparities between the highest and the lowest per capita income groups were quite substantial. For example, the top 10% of the households received 4.5 times more personal income per capita in 1967 than the bottom 10%, as compared with 5.0 and 4.1 times more in 1972 and 1977 (see Table 13).

As the data in Table 13 indicate, changes in relative dispersion of per capita personal income between 1967 and 1972 were minor. But in 1977 we observe a marked decline in relative dispersion in comparison with the previous years, not only for households in total but also for each social stratum except peasants. By and large, the changes from 1967 to 1977 are rather on the egalitarian side, but the scope of changes is moderate. Selected percentiles to the median and other measures of inequality computed in Appendix Table D corroborate this conclusion.

Appendix Table D shows that relative dispersion of personal household income per capita increased between 1967 and 1972 for one group—pensioners. On the other hand, the relative dispersion of per capita household income of manual workers clearly declined in the upper tail of distribution.

Table D also shows that between 1972 and 1977, relative dispersion of per capita household income declined in all categories, and that the level of inequality was even slightly lower than in 1967. This should be considered a success for the state's incomes policy after implementing the reform.

Moreover, the relative dispersion of personal household income per capita is very low by the standards of the capitalist countries, both developed and underdeveloped. For example, as can be seen from Table 13, the ratio of the top to the bottom 20% of per capita household incomes is only about 3:1, whereas in the United States, Canada, and the U.K. this ratio is over 7:1.[13] As far as the less developed capitalist countries of the third world are concerned, the discrepancy is even higher: the ratio is over 10:1.[14] This is more or less the ratio that had existed in Hungary before the war.[15]

## Social Benefits in Cash and Kind

*Family Allowances*

In Hungary all households with two or more children are eligible

Table 13

**Distribution of Household Income per Capita by Social Stratum in Hungary, 1967, 1972, and 1977 (% of household income)**

| | Decile groups | | | | | | | | | | Quotient | Ratio of top to bottom decile groups | Share of total per capita income received by top 5% of households |
|---|---|---|---|---|---|---|---|---|---|---|---|---|---|
| | 1 | 2 | 3 | 4 | 5 | 6 | 7 | 8 | 9 | 10 | | | |
| 1967 | | | | | | | | | | | | | |
| Workers | 4.3 | 6.2 | 7.3 | 8.2 | 9.0 | 9.9 | 10.9 | 12.1 | 13.9 | 18.2 | 1.85 | 4.2 | 10.2 |
| Peasants | 4.0 | 5.9 | 7.0 | 8.0 | 8.9 | 9.9 | 11.0 | 12.3 | 14.1 | 18.9 | 1.94 | 4.7 | 10.8 |
| Double-income group | 4.8 | 6.6 | 7.6 | 8.5 | 9.3 | 10.0 | 10.9 | 11.9 | 13.4 | 17.0 | 1.71 | 3.5 | 9.4 |
| Nonmanual employees | 5.0 | 6.5 | 7.4 | 8.1 | 9.0 | 9.8 | 10.6 | 11.7 | 13.4 | 18.5 | 1.77 | 3.7 | 10.6 |
| Self-employed | 3.3 | 5.7 | 6.8 | 7.8 | 8.6 | 9.6 | 10.8 | 12.2 | 13.9 | 21.3 | 2.09 | 6.4 | 12.5 |
| Total active households | 4.2 | 6.1 | 7.2 | 8.1 | 8.9 | 9.9 | 10.9 | 12.1 | 13.9 | 18.7 | 1.88 | 4.4 | 10.7 |
| Pensioners | 4.2 | 5.9 | 7.0 | 8.0 | 8.9 | 9.8 | 10.9 | 12.2 | 14.0 | 19.1 | 1.93 | 4.5 | 10.9 |
| All households | 4.1 | 6.0 | 7.1 | 8.0 | 8.9 | 9.9 | 10.9 | 12.2 | 14.0 | 18.9 | 1.92 | 4.6 | 10.8 |
| 1972 | | | | | | | | | | | | | |
| Workers | 4.4 | 6.3 | 7.3 | 8.4 | 9.0 | 9.9 | 10.9 | 12.0 | 13.6 | 18.2 | 1.80 | 4.1 | 10.2 |
| Peasants | 4.0 | 5.9 | 6.9 | 7.9 | 8.7 | 9.8 | 10.7 | 11.9 | 14.2 | 20.0 | 1.99 | 5.0 | 11.7 |
| Double-income group | 4.9 | 6.6 | 7.7 | 8.5 | 8.9 | 9.8 | 10.8 | 11.8 | 12.9 | 18.1 | 1.74 | 3.7 | 10.5 |
| Nonmanual employees | 4.9 | 6.4 | 7.3 | 8.1 | 8.6 | 9.5 | 10.5 | 11.8 | 13.7 | 19.2 | 1.84 | 3.9 | 11.0 |

| | | | | | | | | | | | | | |
|---|---|---|---|---|---|---|---|---|---|---|---|---|---|
| Self-employed | 3.9 | 5.7 | 6.7 | 7.7 | 8.6 | 9.6 | 10.4 | 12.0 | 13.9 | 21.5 | 2.05 | 5.5 | 13.5 |
| Total active households | 4.3 | 6.1 | 7.0 | 8.1 | 8.8 | 9.8 | 10.6 | 12.0 | 13.8 | 19.5 | 1.89 | 4.5 | 11.4 |
| Pensioners | 4.0 | 5.9 | 7.0 | 8.0 | 8.9 | 9.8 | 10.8 | 11.9 | 13.8 | 19.9 | 1.96 | 5.0 | 13.0 |
| All households | 4.0 | 5.9 | 7.0 | 8.0 | 8.9 | 9.8 | 10.8 | 11.9 | 13.8 | 19.9 | 1.96 | 5.0 | 11.6 |
| **1977** | | | | | | | | | | | | | |
| Workers | 4.8 | 6.6 | 7.5 | 8.3 | 9.1 | 9.9 | 10.8 | 11.9 | 13.6 | 17.4 | 1.75 | 3.7 | 9.6 |
| Peasants | 4.1 | 6.1 | 7.1 | 7.9 | 8.8 | 9.7 | 10.6 | 11.9 | 13.8 | 20.2 | 1.95 | 4.9 | 12.0 |
| Double-income group | 5.4 | 7.0 | 7.9 | 8.6 | 9.3 | 10.0 | 10.6 | 11.7 | 13.1 | 16.3 | 1.61 | 3.0 | 9.1 |
| Nonmanual employees | 5.3 | 6.6 | 7.4 | 8.1 | 8.8 | 9.6 | 10.5 | 11.7 | 13.6 | 18.5 | 1.78 | 3.5 | 10.5 |
| Total active households | 4.7 | 6.5 | 7.4 | 8.2 | 8.9 | 9.7 | 10.7 | 11.9 | 13.6 | 18.5 | 1.80 | 3.9 | 10.4 |
| Pensioners | 4.5 | 6.0 | 7.0 | 7.9 | 8.8 | 9.6 | 10.7 | 12.0 | 13.8 | 19.7 | 1.92 | 4.1 | 11.4 |
| All households | 4.5 | 6.3 | 7.3 | 8.1 | 8.9 | 9.8 | 10.7 | 12.0 | 13.7 | 18.6 | 1.84 | 4.1 | 10.6 |

*Sources: A.C 1972* (Budapest: KSH, 1975), 65; ibid., *1977* (1980), 96, 98.

7

to receive family allowances. The family allowance is discontinued at the end of the child's secondary education or when the child finishes industrial apprenticeship.

The exclusion of households with one child from the benefit is a peculiarity of Hungary compared to most socialist and capitalist countries.

The original rationale for it was that large families are worse off than small ones even when one includes family allowances, and the majority of children (over 60% under the age of 15) benefit anyway because they are concentrated in households with two or more children. Still, many in Hungary questioned the validity of excluding one-child families from the benefits. The problem has been vigorously debated, and it is likely universalists would win and the allowance system be changed if extra funds were not involved. But considering the lack of funds for social benefits in general due to the economic slowdown in Hungary, it is very unlikely that the family allowance system will in the nearest future include one-child households.

However, we must admit that Hungary did make a lot of progress between 1965 and 1980 in increasing the scope of universality of family allowances. In 1965, 600,000 households received family allowances, whereas in 1980 this figure was over one million, which is about 30% of all households in the country. This increase in the amount of households eligible to receive family allowances stemmed from a deliberate policy to end discrimination against families in which the major bread-earners are not employed in the socialized sector. In 1974 the new Social Security Act equalized the family allowance received by collective farmers with that received by employees of the socialized sector.[16] What is more, to broaden the scope of eligibility for family allowances, the precondition of steady employment of one parent was abolished. Family allowances were granted to households composed of part-time employees and industrial apprentices, university students' households, and households where active members work at home.

In Hungary the size of family allowances is not linked negatively to wages or household per capita income. A flat rate per child is paid to all families eligible, irrespective of their incomes. The rationale for such an approach is: (a) it does not contradict the logic of wage differentiation, and (b) it is the most democratic because it treats equally all children within the group that gets allowances.

It is interesting to note that in Poland Solidarity and the government decided in 1981 to maintain the principle of universality of the allowance but to link it to family per capita income—the lower the per capita income of the family, the higher the allowance per child.

In Hungary family allowances have had some positive influence on the relative position of larger families as far as per capita income is concerned. In 1975 a family with three children had 56% of the per capita income of a childless family, whereas the figures were respectively in 1972—51%, in 1967—53%, and in 1962—52%.[17] The relative position of families with four or more children has not improved at all. Their per capita income has for many years represented approximately one-third of the childless families' per capita income. However, these differences do not fully reflect differences in the living standards of large and small households because the per capita income unit does not take into consideration the age composition of the children in the household and any economies of scale of the household. To maintain three children at a certain standard does not require three times more funds than keeping one child. In other words, if we used an income per *consumer* unit[18] instead of an income per capita unit, the differences at every point of time between a household with three children and a childless household would drop by approximately 20%.[19] However, the differences in real living standards would still be substantial. What is more, those differences do not show a tendency to diminish markedly as time passes. The lack of substantial change here has in part been a result of insufficient increases in family allowances. Although the family allowance per child increased from 1960 to 1980 both in size and as a part of the average monthly earnings, it still represents no more than

11-12% of average monthly earnings.[20]

*Selective Child-Care Allowance*

Another benefit in cash of importance for the welfare of the household is the selective child-care allowance first introduced in 1967. Initially only women with twelve-month full-time employment prior to childbirth were eligible to receive such grants; later the new Social Security Act of 1974 also made eligible for this grant women in part-time employment and students. The major arrangements for the child-care allowance are as follows: The allowance becomes effective at the end of the twentieth week of fully paid maternity leave and is paid up to the child's third birthday. The allowance per child is approximately 40-50% of the average monthly wage of young women. In 1975 the child-care allowance was between 800 and 1,000 forints per month. The allowance has since increased at the pace of the average monthly wage of young women. Indexing kept the ratio of the child-care grant to the average monthly wages of young women more or less constant.

Moreover, the child-care allowance is optional and very flexible in its implementation. Mothers using the child-care allowance retain their jobs throughout the three-year period and can go back to work permanently whenever they want, or they can go back temporarily and take the allowance again before the three years have expired. This program has gradually become very popular; the number of women using the child-care allowance has increased from 34,000 in 1967 to 254,000 in 1980,[21] which represents nearly 80% of all mothers entitled to it.

However, it should be noted that proportionally more women with lower education take the child-care grant than ones with higher education. For example, the proportion of mothers who use the grant for more than eighteen months is 80% for unskilled workers, 50% for skilled workers, and 18-24% for doctors, teachers, and engineers.[22] The main immediate aim of introducing the child-care allowance was to help women in their difficult everyday struggle to combine work with child and household care and provide proper care for the children, especially when child-care institutions outside the family were inadequate in number and quality. However, the long-run objective of the state is also to increase sex equality in terms of workplace opportunities. To this end, discussions are underway to change the child-care grant for women into a parental right with the possibility of switching roles between husband and wife. Such a measure, if implemented, would be conducive to a gradual change in the traditional functions of men and women in the family and would thus improve women's opportunities to advance in economic and social life.[23] Since the allowance was introduced, the proportion of women taking up employment before their first child is born has increased considerably; but as long as it is a *woman's* allowance de jure and de facto, the increase in employment of women will probably be temporary. Some women who take advantage of the allowance will return to work only for a short while and some probably not at all. Only when the allowance changes its character and becomes a genuine parental grant will it become durably and permanently conducive to an increase in employment of women with children.

## Pensions

In 1951 the retirement age in Hungary was fixed at fifty-five years for women and sixty years for men employed in the socialized sector only. In 1980 the retirement age became universal and applied as well to the cooperative sector[24] (both cooperative peasantry and urban cooperatives).

The minimum length of employment to be eligible for a full pension was set at ten years. However, in 1981, with some exceptions, this was increased to twenty years.[25] A full pension is now established as 75% of the highest earnings during the last five years of employment, without an upper limit, as was the case in the '60s.[26]

The minimum old-age pension has gradually increased, and in

1977 it was fixed at 1.040 forints per month, which represented no more than one-third of the average wage. However, pensions from 1960 to 1980 constantly increased both in size and as a part of average monthly earnings. In 1980 an average pension constitutes 55% of the average monthly earnings of the socialized sector, whereas in 1960 it was only 30% and in 1970 and 1975 respectively—33.4 and 42%.[27] Although this is a major achievement, still the weight of pensioners and their households within the lowest per capita income brackets is much higher than active households, whereas the reverse is true as far as the highest per capita income brackets are concerned.[28] For example, about 12% of all pensioners' households had, in 1977, a per capita income below 1,000 forints monthly, whereas only 5% of the active households received such a low per capita income. As far as the high-income brackets are concerned (above 3,200 forints per capita monthly), the shares in it of pensioners and active households are respectively 11 and 16%.[29] There are many reasons for this unfavorable concentration of pensioners' households in the lower and higher per capita income brackets. To mention only a few of them: (a) pensioners' households have a less favorable ratio of members with incomes to those who must be supported; (b) not all people at retirement age have full pensions because they have worked too little, or they have only survivors' rights (widows); (c) pensions are not fully indexed to the increases in the average wage,[30] hence those who have retired earlier have lower pensions than those who retired later. This lag in pension due to different periods of retirement is called the "old portfolio" of pensions. Poverty-stricken pensioners are usually those who lack full pensions or those who, although they get full pensions, retired a long time ago; their relative position vis-á-vis more recently retired "younger pensioners" has eroded due to a lack of indexing to changes in the average wage.

In Hungary, as in most countries, pensions are work related: the higher the earnings, the higher the pension. Retired people who had low earnings during their active life have low pensions. Such a strict link between earnings and pensions is not very conducive to eliminating pockets of poverty among pensioners. In the ongoing debate about how to improve the pension system, some have proposed severing the link between pensions and earnings and establishing instead a flat rate for all pensioners irrespective of the length of their employment prior to retirement age.

Advocates of a flat rate for all pensioners argue that such a system would reduce the degree of inequality of old-age pensions and would improve the material situation of the poor pensioners.

Needless to say, a flat-rate pension would benefit those who before retirement had earnings below the average or no earnings at all and would penalize those who during their active life had average or above-average earnings.

To avoid discrimination against high earners and to guarantee that no one loses too much, the flat-rate pension would need to be settled above the average wage, which is unrealistic given the objective of the incentive system and the limited resources socialist countries face at this stage of development. Although the work-related pension system has its opponents, by and large there is a consensus in the socialist countries that one way or another pensions must be related to earnings. Even the very highly egalitarian program of Solidarity never advocated the abolition of the work-related pension system, asking, rather, to establish minimum pensions based on the concept of a social minimum constantly upgraded in step with the expansion of the nation's wealth.

However, maintaining a work-related pension system does not require that the distribution of pensions be a copy of earnings at a lower level. In some socialist countries there is a sort of inverse relationship between earnings and pension on the margin. Ceilings for the highest and lowest pensions are established in order to avoid very low pensions and to reduce the overall relative dispersion of pensions. However, these minimum pensions are still not sufficient (e.g., in the Soviet Union) to eliminate poverty among pensioners.

Now, how effective are social benefits in cash in reducing inequalities in personal income? In total, social benefits in cash have a very beneficial effect on the relative dispersion of personal income; and some items within the benefits, like family allowances, even reduce absolute differences in per capita income because lower-income groups receive absolutely more in family allowances than higher-income groups. Approximate calculations made in Hungary indicate that in 1977, family allowances alone were responsible for more than 50% of the reduction in households' per capita income disparities.[31] Although social benefits, both in cash and kind, are still quite unevenly distributed in Hungary, as in other Eastern European countries, they are nevertheless less unequally distributed than earned incomes. Therefore, including social benefits in the household income reduced relative disparities in per capita income. By and large, social benefits in cash are distributed according to need and to some degree counteract work-related differentials.

Up to this point our analysis has been based on the personal income unit, which includes all kinds of earnings and social benefits in cash. The question arises whether the inclusion of social benefits in kind would alter the picture of the distribution pattern. Before an answer to this question is attempted, it is worth saying a few words about different parts of social benefits in kind and their specific equalizing character.

Health benefits are the second largest social benefit in kind (after education). (In 1980 they constituted nearly 30% of total benefit expenditures; see *S.E. 1980* [1981], 387.) By and large, the total amount of health benefits is the same on a per capita basis for manual and nonmanual employees. However, the average life-span is substantially shorter for manual than nonmanual employees, and the infant mortality rate is much higher for manual than nonmanual families.[32] This unfavorable state of affairs can be explained by inferior housing conditions, a less-balanced diet, difficulties in getting specialized medical care in smaller communities, and occupational diseases and industrial accidents more prevalent among manual workers.

Some items of social benefits in kind, although designed originally to reduce differences in life-style of different strata, have actually increased those disparities. A good example is rent subsidies in Hungary. After 1945 rent was fixed at a very low level in order to protect low-income groups. However, it has gradually become clear that rent subsidies are more favorable to better-off families than poor ones because the better-off groups more commonly live in rental flats and the quality of their flats is usually better than average: larger size, better facilities. Suffice it to say that in 1967, rent subsidies per annum for flats occupied by professionals and managers were 8 times larger than those for unskilled workers' flats; the subsidy ratio of nonmanual to manual workers in total was nearly 4 to 1.[33] Although rent for better quality flats was raised substantially in 1970, the advantages in rent subsidies of the above-mentioned groups are still enormous.

Another example of subsidies that benefit the better-off income groups is subsidies on such cultural goods as books, theater tickets, and university education.[34]

This highly unequal distribution of some social benefits items in kind has to do with the different positions of different strata in society. The ability to lobby, knowledge of what is available, the awareness of rights to benefits, and the ability to pay even at subsidized rates (for example, for organized holidays, etc.) are very different for different strata in Hungary. Moreover, regional differences intensify social differences. Smaller towns and localities are not as well equipped with health services, kindergartens, and housing and cultural facilities as larger towns. Considering that nonmanual workers live in larger proportions in big settlements than do manual workers (this is especially so as far as the social elite is concerned), this puts them in a favorable position as users of more and better services in kind.

The unfavorable situation in the distribution of social benefits in kind has prompted some sociologists in Hungary to claim that the principle of universal services is, by its very nature, "undemocratic" because better-off groups (better off in terms of money, power, knowledge, connections, marketable skills, etc.) will always utilize social benefits in kind disproportionally to their numbers. Such uneven utilization may be aggravated if the universal right to services goes together with an acute shortage of those services. This is why some affirmative action has been proposed, for example, by Z. Ferge,[35] in favor of the less well-to-do groups.

Now we can return to our general question: What is the impact of social benefits in kind in total on the relative dispersion of total per capita income?

Data in Table 14 and comparisons between Tables 13 and 15 permit the following conclusions:

1. At every point in time the level of relative inequality is reduced when social benefits in kind are included. For example, the ratio of the top decile group to the bottom and the quotient are obviously lower in 1967 and in 1972 for all major population strata in Table 14 than in Table 13. Although social benefits in kind have reduced relative disparities in Hungary, they have a tendency to increase absolute differences in income between the highest and lowest income group. This is so because households with the highest per capita incomes receive in total slightly more social benefits in kind (in absolute terms) than households with lower per capita incomes. Some items of social benefit, like university education, recreation, sport, culture, and housing subsidies, even increase relative income disparities. The "wealthy" receive here not only absolutely but relatively more than the poor.

2. In the postreform years 1967–72 there were no changes in relative disparities of total per capita income of active households. Changes within this broad category of active households (as illustrated in both Table 13 and 14) went in different directions, canceling each other. The relative disparities in per capita income of the workers' households and the self-employed declined over time, whereas the disparities in per capita incomes of the households of nonmanual employees, double-income families, and peasants increased in this period. A substantial increase in relative disparities in pensioners' per capita household income (personal and total) resulted in a moderate increase in relative disparities in the household per capita income distribution of the whole population (see Table 14). The fact that there were no changes in 1972 in comparison with 1967 in relative dispersion in

per capita income of active households (excluding and including social benefits in kind) would logically suggest that relative dispersion of social benefits in kind did not change over time; this factor, by and large, was rather neutral as far as changes in per capita household incomes are concerned. Data in Appendix Table E support this conclusion. The neutrality of social benefits in kind is also confirmed by data for 1972 and 1977. As can be seen from Table 15, all decile groups get on average more or less the same amount of social benefits in kind (around 10%), and between 1972 and 1977 there were no changes in this regard.

A completely different picture emerges as far as social benefits in cash are concerned. This time is far from neutral as far as the distributional changes in relative dispersion of per capita household income over time are concerned.

Table 15 shows that not only were social benefits in cash more equalizing than social benefits in kind, but its equalizing influence on relative dispersion of per capita household income was also much stronger in 1977 than in 1972; differences between relative dispersion of personal and earned per capita household income (measured by the ratio of top to bottom decile groups and by the quotient) were much more pronounced in 1977 than in 1972. It follows, therefore, that social benefits in cash were more equally distributed in 1977 than in 1972, contributing to a decline over time in the relative dispersion of per capita household income.

Although the relative inequality of per capita household income did not increase after the reform was instituted in 1968, there were, however, certain phenomena worth mentioning that were not conducive to the egalitarian trend. The differentiating effect of the size of the household and earner-dependent ratio on per capita household incomes has not been reduced by proper social policies. It is difficult to claim much progress in improving the lot of poor families when, according to statistical data, nearly all households with four or more children and nearly half (45%) of all households with three children have less than 1,000 forints per capita income a month.[36] It would be no exaggeration to say that large pockets of poverty still exist among these families since

Table 14

**Distribution of Household Total per Capita Income (including Social Benefit in Kind) by Social Stratum in Hungary, 1967 and 1972 (% of household income)**

| | Decile groups | | | | | | | | | | Quotient | Ratio of top and bottom decile groups |
|---|---|---|---|---|---|---|---|---|---|---|---|---|
| | 1 | 2 | 3 | 4 | 5 | 6 | 7 | 8 | 9 | 10 | | |
| **1967** | | | | | | | | | | | | |
| Workers | 4.8 | 6.6 | 7.5 | 8.4 | 9.2 | 10.0 | 10.9 | 11.9 | 13.4 | 17.3 | 1.73 | 3.6 |
| Peasants | 4.4 | 6.3 | 7.3 | 8.2 | 9.1 | 10.0 | 10.9 | 12.1 | 13.7 | 18.0 | 1.82 | 4.09 |
| Double-income households | 5.3 | 7.0 | 8.0 | 8.6 | 9.3 | 10.0 | 10.8 | 11.8 | 13.0 | 16.2 | 1.61 | 3.05 |
| Nonmanual employees | 5.4 | 6.8 | 7.6 | 8.4 | 9.1 | 9.8 | 10.6 | 11.6 | 13.1 | 17.6 | 1.68 | 3.26 |
| Self-employed | 3.9 | 6.0 | 7.1 | 7.9 | 8.7 | 9.5 | 10.6 | 11.9 | 13.8 | 20.6 | 1.98 | 5.28 |
| Total active households | 4.7 | 6.5 | 7.4 | 8.3 | 9.1 | 9.9 | 10.8 | 11.9 | 13.5 | 17.9 | 1.78 | 3.80 |
| Pensioners | 4.2 | 5.9 | 7.0 | 8.0 | 8.8 | 9.8 | 10.9 | 12.1 | 14.0 | 19.3 | 1.93 | 4.59 |
| All households | 4.5 | 6.3 | 7.4 | 8.2 | 9.1 | 9.9 | 10.9 | 12.0 | 13.6 | 18.1 | 1.81 | 4.02 |

1972

| | | | | | | | | | | | | |
|---|---|---|---|---|---|---|---|---|---|---|---|---|
| Workers | 4.7 | 6.6 | 7.6 | 8.8 | 9.5 | 9.8 | 10.9 | 12.1 | 13.0 | 17.0 | 1.69 | 3.61 |
| Peasants | 3.7 | 6.5 | 7.7 | 8.1 | 8.9 | 9.7 | 10.6 | 11.5 | 14.3 | 19.0 | 1.87 | 5.13 |
| Double-income households | 5.0 | 7.0 | 7.9 | 8.8 | 9.3 | 9.9 | 10.4 | 11.7 | 13.3 | 16.7 | 1.63 | 3.34 |
| Nonmanual employees | 5.3 | 6.6 | 7.4 | 8.4 | 9.0 | 9.8 | 10.2 | 10.6 | 13.4 | 19.3 | 1.73 | 3.64 |
| Self-employed | 4.0 | 6.1 | 7.2 | 8.4 | 8.8 | 9.4 | 10.2 | 11.9 | 13.3 | 20.7 | 1.91 | 5.17 |
| Total active households | 4.9 | 6.1 | 7.5 | 8.1 | 8.7 | 9.9 | 10.9 | 11.9 | 13.5 | 18.5 | 1.78 | 3.77 |
| Pensioners | 4.0 | 5.3 | 6.7 | 7.7 | 8.5 | 9.7 | 10.5 | 12.1 | 14.2 | 21.3 | 2.09 | 5.32 |
| All households | 4.1 | 6.2 | 7.4 | 8.2 | 8.8 | 10.0 | 11.3 | 11.9 | 13.6 | 18.5 | 1.85 | 4.51 |

*Sources: A.C 1972* (Budapest: KSH, 1975), table 4, 2, 66.

Table 15

# The Influence of Social Benefits in Cash and Kind on the Distribution of Personal and Total per Capita Income in Hungary*

|  | Decile groups | | | | | | | | | | Top 5% | Quotient | Ratio of top and bottom decile groups |
|---|---|---|---|---|---|---|---|---|---|---|---|---|---|
|  | 1 | 2 | 3 | 4 | 5 | 6 | 7 | 8 | 9 | 10 |  |  |  |
| A. Distribution of per capita income 1972. | | | | | | | | | | | | | |
| Manual worker households | | | | | | | | | | | | | |
| IE | 3.2 | 5.4 | 6.7 | 7.8 | 8.8 | 9.9 | 11.1 | 12.6 | 14.6 | 19.7 | 11.1 | 2.10 | 6.16 |
| IP | 4.4 | 6.4 | 7.3 | 8.2 | 9.1 | 9.9 | 10.9 | 12.0 | 13.7 | 18.1 | 10.2 | 1.81 | 4.11 |
| IT | 4.8 | 6.7 | 7.7 | 8.5 | 9.2 | 10.0 | 10.8 | 11.9 | 13.3 | 17.1 | 9.5 | 1.70 | 3.56 |
| Nonmanual worker | | | | | | | | | | | | | |
| IE | 3.7 | 5.4 | 6.6 | 7.6 | 8.5 | 9.6 | 10.8 | 12.3 | 14.5 | 21.0 | 12.2 | 2.13 | 5.68 |
| IP | 4.9 | 6.3 | 7.2 | 7.9 | 8.7 | 9.5 | 10.5 | 11.8 | 13.7 | 19.5 | 11.3 | 1.87 | 3.98 |
| IT | 5.2 | 6.6 | 7.4 | 8.2 | 8.9 | 9.7 | 10.5 | 11.7 | 13.4 | 18.5 | 10.5 | 1.76 | 3.56 |
| All active households | | | | | | | | | | | | | |
| IE | 3.3 | 5.4 | 6.6 | 7.6 | 8.7 | 9.7 | 10.9 | 12.4 | 14.6 | 20.8 | 12.1 | 2.14 | 6.30 |
| IP | 4.3 | 6.1 | 7.1 | 8.0 | 8.9 | 9.7 | 10.7 | 11.9 | 13.8 | 19.3 | 11.2 | 1.89 | 4.49 |
| IT | 4.7 | 6.5 | 7.4 | 8.2 | 9.0 | 9.8 | 10.7 | 11.8 | 13.4 | 18.4 | 10.6 | 1.78 | 3.91 |

1977

| | | | | | | | | | | | | | |
|---|---|---|---|---|---|---|---|---|---|---|---|---|---|
| **Manual worker households** | | | | | | | | | | | | | |
| IE | 3.5 | 5.4 | 6.7 | 7.7 | 8.8 | 9.9 | 11.2 | 12.2 | 14.7 | 19.5 | 10.9 | 2.08 | 5.57 |
| IP | 4.8 | 6.6 | 7.5 | 8.3 | 9.1 | 9.9 | 10.8 | 12.0 | 13.6 | 17.4 | 9.6 | 1.74 | 3.63 |
| IT | 5.2 | 6.9 | 7.8 | 8.6 | 9.3 | 10.0 | 10.8 | 11.8 | 13.2 | 16.5 | 9.0 | 1.64 | 3.17 |
| **Nonmanual worker** | | | | | | | | | | | | | |
| IE | 3.7 | 5.5 | 6.6 | 7.6 | 8.5 | 9.6 | 10.8 | 12.3 | 14.6 | 20.8 | 12.0 | 2.12 | 5.62 |
| IP | 5.2 | 6.6 | 7.3 | 8.1 | 8.8 | 9.6 | 10.5 | 11.7 | 13.6 | 18.6 | 10.6 | 1.79 | 3.58 |
| IT | 5.5 | 6.8 | 7.6 | 8.3 | 9.0 | 9.7 | 10.5 | 11.7 | 13.2 | 17.6 | 9.9 | 1.70 | 3.20 |
| **All active households** | | | | | | | | | | | | | |
| IE | 3.5 | 5.4 | 6.6 | 7.7 | 8.7 | 9.7 | 11.0 | 12.5 | 14.6 | 20.4 | 11.7 | 2.11 | 5.83 |
| IP | 4.7 | 6.5 | 7.4 | 8.2 | 9.0 | 9.8 | 10.7 | 11.9 | 13.6 | 18.3 | 10.4 | 1.79 | 3.89 |
| IT | 5.1 | 6.8 | 7.7 | 8.4 | 9.1 | 9.8 | 10.7 | 11.7 | 13.2 | 17.4 | 9.8 | 1.69 | 3.41 |

B. Distribution of social benefits in kind—all households

| | | | | | | | | | | |
|---|---|---|---|---|---|---|---|---|---|---|
| 1972 | 9.0 | 9.8 | 10.2 | 10.3 | 10.6 | 10.1 | 10.2 | 10.1 | 9.7 | 10.0 |
| 1977 | 9.0 | 9.7 | 10.0 | 10.6 | 10.4 | 10.8 | 10.2 | 10.0 | 9.8 | 9.6 |

*Source: A.C 1977* (Budapest: KSH, 1980), 106-9, 162.

*IE—earned income per capita, IP—personal income per capita, IT—total income per capital.

by any definition they would fall below the poverty line in Hungary.[37]

A long-run commitment was made by the leadership in the middle of the '70s to reducing slightly the relative dispersion of per capita household income via a more rapid increase in social benefits than in the previous years; but at the same time, the existing dispersion of earnings was to be maintained. Many economists in Hungary, however, were aware of the need to reduce existing income inequality. Otherwise absolute differences in per capita income would become socially unacceptable.[38] This is why it was proposed that the government reduce relative differences in per capita household incomes over the next ten years. This should be achieved mainly by a much faster increase in family allowances, pensions, and other benefits. But a substantial increase in social benefits in the '80s is very unlikely given the serious slowdown in the rate of growth to near stagnation from 1978 to 1981 and the projection for slow growth in the '80s in general due to heavy indebtedness and other economic difficulties that represent major obstacles for expansion of the welfare system. We can expect that the authorities will, as in most countries with tendencies to stagnation both in the East and the West, cut into the welfare system and adapt its size to the more slowly growing economy.

As long as the Hungarian economy was developing rapidly, practically everyone gained from the constantly growing social benefits fund. The only issue under these favorable circumstances was who is going to gain more and who is going to gain less. But if resources for social benefits funds in the '80s can grow only very slightly or not at all, two options are formally open to the authorities. Either they make very modest improvements for everybody, or they play the zero-sum game, where one's gain is the other's loss. Needless to say, under these circumstances the better-off groups, which have better knowledge about accessibility to benefits and more lobbying power, would be the winners.

Therefore, if the state does not make a major effort to prevent an absolute deterioration in the weakest group in society, spontaneous forces reflecting the strength of different strata will push toward an inegalitarian solution.

Assuming a slight increase in social benefits and, at best, stability in their relative dispersion, we cannot expect the welfare system to be a countervailing force against further differentiation of earnings, because under these circumstances any increase in relative dispersion of wages, everything else equal, will lead to an increase in the overall inequality of per capita household income. Such an outcome would probably be politically unacceptable, and the Hungarian leadership would then not be able to change course as promised in 1980 and increase relative disparities in earnings.

•  •  •

To conclude our analysis, we will turn to the question of how the decline in the dispersion of per capita income of active households can be explained in view of the stability in relative dispersion of earnings from 1966 to 1980. As mentioned before, there are insufficient data for us to estimate changes in relative dispersion of households' activity rates (K/N) and social benefits (Y/W) over time, although *a priori* reasoning is suggestive.

Demographic factors by their very nature do not change noticeably over a short period of time. It is, however, reasonable to assume, given the overall increase in the K/N ratio in Hungary,[39] that big households (usually with low per capita incomes) would have increased their activity ratio faster than small households (with higher per capita incomes) either by reducing their size relative to small households or by increasing the ratio of earners to nonearners.[40] Indeed, in Hungary, apart from economic pressure that is likely to work in this direction, opportunities to increase the activity rate are now virtually confined to large households. If this is so, it is likely to have acted as a factor reducing the relative dispersion of household per capita income.[41]

As far as social benefits are concerned, the evidence indicates that the relative dispersion of social benefits combined has declined in time and has become another factor reducing the inequality of the distribution of household per capita income.

CHAPTER IV

# The Distribution of per Capita
# Household Income in Poland

In Poland as in Hungary, family size and the ratio of earners to dependents are major sources of differences in per capita household income. The larger the household, the smaller the probability of belonging to the higher income brackets. According to household budget statistics,[1] in Poland 32% of households with six persons are in the lowest per capita income bracket, whereas one-person households are not represented in this bracket at all. The difference between per capita incomes of one- and six-member Polish households in 1978 was 2.7:1. There is also a negative correlation between the size and the activity ratio of households. Although the absolute number of earners increases with the size of the households, the activity ratio (the ratio of earners to household members) declines with the size of the household. Large households have proportionally more inactive members to maintain than small households.

In Poland, as in other socialist countries, the level of the average wage per earner contributed only slightly to the differentiation of households' per capita income. Econometric analysis in Poland has shown a weak correlation between per capita household income and earnings of its members;[2] the correlation ratio is 0.26 for nonmanual employees and 0.32 for manual ones, with the total figure for all employees at 0.30.

The strong influence of demographic factors on differences in per capita household income leads to a situation in which a highly skilled worker can belong to the highest wage bracket but his household to the lowest per capita income bracket if the household has many children and, for that reason, an unfavorable earner-dependent ratio.[3]

Although distributional data on per capita household income in Poland are very scarce and incomplete, the available figures indicate that by and large the status quo in relative dispersion was maintained in the pre-Solidarity period. Data in Appendix Table F show that changes in relative dispersion in per capita household income, in the total socialized sector, were rather small from 1967 to 1978. Only in 1980-82, as a consequence of strong egalitarian measures taken under pressure from Solidarity did relative disparities of per capita household income markedly declined.

Manual workers' per capita household income is more unequally distributed than nonmanual, but the former's relative position measured by the median and the mean per capita annual household income improved both in the Gierek and Solidarity periods vis-à-vis the nonmanual stratum, as can be seen from Table 16 below.

The official data on relative dispersion for the whole economy expressed in deciles, published only for some years, corroborated the findings of Appendix Table F.

From Tables 11, 12, 13, Appendix F, and 17 combined we can infer that:

1. The relative dispersion of employee households' per capita income in the Gierek period declined but was partially offset by increases in relative dispersion among mixed households and among households of pensioners and those unable to work. However from 1980 to 1982 relative disparities in per capita income of all categories of households in Poland declined.

2. By all measures used in this book, the degree of inequality of distribution of per capita income is substantially higher in Poland than in Hungary. The quotient in 1976 for the households of the socialized sector in Poland is higher than in Hungary by approximately 13%; for the peasant households the corresponding figure is 47%; the ratio of the top decile to the bottom decile for the socialized sector is higher in Poland than in Hungary by approximately 43%; for the peasant household the figure is approximately 47%. Unfortunately we do not have figures for per

Table 16

**Per Capita Income of the Nonmanual Strata in Proportion to Manual Workers in Poland (Per capita income of manual workers = 100)**

| Year | Means | Medians |
|------|-------|---------|
| 1967 | 132.8 | 131.4 |
| 1968 | 131.3 | 131.7 |
| 1969 | 131.3 | 130.5 |
| 1970 | 132.3 | 130.1 |
| 1971 | 124.9 | 124.4 |
| 1980 | 125.8 | 124.2 |
| 1982 | 118.0 | 116.0 |

*Source*: See Appendix Table F. Separate data for manual and nonmanual household per capita income were published until 1971 but resumed only in 1981. Unfortunately, apart from incomplete data on manual and nonmanual per capita income, no figures are published about incomes of the more specific social strata of the socialized sector, such as: (a) leading managers and top professionals, (b) skilled and unskilled workers, (c) clerical employees, etc. This shortcoming is a real obstacle to grasping the stratification map of Polish society.

The only average per capita income data available are for selected occupations and only for one year. Nevertheless, these data are of some interest. According to figures given by the Central Statistical Office (*Tendencje rozwoju społecznego* [Tendencies of Social Development] Warsaw: GUS, table 3, 265), engineers' households have twice as much per capita income on the average as unskilled households; skilled workers about 23% more than unskilled; and administrative personnel and accountants 51% more than unskilled workers.

capita household income distribution in Hungary for any years in the '80s. But considering the decline in the inequality of per capita income distribution in Poland in 1980-82, we can logically infer that in this period the discrepancies in relative dispersion narrowed between these two countries.

3. The peasant household per capita income is substantially more unequally distributed than that of households in the socialized sector. Twenty-five percent of peasant households belong to the lowest per capita income bracket, compared with 7% of employee households. A very high degree of inequality of distribution in the Polish village is linked with the fact that those peasants with small, badly located, and infertile land are often burdened with large families. Their per capita incomes are very different

from those farmer-millionaires whose land is located around Warsaw or another substantial urban center, and who grow highly intensive agricultural products.

Although the differences in earnings and in per capita incomes between peasant households and employee households has declined since 1945, they are still substantial. Although income per employee in the village has grown faster in the last decade than in town, the earnings of the peasantry in 1982 were still not more than 0.92 of the earnings of the nonagricultural sector. What is more, this indicator does not reflect the real renumeration of labor in agriculture compared with the nonagricultural sector because in agriculture we observe a lengthening of the workweek, whereas in nonagricultural activities the opposite is true; the working day and week have become shorter (free Saturdays, longer holidays, etc.).[4]

As far as household income per capita is concerned, in spite of progress made in this area in recent years (1970-82), the peasant population still lags behind in material welfare vis-à-vis nonagricultural households.[5] This is not only because of smaller earnings but also because social benefits both in money and in kind still represent a comparatively small amount of peasants' total income.

In 1980 the share of social benefits in cash in total personal household income of the peasants was only 4%, compared with over 10% in the case of employees' households. The relative situation is even less favorable for the peasantry as far as social benefits in kind are concerned. Their access to health care, kindergarten nurseries, and holidays cannot even be compared to urban households.[6] This handicapped position will not be alleviated in the near future because the deep economic crisis has forced the authorities to reduce absolutely social benefits in kind on a national scale.[7]

The inferior situation of peasant families is also evident from the number of people living below the poverty line (measured by the so-called social minimum).[8] In 1980, 45% of all peasant households received per capita income below the social mini-

Table 17

## The Distribution of per Capita Household Income in Poland according to Decile Groups (% of household income)

| | Decile groups | | | | | | | | | | Coefficient | Quotient | Ratio of top to bottom decile groups | Decile ratio |
|---|---|---|---|---|---|---|---|---|---|---|---|---|---|---|
| | 1 | 2 | 3 | 4 | 5 | 6 | 7 | 8 | 9 | 10 | | | | |
| **1973** | | | | | | | | | | | | | | |
| Households of employees | 4.2 | 5.7 | 6.7 | 7.6 | 8.5 | 9.5 | 10.6 | 11.7 | 13.7 | 21.8 | 18.0 | 2.06 | 5.20 | — |
| Mixed households of workers and peasants | 4.4 | 5.8 | 6.8 | 7.7 | 8.5 | 9.4 | 10.5 | 12.1 | 14.0 | 20.9 | 17.7 | 2.02 | 4.75 | — |
| Peasant households | 3.8 | 4.8 | 5.7 | 6.6 | 7.6 | 8.6 | 9.8 | 11.6 | 14.2 | 27.3 | 23.4 | 2.51 | 7.20 | — |
| Inactive households | 4.7 | 6.3 | 7.1 | 8.0 | 8.8 | 9.6 | 10.5 | 11.7 | 13.8 | 19.5 | 15.8 | 1.87 | 4.15 | — |
| **1976** | | | | | | | | | | | | | | |
| Households of employees | 4.3 | 5.9 | 6.9 | 7.8 | 8.7 | 9.7 | 10.6 | 11.9 | 13.9 | 20.3 | 16.8 | 1.98 | 4.72 | — |
| Mixed households of workers and peasants | 3.8 | 5.6 | 6.7 | 7.7 | 8.6 | 9.6 | 10.7 | 12.1 | 14.1 | 21.1 | 18.1 | 2.09 | 5.55 | — |
| Peasant households | 3.4 | 4.9 | 5.9 | 6.8 | 7.9 | 9.1 | 10.5 | 12.3 | 14.7 | 24.5 | 22.3 | 2.46 | 7.20 | — |
| Inactive households | 4.2 | 6.1 | 6.9 | 7.8 | 8.7 | 9.7 | 10.8 | 11.9 | 13.8 | 20.1 | 16.7 | 1.98 | 4.80 | — |

| | | | | | | | | | | | | | | |
|---|---|---|---|---|---|---|---|---|---|---|---|---|---|---|
| **1980** | | | | | | | | | | | | | | |
| Households of employees | 4.5 | 6.0 | 7.0 | 7.9 | 8.8 | 9.7 | 10.9 | 12.1 | 13.9 | 19.2 | 16.1 | — | 4.30 | 2.84 |
| Mixed households of workers and peasants | 4.3 | 5.7 | 6.7 | 7.7 | 8.6 | 9.5 | 10.6 | 12.2 | 14.3 | 20.4 | 17.5 | — | 4.75 | 3.10 |
| Peasant households | 3.2 | 4.6 | 5.8 | 7.0 | 7.9 | 8.8 | 10.1 | 12.0 | 15.0 | 25.6 | 22.7 | — | 8.00 | 4.22 |
| Inactive households | 4.4 | 5.9 | 7.0 | 7.9 | 8.7 | 9.6 | 10.8 | 12.1 | 13.8 | 19.8 | 16.5 | — | 4.50 | 2.86 |
| **1982** | | | | | | | | | | | | | | |
| Households of employees | 5.5 | 6.8 | 7.5 | 8.2 | 9.0 | 9.8 | 10.6 | 11.7 | 13.3 | 17.6 | 13.2 | — | 3.20 | 2.28 |
| Mixed households | 4.7 | 6.1 | 6.9 | 7.8 | 8.5 | 9.4 | 10.5 | 12.0 | 14.0 | 20.1 | 16.6 | — | 4.28 | 2.80 |
| Peasant households | 3.4 | 5.3 | 6.3 | 7.1 | 8.1 | 9.3 | 10.5 | 12.3 | 14.9 | 22.8 | 20.5 | — | 6.70 | 3.65 |
| Inactive households | 5.3 | 6.9 | 8.1 | 8.9 | 9.4 | 9.9 | 10.5 | 11.4 | 12.7 | 16.9 | 11.3 | — | 3.20 | 2.17 |

Source: *Tendencje rozwoju społecznego*, table 40, 90; *R.S 1983*, (Warsaw: GUS), table 19(186), 114.

mum, whereas for families outside agriculture, this figure was only 25%.[9]

The inferior position of Polish peasants vis-à-vis their Hungarian counterparts is clear not only in the realm of relative earnings but also in the scope of social benefits in kind granted to the peasantry.

The Polish peasantry were granted free health care only in 1972. Only in 1974 were old-age pensions granted to the Polish peasants, but with special strings attached for getting them. For example, a transfer of land to the state will yield a higher pension than a transfer to an heir in the family. One of many other restrictions on land transfer to an heir was the requirement that he must be a qualified farmer. No wonder that this policy of the Gierek regime was perceived by the peasantry as one way to expand the state sector in agriculture at the expense of the private sector.

In contrast to its Hungarian counterpart, the Polish peasantry is still deprived of family allowances and other welfare payments. The better position of the Hungarian peasants than the Polish ones does not of course exclude the fact that Hungarian peasants do lag behind the Hungarian urban population in material welfare. The situation of the Hungarian peasants is far from idyllic. The process of equalization of social benefits between the town and village is far from complete, especially as far as social benefits in kind are concerned. Nevertheless, we can say that Hungary has reduced the difference in material well-being between the village and towns much more persistently and coherently than Poland.

We can expect in Poland a significant "appeasement" of the peasantry in order to increase agricultural production and sales of produce to the state as a major step in overcoming the deep economic crisis.

Although the relative inequality of per capita income in the whole economy did not change markedly in Poland in the pre-Solidarity period, certain negative developments should be mentioned which were not very conducive to the egalitarian trend. The Central Statistical Office has confirmed that in 1976, 46% of all households with three children and 77% of all households with four children had a monthly per capita income below the required minimum consumption standard.[10] It is known that large households react to a decline in real income, triggered by price increases, by first reducing expenditures on culture, education, sport, and recreation. The children of these families have on average a shorter period of schooling; and although over 50% of their income is spent on food, the consumption of vegetables, fruit, butter, and even milk is below the required nutritional norm, whereas the consumption of basic fat, flour, bread, and potatoes is excessive. Incomes below the so-called social minimum take their toll as well in terms of infant mortality. Infant mortality is also related to the low per capita incomes of large households; the mortality rate for the six-child families is 35 per thousand, whereas the average for the country is only 22 per thousand.[11]

An improvement in the living standard of these underprivileged households could be achieved by progressively increasing family allowances for children, which up to now have been too negligible a part of their budget to influence their material position. Although family allowances did increase from (1970 to 1978) by approximately 50%, average money wages, however, increased by 100%. As a result, family allowances represent a smaller and smaller part of household income and of all social benefits in cash.[12] A further erosion of the role of family allowances, especially in the budgets of large households, is linked to increases in consumer prices. The official consumer price index rose by 35% from 1970 to 1978; thus the purchasing power of the increased family allowances was nearly unchanged in this period.

Pockets of poverty further increased in the last years of Gierek's regime. On the wave of widespread unrest in the summer of 1980, the authorities gradually agreed under pressure from Solidarity to liquidate pockets of poverty via substantial increases in family allowances and an overhaul of the pension system.

Until 1981 family allowances were a rather token sum without serious bearing on the standard of living of the household. In

negotiations with Solidarity the government agreed to differentiate family allowances in accordance with the size of per capita
household income; lower-income groups would receive much
higher family allowances per child than higher income groups.

The government proposed to distinguish three groups of
households by size of per capita income: up to 2,000 zl, between
2,000 and 2,500 zl, and 2,500-3,500 zl per month. The poorest
families would receive family allowances in 1983 of 500 zl for
each child per month, the middle-income group 350 zl, and the
highest 180 zl. Solidarity demanded that these differences be
even more in favor of poor families, and it asked that family
allowances be linked to an objective base, namely: the cost of
maintaining a child. Other objections to lower family allowances
fo so-called mixed peasant-workers families were put forward by
Solidarity.[13]

According to a recent inquiry, the material situation of a substantial portion of pensioners is very grave. In 1979 a quarter of
all pensioners (both old-age and disability pensions) had incomes
below the social minimum.

In November 1981, when a substantial increase in pensions
took place, the government agreed, for the first time in socialist
Poland, to use the concept of social minimum as a criterion to
establish the lowest possible pension.[14] A minimum old-age pension cannot be lower than 3,000 zl[15] and the lowest disability
pension cannot be lower than 2,200 zl per month. Needless to
say, this social minimum covers only essential needs.

In spite of the substantial increase in pensions in November
1981, the situation of pensioners has not improved. In April
1982, 50% of all pensioners (elderly and disabled) still got less
than 3,000 zl per month, and 80% less than 4,000 zl, whereas a
year earlier, before the November 1981 increase, the figures were
only slightly lower.[16] It is very difficult to judge whether the
material well-being of the pensioners has improved or deteriorated over the period of 1980-1983 because we do not know how
price increases and shortages have specifically affected and eroded the real incomes of pensioners. However, all indications point

to the relative incomes position of pensioners deteriorating. This is clear when we measure the differences between the average wage and average pension. The ratio of the average pension to the average wage was:

51.2 in 1970
47.0 in 1980
42.1 in 1981
33.7 in 1982
40.2 in 1983

We can also measure the relative position of the pensioners by comparing pensions granted recently and pensions granted in the past (the so-called old portfolio of pensions). Here again regression is evident. The differences between new and old pensions have constantly increased between 1978 and 1982. A consensus between Solidarity and the government had emerged in August 1981 that a far-reaching reform of all the pension systems had to take place. The old portfolio of pensions had to be abolished and these pensions brought up to the current level, and a systematic escalation year by year of all pensions had to take place by increasing them in step with average wages in the socialized sector as a whole.[17]

Reform of the pensions system, neglected for so many years, will be an extremely expensive project. An extra injection of money, in an economic environment of declining output and acute shortages, can only make the general inflationary pressures even more serious. Despite the unfavorable economic situation in 1982, the government decided that abject poverty among a substantial part of pensioners required immediate action.

The government openly admitted that the existing pension system had not allowed the elderly and disabled to live a decent life, and that there had been an absolute and relative pauperization of a substantial segment of pensioners. Once more historical experience had proven that an inefficient economy, even if it is committed to an egalitarian welfare system, cannot provide the funds; and when such a system faces acute "budget balancing" problems, one way or another it neglects the interests of the weakest section in society. Commitments to an improved welfare system will always remain a slogan without a healthy economy. A stagnant economy, be it in the East or West, usually means a decline in the welfare system.[18]

### Factors determining per capita income distribution

We now turn to two variables that affect the distribution of per capita income:

a) relative dispersion of the household activity ratio (the ratio of working members to the size of the household), and

b) relative dispersion of all social benefits both in cash and in kind.

Adequate time series of activity ratios exist only for those house-holds whose main source of earnings is work in the socialized sector. We present below calculated activity ratios for 1963 to 1978.

As we can see from Table 18:

1. The average size of the household, which continues to be large by Western standards, shows no real trend, declining slightly in the 1960s and then increasing slightly in the 1970s. Only more affluent families (households in the highest income brackets) have measurably increased in size.

2. The overall activity ratio rose slightly in the period under investigation. This increase is mainly the result of the average increase in the number of people working in the households. However, the households in the extreme per capita income brackets have not participated in this increase at all. Households in the highest income brackets have actually reduced substantially their already very high activity ratio.

The fact that the families in the extreme lowest income bracket have not increased their activity ratios is quite surprising and against common expectation. Although there is a much larger reserve of female labor in the low-income groups than in the upper-income ones,[19] up to now they have not yet been drawn

Table 18

# Activity Ratios of the Total Household Population and for Extreme per Capita Income Brackets

| | Size of households in:* | | | Activity ratios of households in:* | | |
|---|---|---|---|---|---|---|
| | Total | lowest bracket | highest** bracket | Total | lowest bracket | highest** bracket |
| 1963 | 3.41 | 5.21 | 1.67 | 0.44 | 0.24 | 0.84 |
| 1964 | 3.40 | 5.30 | 1.64 | 0.44 | 0.24 | 0.83 |
| 1965 | 3.38 | 5.48 | 1.68 | 0.45 | 0.23 | 0.85 |
| 1966 | 3.30 | 5.56 | 1.59 | 0.46 | 0.23 | 0.85 |
| 1967 | 3.23 | 5.10 | 1.65 | 0.47 | 0.23 | 0.84 |
| 1968 | 3.22 | 5.18 | 1.54 | 0.48 | 0.23 | 0.83 |
| 1969 | 3.24 | 5.19 | 1.78 | 0.49 | 0.23 | 0.81 |
| 1970 | 3.20 | 5.29 | 1.85 | 0.50 | 0.23 | 0.79 |
| 1973 | 3.51 | 5.27 | 2.00 | 0.47 | 0.22 | 0.78 |
| 1974 | 3.49 | 5.05 | 2.20 | 0.47 | 0.25 | 0.75 |
| 1975 | 3.46 | 5.28 | 2.35 | 0.47 | 0.24 | 0.78 |
| 1976 | 3.45 | 5.08 | 2.49 | | | |
| 1978 | 3.46 | 5.12 | 2.43 | | | |

*Sources:* Calculated on the basis of *R.S—Budżety gospodarstw domowych* [Household Budgets];—*Budżety gospodarstw domowych* [Household Budgets], *Statystyka Polski No. 57, 81, 99*, (Warsaw: GUS, 1971, 1975, 1976).

*The average manual and nonmanual households are not substantially different in size. In 1970 and 1971 the average manual household in Poland was larger than the nonmanual one by approximately 8-15%. The activity ratio of these two strata is however larger for the nonmanual than for the manual by approximately 18-20%. The larger activity ratio of the nonmanual workers is a result both of the smaller size of the household and larger absolute number working in the household.

**The figures for the highest and the lowest income brackets are not fully comparable for the '60s and '70s because the magnitudes of the open-ended extreme brackets are different for these two periods.

into the active labor force because low per capita income households usually have a lot of children to take care of. On top of that,
the women in such families have low qualifications. In the future
more social facilities and proper job training could very quickly
increase the activity ratio, provided of course that this becomes
an objective of the state.

According to data published by T. Komorniczek,[20] the least
affluent first decile of households increased its activity ratio in the
'60s much more than the most affluent tenth decile of households
(the first decile by 20%; the tenth decile by only 4%). The same
tendency can be observed if we compare changes in the activity
ratio of the top five deciles with changes in the lowest five. The
figures are 8 and 17%. So we can conclude that bigger families,
less affluent under pressure of material difficulties, have increased their activity ratio faster than smaller and usually more
affluent families. As a result of these changes, the overall relative
dispersion of the activity ratio of the households has declined.
Hence changes in the relative dispersion of the activity ratio in
favor of the less affluent part of society have become a countervailing force to the increases in relative dispersion of earnings
from 1967 to 1978.[21]

However, if we measured the activity rates of the less and more
affluent households not by the extreme per capita income bracket,
which comprised only a small fraction of all households (e.g., in
1972, 3% in the bottom and 5% in the top bracket), but by the
decile distribution of per capita income, then it would become
apparent that the less affluent households have increased their
activity ratio. What is more, this increase was larger than for the
well-to-do households.

Now let us turn to the second variable that can affect the
relative dispersion of per capita household income, namely, social benefits. Unfortunately, data indicating how the overall distribution of social benefits in general and social benefits in kind,
in particular, changed are far from complete for the whole period
under investigation. The only published figures about changes in
the overall distribution of social benefits can be found in

Table 19

**Social Benefits in Cash per Person Received by Households of Employees in the Lowest and Highest per Capita Income Bracket as a Ratio to Average Social Benefits in Cash Received by all Employees' Households**

|      | Lowest income bracket | Highest income bracket |
| --- | --- | --- |
| 1963 | 0.95 | 1.25 |
| 1967 | 0.87 | 0.96 |
| 1968 | 0.86 | 1.09 |
| 1969 | 0.79 | 1.01 |
| 1970 | 0.74 | 0.99 |
| 1973 | 0.79 | 0.97 |
| 1974 | 0.84 | 0.96 |
| 1975 | 0.87 | 1.10 |
| 1976 | 0.84 | 1.07 |
| 1980 | 0.72 | 1.42 |

*Source: R.S—Budžety gospodarstw domowych.* Data for 1963–70 are not fully comparable with data for 1973 and for 1974–80. The lowest and highest per capita income brackets for 1963–70 are up to 7,200 zl. and above 24,000 zl.; for 1973 they are 9,600 and 36,000 zl.; for 1974–76, 12,000 and 36,000; for 1980, 18,000 and 60,000.

T. Komorniczek[22] and only for 1963 to 1969. According to his figures the bottom decile group got 8.6% of the social benefits and the top got 10.1%. The distribution is nearly perfectly equal; every decile group gets nearly 10% of the benefits. However, the less affluent half of the population (the bottom five decile groups) receive slightly fewer social benefits than the more affluent half of the population (the top five groups). Moreover, the share of the less affluent half of the population has lagged over time. In 1963 they received 49.2%, and in 1969 only 47.6% of all social benefits. This increase in relative dispersion of social benefits in the '60s is even more evident if we compare the changes in the share of the top two decile groups in the total social benefits with the changes in the share of the bottom two. This share has declined for the poorest 20% of the families from 19.2 to 17.9%, whereas for the wealthiest 20% of the families it has increased from 20 to 21.1%.

This inegalitarian trend in the distribution of social benefits is unique for Poland. At variance with the situation in other socialist countries, notably Hungary, changes in the relative dispersion of social benefits in the '60s in Poland did not offset the increase in inequality of earnings.

All partial data available for the 1970s indicate clearly that in employee households, the higher the per capita personal income, the higher the sum of social benefits received.[23] In nearly all major categories of social benefits, education, health, culture, pension, etc., the more affluent groups get more in absolute terms in social benefits than less affluent households. The figures in Table 19 make this very clear.

From Table 19 we can see that not only are the poorest households getting fewer social benefits in cash annually per capita than the most affluent ones, but the difference is growing over time. From 1963 to 1970 there is even an absolute decline in the amount of social benefits received by households in the lowest per capita income bracket. Even family allowances, the only item of social benefits in cash for which the less affluent get more than the more affluent, increase more rapidly for the more affluent than the less affluent.[24] Considering the fact that average family allowances have grown much slower than wages and represent a much higher proportion of social benefits in cash received by the less affluent than by the more affluent households, the rigidity of family allowances has mainly hit the poor families.

If this inegalitarian trend in distribution of social benefits in cash continues in the future, social benefits in cash will largely be correlated with earnings per person in the family and will gradually cease to be a mitigating factor in the relative dispersion of per capita income. A tendency to divide benefits in accordance with income from work distorted the functions and nature of social benefits in cash. Social benefits in cash should be differentiated to a great degree according to the specific needs of the household and according to its material conditions.

Although social benefits both in cash and in kind have increased absolute differences in per capita household income, they have nevertheless markedly reduced the relative dispersion of household per capita income.[25]

There is a lack of consensus in the Polish literature about the degree to which social benefits should reduce absolute disparities in per capita income. The main points of view are naturally ideologically heavily loaded and reflect major differences in personal approach to the philosophy of egalitarianism. Three general points of view can be distinguished briefly:

1. Social benefits should not be used as a tool for reducing income disparities. To take away with one hand what the state provides with the other is inconsistent with the principle of distribution according to work and is a hindrance to improving labor productivity. If the state wants to reduce inequalities, it should use wage differentials or the tax mechanism. The major function of social benefits is not egalitarianism but to provide as much as possible to everyone to ensure equal opportunity. Those who contributed more to society in terms of work and hence have higher earnings should receive more in total social benefits.[26]

2. The most desirable situation from a social point of view is that benefits in total have a neutral impact on absolute income disparities. Some items of social benefits should increase and others should reduce absolute differences in per capita incomes; in other words, every income group should receive in total proportionally the same amount of social benefit.[27]

3. Social benefits should go mainly to those who are in need, especially to big families with low per capita income. Equal opportunity is an empty slogan if we do not reduce not only relative but also absolute differences in per capita income.[28]

In the pre-Solidarity period the prevailing point of view, shared as well by the Gierek government, was the neutral approach to social benefits. However, since the downfall of Gierek the authorities in Poland, under pressure from the workers in Solidarity, have moved to implement a more equal distribution of social benefits. Whether this trend will last in the second part of the eighties and beyond remains to be seen.

Unlike in Hungary, changes in the share of social benefits of

Table 20

**Percentage Distribution of total per Capita Income by Major Source of Income**

| | Income from work and other work-related incomes | Income derived from social benefit in cash | in kind | Total social benefits | Total income |
|---|---|---|---|---|---|
| 1960* | 81.6 | 7.9 | 10.5 | 18.4 | 100.0 |
| 1965 | 81.7 | 7.6 | 10.7 | 18.3 | 100.0 |
| 1969 | 79.0 | 9.2 | 11.8 | 21.0 | 100.0 |
| 1970 | 80.2 | 9.0 | 10.8 | 19.8 | 100.0 |
| 1971 | 79.2 | 9.4 | 11.4 | 20.8 | 100.0 |
| 1972 | 79.3 | 9.1 | 11.6 | 20.7 | 100.0 |
| 1973 | 79.6 | 8.9 | 11.5 | 20.4 | 100.0 |
| 1974 | 80.4 | 8.9 | 10.7 | 19.6 | 100.0 |
| 1975 | 80.9 | 8.4 | 10.7 | 19.1 | 100.0 |
| 1976 | 80.3 | 8.6 | 11.1 | 19.7 | 100.0 |
| 1977 | 80.0 | 9.0 | 11.0 | 20.0 | 100.0 |
| 1978 | 79.3 | 9.6 | 11.1 | 20.7 | 100.0 |
| 1980 | 78.4 | 10.1 | 11.5 | 21.6 | 100.0 |
| 1981 | 79.0 | 10.7 | 10.3 | 21.0 | 100.0 |
| 1982 | 74.0 | 15.0 | 11.0 | 26.0 | 100.0 |

*Sources*: Calculated on the basis of (a) *R.S 1976*, table 1 (121), 79; ibid., *1978*, table 1 (99), 63 and table 1 (134), 90; ibid., *1983*, tables 1(168), 99 and 1 (212), 150; (b) Miedzynarodowe poró̇wnanie struktury spożėycia [International Comparisons of the Consumption Structure], (Warsaw: GUS, 1974, No. 69), 45; (c) *Tendencje rozwoju społecznego* (Warsaw: GUS, 1979, table 42, 91).

*Data for the '60s are not fully comparable with those for the '70s due to some minor methodological and classification changes.

total income are much less pronounced in Poland.

From the data in Table 20 we can see that the share of social benefits in total per capita household income has not changed very much from 1960 to 1978 and has fluctuated around 20%. Only between 1980 and 1982 did this ratio rise to 26%. The proportion of social benefits in cash to social benefits in kind was also more or less stable between 1960 and 1978. The predominant form of benefit in this period was the less equally distributed social benefits in kind. This tendency was reversed in 1981 and

1982, when social benefits in cash became the dominant form of social benefit. Poland in the '60s and '70s had one of the worst records among the CMEA countries as far as the share of social benefits in total income is concerned. In Hungary, for example, the share of social benefits in total income was much higher than in Poland and reached 32% in 1980, whereas in Poland this ratio was only 21.6%; moreover, the predominant form of social benefits in Hungary from 1974 on was in cash and not in kind.[29] As we have noted, this had more equalizing consequences.

Although our data about distribution of social benefits is incomplete for part of the period under investigation, on the basis of partial statistical figures we can argue that the relative dispersion of social benefits has not declined; hence it has not been a countervailing force to increases in relative dispersion of earnings. The main factor that has offset the increase in inequality of earnings was the more rapid increase in the activity ratio of the less affluent than the more affluent households. As a result, the overall relative dispersion of per capita household income was more or less stable in Poland from 1967 to 1978.

# CHAPTER V

# Conclusions

Now that we have completed the statistical analysis, it is time to answer the question that was posed at the beginning of the book: Has the gradual increase in the role of the market mechanism in Eastern Europe affected the distributional pattern? Has it been conducive to more inequality?

The comparative analysis of Poland and Hungary permits us to conclude that the claim of some economists and sociologists that market reforms always mean an increase in the inequality of earnings is not justified. We observe, rather, the lack of an automatic correlation between economic reforms and the dispersion of earnings. Our analysis has shown that a socialist country with a highly centralized system of management can have larger inequalities in the distribution of earnings and in per capita income than a more decentralized market-oriented economy. Relative disparities of earnings in Poland and in Hungary are a case in point.

The level of inequalities depends on many factors, and the degree of decentralization is only one of them. Inequality in the distribution of earnings in the socialist countries is a complex phenomenon. We mention here only a few factors besides the degree of decentralization:

a) The kind of differentials that the country has inherited from the old regime;

b) the stage of development and affluence. This variable seems positively correlated with egalitarianism in Eastern Europe. The more developed socialist countries in Eastern Europe like East Germany and Czechoslovakia have more equally distributed earnings than the less developed countries like Poland, Hungary, and the USSR;[1]

c) political tradition in general and the socialist tradition of egalitarianism in particular. Those traditions are not the same in Moscow, Prague, Warsaw, or Budapest;

d) the nature and quality of the economic policy of the state.

Whatever factors determine the degree of inequality in a socialist country, changes in this variable can be brought about either by market forces or directly by the center. Which instrument is used is a matter of economic policy of the state. When an increase in inequalities is desired, the market mechanism can be used rather than direct orders from the center. However, the possibility of rapid and drastic changes in the relative positions of different strata and occupational groups through state actions or through market reforms is limited despite the powerful tools at the state's disposal. These limitations are important in understanding why there has not been a dramatic increase in income inequalities with the introduction of market reforms.

In all socialist countries, irrespective of their managerial system, there are serious sociopolitical constraints that restrict the role of the material incentive system and, linked with it, the differential pay system. Only a few of these constraints will be mentioned here.

First, the degree of transparency, as Parkin called it, of the reward system is much more pronounced in socialism. It is much easier for the people to perceive a direct link between their rewards and political decisions and power under socialism than under capitalism. Inequalities stemming from the market have a smaller degree of transparency. The market seems to be a highly impersonal mechanism of distribution, ruled by some principles that have nothing to do with the will of the parties involved. But not so in a socialist economy. Instead of the invisible hand, here the hand is very visible as far as distribution of rewards is concerned. It is done, to a large extent, directly by political authority. So the political bodies are directly blamed or praised for their decisions. The perception of inequality is therefore much sharper. As well, and not without importance, there is the fact that Marxist ideology creates a commitment, at least in words, to egalitarianism and to a classless society.

Second, in countries where full employment is a social imperative, a substantial increase in wage differentials is blocked when there can be no large pockets of unemployment because in an environment of full employment and shortages of labor, large differentials between enterprises would result in excessive movement of workers. As a result of this movement, weak enterprises would lose qualified manpower to enterprises offering higher pay and hence further weaken those enterprises.

Third, workers in all socialist countries oppose substantial differences in average wages between enterprises of the same industry or branch and even between employees of the same category in different industries, whether or not such differences are justified by higher productivity. This kind of egalitarianism was manifested especially strongly by the Polish workers' demands in 1980-81 to increase the lowest wages the most and to implement the principle "the same wage for the same job irrespective of the enterprise or industry in which someone works." This egalitarian tendency reflects the belief of the workers that differences in productivity due to differences in quality of machinery and equipment should not influence differences in pay for the same job, because under socialism, the workers should be the owners of all the capital stock and not only of the capital of a specific factory. Hence the fruits of more productive machines should belong to all workers wherever they work.

Fourth, in socialist countries open inflation leads to a reduction in the dispersion of earnings. In keeping with the egalitarian ethos of protecting low-income families, compensation in wages for price increases of consumer goods is deliberately more beneficial to low-earning groups. Price rises are compensated to a larger degree for low-wage groups than for more affluent ones, thus leading to a reduction in wage dispersions. This tendency is especially strong when the average real wage in a socialist country is declining. In this case the real wage of the low-income groups will be protected, and the biggest burden will be put on the highest-income groups.[2]

Fifth, lasting extreme difference in earnings and income would end up in substantial differences in wealth, which cannot be permitted. Although the extremes of earnings between the highest- and lowest-paid employees within the state enterprises are quite substantial, these differentials have by and large gained some social acceptance, whereas differences in consumption standards are strongly resented. This is obviously inconsistent, but it is the reality of today's socialist countries.[3]

The reason why substantial differences in personal consumption are not socially acceptable, and why social tension has intensified in recent years around this issue, has to do partially with the stage of development. At a lower level of development in the '40s and '50s, differences in consumption among various social groups were reflected in the standards of food and clothing. Now, when basic needs have been met, the differences manifest themselves more conspicuously in cars, summer residences, etc. Differences in wealth and property have therefore emerged, and a high proportion of top incomes are saved and invested in durables, houses, paintings, or other kinds of tangible wealth. Sooner or later this fact may force the governments to establish a limit on how many immovable goods one family can possess and to use measures against wealth inheritance.[4] These measures obviously reflect a contradiction. On the one hand, the state allows some groups to have high levels of income, out of which a substantial part can be accumulated. On the other hand, the state is forced to limit the accumulation of capital assets on the part of these groups. Until now the authorities have very often wanted to believe that the affluent would spend their incomes mostly on luxuries—consumer goods (expensive alcohol, expensive clothing), which are highly burdened with turnover taxes—so that the amount left for accumulation in tangible assets would be small. But unfortunately for the authorities, the top income groups are able to acquire both traditional luxury consumer goods and tangible wealth. This is why the state will be forced to put a limit on the accumulation of tangible assets in private hands.

Because the socialist system must limit differences in income and wealth, the effectiveness of the material-incentive system in stimulating productivity is reduced. This is why material incentives alone cannot be relied on to induce work motivation.

Sixth, how effective the material-incentive system is in stimulating good work and increases in productivity depends not only on earnings and differential pay but also on what one can buy for one's earned income. In this respect different systems perform quite differently. It is my firm belief that socialism cannot, due to certain systemic features, develop such a variety of goods as capitalism can, irrespective of the stage of development. It is true that the variety of goods in a capitalist society is sometimes excessive, frivolous, and hence wasteful. However, this situation does not change the fact that the variety of consumer goods in a capitalist society is much broader than in even the most developed socialist countries. Therefore the seductive force of the supermarkets cannot be as strong in socialism as in capitalism. Moreover, the acquisitive instinct cannot be as strong under socialism as under capitalism because acquisition of capital on a substantial scale is excluded. As we know, the incentive to acquire and pass on capital is still a powerful engine of hard work and drive in the capitalist world. The myth that everyone can make it big through hard work and ingenuity is dying hard, especially since we can still find examples of those who have made it. This myth is not shattered by the fact that for every person who has made it there are a thousand who have failed.

It is not, therefore, unjustified to say that for systemic reasons, both the carrot (in the form of material rewards) and the stick (in the form of unemployment and bankruptcy) are not and cannot be as strong under socialism as under capitalism.[5]

The last but not least important aspect that limits the stimulative effect of the material-incentive system is the fact that the link between wages and productivity is not unambiguously clear at all levels of the economy: only on the national scale is this link clear. The opportunity to increase wages (on a national scale) depends on the increase in productivity, but this is not always so in an enterprise. Changes in the level of wages by an enterprise or branch do not necessarily follow changes in their own productivity, because the opportunity to increase productivity is very different in different enterprises and to a considerable extent depends on factors independent of the workers (natural conditions, technology, market position, etc.).[6] In a market framework the same amount of work can bring completely different results. It is practically impossible to separate profits or incomes that result from enterprise labor from those that are the result of market forces.

This problem comes strongly to the fore when prices are used as the instrument to allocate resources with the present level of concentration of production. In most socialist countries the chances for price competition are marginal. Most enterprises in the socialist countries, including those in Hungary and Yugoslavia, have a monopolistic or strongly oligopolistic position.[7] Only imported products can compete with domestic products. Considering the serious difficulties that all socialist countries have, and will have in the future, with their balance of payments, imports are a rather weak substitute for domestic competition. The tendency for enterprises to increase profits or incomes by raising prices, instead of reducing costs, is a major one in socialist decentralized market economies, where control over prices is not marginal at the enterprise level.

Naturally, enterprises that are less successful in terms of income due to factors outside their influence will pressure the authorities to level off the incomes of different enterprises by different redistributive means available to them. That makes the incentive system less transparent and effective. Successful firms know that sooner or later their uncommonly high profits will be skimmed by the state; hence they know that their performance, whatever it is, will not bring large gains or large losses, and that eventually if they are in trouble, they will be bailed out by the state. Needless to say, such awareness will have negative consequences for risk taking, innovations, etc. These consequences are a result of the "soft budget constraints," using Kornai's term, under which most socialist enterprises operate even in Hungary. This "softness" of the budget is not accidental or an aberration caused by the bureaucrats. It is a systemic feature of socialism.

All socialist countries suffer, according to Kornai, from a chronic shortage of production and goods.

These shortages are a result of a natural hunger for resources, especially investment funds, by the socialist manager. He identifies himself with the cause of rapid development because his power and prestige are enhanced by it and because his income and the income of others will increase. At the same time, because of the soft budget constraints, his ''hunger'' for resources is not limited by a fear of losses or of failure.

Shortages make output unresponsive to changes in demand. We therefore usually have a seller's market, with its lack of pressure to save both labor and material inputs, to innovate and produce high-quality goods. This feature of socialism does not result from a particular stage of development, as many writers used to believe, but has systemic roots in the soft budget constraints under which socialist firms operate; the state guarantees that enterprises will continue to produce or even expand even when they do not yield sufficient financial returns.[8] The obvious remedy would be to harden the budget, to subordinate the enterprise to the discipline of the market, with its full financial responsibility, layoffs when warranted by market economic criteria, etc. But according to Kornai there is a limit to how far the budget can be hardened because doing so would clash with the egalitarian and ethical principles of socialism.[9] Profit incentives, writes Kornai, ''clash with the ethical principle which prescribes that everybody should have his share in material goods according to his work and that there should be equal pay for equal work.''[10]

This contradiction prevents a far-reaching hardening of the budget. As a result, a compromise between efficiency and ethical requirements emerges. Kornai believes that such a compromise is workable and desirable. Socialism must admit its limitations in terms of efficiency and look for its strength somewhere else. A claim that one social system must be better than another from every point of view is utopian. It is reminiscent of perfect models that combine all the best features from all systems. In every system, Kornai claims, we must take the good with the bad. Although socialism will always be to a certain degree an "economy of shortages," this fact does not mean that these societies cannot function and develop if the right compromise can be struck between the contradictory elements of the system.

Needless to say, the difficulty in reaching such a "successful" compromise is enormous. Kornai quietly assumes that the contradiction between efficiency and the socialist value system does not prevent some continuous equilibrium between these two elements. More specifically, it means that efficiency can continue to improve, although not as fast as it would without socialist ethical requirements. Hence Kornai assumes that there will be sufficient material means to support socialist values. We cannot, however, exclude the possibility that this equilibrium of countervailing forces, as Brus and Kowalik call it,[11] will not hold, and a deterioration of efficiency will not only prevent the growth objectives of society from being achieved but will also make it impossible to materially support the realization of the ethical and egalitarian values of socialism. Recent developments in the socialist countries, especially in Poland, support this view.

## Solidarity and Economic Reform

In this context it is worth considering what can be learned from Solidarity's approach to egalitarianism and economic reforms.

Although it is premature to fully assess the legacy of the Solidarity movement, one thing is clear: it has left a great imprint on Polish society in particular and probably on other Eastern European countries as well. The ideas formulated by this movement remain an important source for the debate on how to transform "existing socialism" into "socialism with a human face."

A full description and analysis of the program of Solidarity go beyond the aim of this work. We would like to concentrate on the question of egalitarianism and its link to economic reforms.[12]

From its inception the Solidarity movement was strongly egalitarian. Demands for more equality were first formulated in the so-called Gdansk Accord of August 31, 1980, and later in various other Solidarity documents.[13]

The incomes policy package of Solidarity is one of the most egalitarian programs ever formulated in a socialist country. No communist party in the last fifty years, including the Maoist,[14] has gone as far in its egalitarian postulates. It is true that some Solidarity demands were linked simultaneously with open inflation and declining output as well as a declining level of consumption. Under such circumstances compensation for price increases was designed to provide greatest protection to the lowest wage earners. However, there are elements of the program that go beyond the "temporary" acute lack of equilibrium on the consumer market. Certain egalitarian demands, as can be seen from the package, were a major ideological feature of Solidarity.

The egalitarian ethos of Solidarity, and hence the workers, reflects the ideological roots and traditions of the movement. The official rhetoric that socialism is about equality and justice is taken very seriously by the workers (especially the young ones). Some authors explain the egalitarian tendencies of the Polish working class in terms of the Catholic ethic of moderation in consumption and the rustic character of the Polish nation.[15]

However, I do not believe that the Polish nation has a special organic predilection for egalitarianism that is not observable in other nations in the socialist orbit. It is rather the intensity of special circumstances that has made this sensitivity to social justice more acute in Poland than elsewhere.

The enormous disparity between deeds and words, manifested in the exorbitant privileges granted to the ruling elite, especially in the period of the Gierek regime, created an especially fertile ground for opposition to any privilege or social inequality. It is no accident that the quest for social justice is so strongly represented in Solidarity's program. It is symptomatic that by July of 1980, when a wave of strikes hit Poland, in many factories the first workers' demand was to eliminate such privileges as summer houses, luxurious flats, and private villas, very often built with social funds. The egalitarianism of the workers and of the Solidarity movement was a reaction to the intolerable elitism of the '70s. The strong demand for equality was a reaction to a high degree of social inequality.

The advocacy of equalitarianism, social justice, and democratic values has a long tradition in Poland, as in other socialist countries, which predates the Solidarity movement. In spite of the fact that the overwhelming majority of Poles remain Catholic and only a very few identify themselves with Marxism in one form or another, they accept the most fundamental socialist values, especially the idea of real equality of life opportunities. A leading Polish sociologist, S. Nowak, has generalized more than 150 surveys conducted by sociologists since 1956 (out of which six are his own) and has concluded that:

> The great changes in social and economic organization of the society—the nationalization of industry, land reform, economic planning, the abolition of the pre-war class structure—were accepted by the people. As a reflection of the strong propagation of egalitarian ideology in those formative years, the people embraced the idea of equality of life opportunity for all citizens and even the idea of preferential opportunity for the underdog. Their egalitarianism was more moderate when it came to the distribution of income; the majority accepted some inequality. What the people held to be a morally acceptable spread between the top and the bottom, however, would seem fairly radical by the standards of Western Europe. Indeed, the majority held that there was not enough equality in the social stratification of socialist Poland. Most people also shared in the fairly strong conviction that society as a whole and the state in particular are responsible for the equalisation of life opportunities and for the development of the potential of all citizens as well as for the satisfaction of people's basic needs.[16]

Another interesting finding in the work of Nowak and other sociologists is that inequalities in income and wealth are perceived as the major cause of social disintegration and tension. As would be expected, all studies about egalitarianism find that the level of income is inversely related to egalitarian attitudes. The more affluent members of society are more prone to accept differentiation of income and privileges than the less affluent ones. This explains as well why more educated people are less egalitarian, as income in Polish society is increasingly related to education.

However, the more educated strata, according to Nowak's findings, are more strongly attached to democratic values. Hence he concludes that "The higher up the social ladder the respondents were, the more democratic and less egalitarian they were."[17]

The egalitarian aspect of Polish society requires, however, some qualification. We should not overlook the fact that the demand for egalitarian changes by social groups and their will to implement them are not necessarily the same in any society. It is interesting to note that egalitarian statements are usually much stronger when equality is discussed on a general level.[18] But when questions are asked on a lower level of generality and have a bearing on actual privileges and differentials, then egalitarian inclinations are much less pronounced. Even top Solidarity activists have not escaped this human inconsistency. The regional leaders of Solidarity received salaries six times larger than the minimum wage and nearly three times larger than the average monthly wage, despite the fact that as an organization, Solidarity has found such salaries in general too excessive.

Most blue-collar workers, decades before Gierek declared his "enrichment program" for the elite, complained that there was too much privilege, that the party had reneged on its basic ideological promise of equality and justice. This kind of complaint has had serious consequences because the legitimacy of the communist regime in the eyes of the workers has been based on the commitment of the state to social equality and justice. By not fulfilling its own ideological promises, the regime has lost its legitimacy.[19] In addition, inequalities and privileges, together with corruption and mismanagement, were perceived by the workers to be the major cause of the country's economic and social malaise. Many privileges granted by the Gierek regime to the elite (special allowances, pensions, tax exemptions, etc.) were considered by the workers to be deeply unjust and an insult to the dignity of manual work, to the dignity of labor so loudly professed by the communist leaders. The egalitarian ethos of the workers, accumulated for so many years, was expressed with great force by the Solidarity movement. It is quite evident in the Solidarity Program, where egalitarianism and justice are considered one of the fundamental values of the movement, despite the fact that Solidarity does not link those values with the socialist heritage.

It should also not be overlooked that the demand for equality and social justice has provided the Solidarity movement with a basis on which to construct a new labor identity and a new social consciousness. Solidarity has used this ground to effectively oppose the privileges and corruption of the communist regime.

The egalitarian ethos of the Polish workers was also strengthened by the economic crisis. The ruling elite, the managerial privileged group, was blamed for mismanaging the economy. The belief that "they" (the rulers of the country) are responsible created an antimanagerial sentiment among the workers. The workers did not see any reason why managers and other parts of the ruling strata should get privileges when they were performing so badly.

Moreover, substantial wage differentiation was compromised by the chaotic and illogical system of wages, which did not promote good work and efficiency but instead further emphasized the amount of privileges. The link between productivity and pay was completely blurred by this wage system.

Intense disturbances on the consumer market in 1980-81 were also conducive to egalitarian tendencies in Polish society. In an atmosphere of acute shortages, the ability to get scarce goods and certain nonwage benefits, through connections and privileges, became more and more important to the material well-being of the family. More and more, differences in standard of living were not linked to earnings from work. The acute economic crisis and the measures to get out of it also raised the problem of who was going to pay for the austerity program. The workers correctly decided that those who had benefited the most in the time of the Gierek regime should also pay the most when the consequences of that regime were felt.

It is very difficult to judge what part of the Solidarity program on income policy was implemented. The official statistical data for this period of turmoil are particularly unreliable due to the chaos of open and hidden inflation as well as wild speculation caused by shortages. Actual income disparities probably did not conform with the official statistics on income inequalities. Thus skepticism concerning the spectacular reduction of income inequalities that is claimed in the official statistics is well-founded. In addition, some economic steps the government agreed to were not egalitarian in intent, namely, rationing of many goods. This measure resulted from a catastrophic decline in production. Although it is true that rationing is a great leveler, there is no reason to make a virtue out of necessity. It is to be expected that while some equilibrium on the consumer market and some extension of economic reforms will occur, differentials will probably gradually increase. It is, however, difficult to prejudge how the pendulum will swing back. The authorities in Poland, although they are committed to marketization of the economy, must also realize that the egalitarian ethos of Solidarity is well entrenched in Polish society, and thus they must recognize that the clock cannot be entirely turned back.

Having explored the strong egalitarian character of Solidarity, it is valid to ask in what sense it is related to the movement's general concept of reforming the economic system.

Initially, immediately after signing the Gdansk Accord, the new independent unions formulated very moderate positions concerning changes in the functioning of the economic system. Apart from some general principles calling for more independence on the part of enterprises and more genuine participation by workers, Solidarity did not present a comprehensive program of economic reforms; this task was left to the government. The new trade unions only wanted to have some input into decisions by the government that affected workers' well-being. In accordance with the Gdansk Accord, Solidarity wanted to be consulted and to have some say on such questions as: how the national income is divided between consumption and accumulation, what the size and structure of public consumption should be, how wages and incomes should be divided, etc.

At the enterprise level, in order to protect the interests of the workers, the independent unions wanted to have some influence in the areas of work conditions, job security, and level of pay. But the unions did not want to take over management functions or responsibilities. We have here a clear echo of the division of power concept. The new independent unions strongly stressed in this initial period the following division of functions in society:

1. The government through their directors should run the enterprises and manage the economy.

2. The party should deal with sociopolitical problems of a strategic nature and with ideology.

3. The trade unions should control how the product is distributed, without being absorbed in day-to-day managing of the enterprise. The accent was more on distribution than on production. The workers rejected direct participation and responsibility in decisionmaking at the enterprise level because they feared that (a) to take responsibility for the production process would not be effective in an environment of shortages of raw materials and energy, and (b) they would lose popularity by cooperating with management, which was considered to be a part of the ruling apparatus: in the latter situation they would share the blame for waste and mismanagement. This is why their approach to self-management was rather lukewarm. Even when the Solidarity activists did not oppose the formation of workers' councils, the workers made it clear that these councils should be entirely separate from the new unions. Needless to say, their cautious approach to self-management was also shaped by the bad experience of the old workers' councils which, corrupted by the managerial process, had become servants to the party bosses in the enterprise

or served merely to rubberstamp everything that management decided.

The decision to delegate so many economic functions and responsibilites to the government was based on the belief that the existing government, with some major changes, would be able to run the economy and would be able to organize the production process. Solidarity at this time was not yet aware of the depth of the economic and political crisis. But soon the workers realized that the government was incapable of running the economy and of overcoming the economic crisis, and they realized that the economic situation was rapidly deteriorating. By the end of 1980 we can see changes in workers' attitudes toward self-governing bodies. It became apparent to them that unless they took factory reforms into their own hands, the economic situation would never improve. This perception was strengthened by the complete paralysis of the government and the lack of any positive state program for reforms.[20]

As a result of this shift in workers' attitudes, many large enterprises started to organize in the early spring of 1981. These founding enterprises held a national conference and created NSZZ, the Solidarity Network of Enterprises (Sieć)[21] as a consulting advisory body to the Solidarity Union with respect to economic reforms and workers' self-government in the enterprises. The Network of Enterprises became a very powerful body that pressured not only the government but also the leadership of Solidarity to advance socioeconomic reforms. Gradually the proposals of the "Network" became a part of the broader program of the "Self-governing Republic" presented to the First Congress of Solidarity in September-October 1981. At this congress a far-reaching decentralization was proposed which, if implemented, would have swept away nearly the entire superstructure of the economic state bureaucratic apparatus.

The first draft of economic reforms, presented in the spring of 1981 by a group of advisors acting as a Program-Consulting Council for Solidarity, was not very different from the draft of the government commission for economic reforms. Both these proposals for economic reform were similar to Lange's and Brus's[22] model in which an attempt is made to reconcile central planning, the market, and producers' self-government. Both the program of the Advisory Council of Solidarity and that of the government commission for reform worked out a model that could, as T. Kowalik expressed it, ". . . be placed midway between Hungarian New Economic Mechanism and the Yugoslav self-governing market economy."[23] The differences between the two proposals centered on political questions rather than purely economic issues. Solidarity's program demanded a simultaneous introduction of some political changes as a precondition for the success of the economic reforms, whereas the government program is totally silent about such political changes.

As the general sociopolitical situation in the country deteriorated and more hostility between Solidarity and the government came to the fore, both programs grew more and more apart. The "Network" at the time was very instrumental in the formulation of a counterproposal to the government approach. This document was vigorously debated within the Solidarity movement. As a result of this heated debate, the concept of "social enterprises," as distinct from state and cooperative enterprises, was crystalized by the Solidarity movement. The "social enterprise" has three major characteristics that have been labeled the "three selfs." They are:

1. *Self-dependence*. The enterprise is independent from the state administration, which has no right to impose its preferences concerning output, inputs, etc. The autonomous enterprise decides what and how to produce and sets prices for its goods and services. The state can pass antimonopoly laws to check unfair price practices. Here we see a major departure from the model of Lange and Brus, where a substantial part of prices is either established or controlled by the authorities, whereas in the Solidarity program, only a few basic consumer goods and services, like milk, bread, schoolbooks, and apartment rents, should be priced by the state. Prices of all other goods and services, according to the Solidarity program, would be set by the self-governing

enterprises. Another major departure from Lange's and Brus's model centers on central control of investment. In the Solidarity program the enterprise has full decision-making power and control over the investment process. The state would have control over investment only in infrastructure, defense, etc. In accordance with this approach the state, as in the Yugoslav model, tries to achieve its macroeconomic goals only through taxation, custom duties, and credits. In other words, the state would rely only on indirect economic methods and tools.

2. *Self-government*. The enterprise is managed by the work force directly or by a workers' council. Directors would be hired and fired by the council. This point has become the major bone of contention between the government and Solidarity. After a lengthy debate in September 1981, a compromise was reached, not well received by the rank and file of Solidarity, in which directors of enterprises would be nominated by the self-governing bodies, but the authorities could veto their decision. In key enterprises the rule would be reversed: the authorities nominate the director, and the self-governing enterprise has the right to veto the authorities' decision.

3. *Self-financing*. Wages and salaries are strictly related to the performance of the enterprise. Only a minimum wage fixed by the state in negotiation with the unions would be guaranteed. Inefficient enterprises would be threatened with bankruptcy. Here again, in contradistinction with the Lange-Brus approach, the state does not establish *ex ante* the major differentials. The role of the state in shaping the distributional pattern is limited to a minimum and maximum wage.

Obviously these three major rules of behavior of the enterprise require a complete overhaul of the state administration. The economic state bureaucracy would be drastically reduced due to the obsolescence of its functions. In line with this approach the Solidarity program proposed abolishing compulsory associations and branch ministries and replacing them with one Central Ministry of Industry and Trade. The Central Planning Commission as well would be transformed into a Bureau of Economic Analysis and

Planning, which would be subordinate to parliament rather than to the government.

This brief description of the Solidarity proposals for economic reform indicates very clearly that a full-fledged market economy of a Yugoslav type was suggested in Poland. The initial attempt to reconcile central planning with the market and with workers' councils was ended, and the Solidarity movement increased its support for a free market structure.

How could such a fascination with the market be explained in a country that has produced such distinguished economists as Kalecki, Lange, Brus, and others, who have deeply analyzed the limits of the market mechanism in a socialist economy and have been profoundly concerned with the possibilities of incorporating this mechanism into a system of central planning? It seems this tradition was momentarily forgotten in Poland, and no one seriously questioned whether a full-fledged market economy could provide an effective mechanism for the allocation of resources under conditions of social ownership of the means of production. There was little discussion of how such a far-reaching decentralization of the economy would guarantee the macroeconomic objectives of a socialist society, such as, for example, full employment—an objective Solidarity has always supported as an unquestionable imperative. Solidarity very strongly advocated an expansion of the welfare system, absolute job security, and an expansion of the paternalistic role of the state but never questioned how this role could be reconciled with extensive marketization of the economy. From all the writings and documents in the Solidarity movement, it is apparent that Solidarity did not perceive the negative consequences of a full marketization of the economy, particularly its incompatibility with the extensive egalitarianism it favored.

Solidarity shared with some other left-wing populist movements the naive view that only the beneficial aspects of the market would be present. There was little discussion of the impact of market reforms on income distribution, job security, bankruptcies, etc. Although in its program Solidarity admits that some "public cost" will be incurred due to reforms, no consistent remedies are proposed to mitigate the increased inequalities of income that would arise among regions and branches of the economy. Neither are there consistent remedies for the consequences of bankruptcies and the job losses they would imply.[24] Solidarity's denial of any major role for the central state in redistributing incomes and resources goes further, in my opinion, than any program formulated by liberal or social democratic governments in Western Europe. This ambivalence in the Solidarity program stems not only from its populist antistate bias but also from its profound distrust of the existing Polish state.[25]

There is no question that this fascination with the market mechanism was a reaction to the abuses and shortcomings of the command economy and its extremely centralized nature. A more extreme variant of decentralization was favored by Solidarity not only because it was considered to be very efficient in an economic sense but also because it was a Trojan horse designed to break the backbone of the bureaucratic structure—a tool to reduce the power of the state. This justifiable preoccupation with a reduction of state power as a way to enhance democracy obviously blinded Solidarity to the economic consequences of extreme decentralization.

Another ambivalent point in the Solidarity program is a lack of clarity concerning how sociopolitical pluralism is related to egalitarianism.

There was a consensus in Solidarity that the new system be based on a diversity of social forces that obviously do not have identical interests. All these different stratas and groups were to have the right to organize and defend their interests. But the ability to organize and apply pressure is not the same for all groups. Who, therefore, will defend the interests of the weak groups in society, especially in the field of income distribution? How will the interests of different groups be reconciled? Is there not a danger that in the process of bargaining between different interests, the outcome will be beneficial to the strongest group?

I do not share the extreme point of view expressed by some

writers[26] that egalitarianism is incompatible with democracy under all systems, that only by denying to the strong groups in society the right to organize and apply pressure can one impose some form of egalitarianism. In defense of sociopolitical pluralism under socialism, it can be argued that the ability to organize and apply pressure is not related to wealth and property, as in a capitalist society, at least not to the same degree. This is obviously a valid point; however, it does not clearly acknowledge that access to power and hence decision making in the framework of socialism is also differentiated—although in different ways. The ability of the workers to organize is not the same, for example, in the state industries as in the urban cooperative sector, nor is it the same in large or small enterprises. Different local unions and associations do have and will continue to have different strengths, different clout, and different importance. Credit must be given to Solidarity that it perceived the diversity of strengths in the various unions and groups. The leadership and rank and file grasped the fact that unions organized on an industrial-branch basis would become an easy target for the government. Hence a territorial organizational structure was prepared and implemented by Solidarity in order to be able to confront the centralized body of the government with Solidarity's own centralized organizations and thus avoid dissipation of its forces. However, Solidarity saw this problem in the context not of how pluralism is linked to egalitarism but how its diversity affects the confrontation with the government.

We do not claim that this kind of contradiction between different group interests cannot be favorably resolved. It can be successfully done if government and unions are committed ideologically to some form of egalitarianism. However, the Solidarity leadership never saw this contradiction clearly nor did they address this problem.

The Solidarity program, despite its lack of clarity and its ambiguities about the relationship between egalitarianism and pluralism, and about the limits of decentralization of the economy, aptly perceived that the cure for the socioeconomic malaise in Poland

and elsewhere did not lie in increasing differentials and privileges. The solution to the Polish crisis is a broad democratization of Polish society and a reduction of differentials and privileges as a part of this process. The Solidarity movement, like its progressive predecessors in Poland and in other socialist countries, was aware that economic democracy confined solely to the workplace would not do. Socialism with a human face can come only from pluralistic political institutions able to control the state. Solidarity's contribution in this matter is not so much in producing pioneering ideas as in its unique attempt to implement them.

Our analysis has already indicated that all socialist countries, irrespective of their management systems and of their degree of centralization or decentralization, have always faced a conflict (or tension) between distributional justice as a part of the socialist value system and the requirements of efficiency. This conflict is bound to increase in the '80s and will create serious socioeconomic problems for them. The major reason for this unfavorable trend is the economic stagnation that is observable, with some variations, in all socialist countries.[27]

What is the way out of this predicament? Will, for example, more inequality improve the efficiency of the economy? Our answer is no. The experience of the socialist countries, and specifically that of Poland, has shown that increased differentials and privileges without broader sociopolitical measures make the situation even worse. The discontent that is created by a lack of justice further undermines the will to work, further reduces the so-called X-efficiency, and further alienates the workers from management and the state. The events in 1980 in Poland strongly support this view. The Gierek enrichment program and the vast privileges that were granted to top state and party bureaucrats (including the top managerial strata) did not and could not increase the efficiency of the economy. On the contrary, this program created broad dissatisfaction among factory workers and eventually led to the outburst in the summer of 1980 and the rise of the Solidarity movement.

It is the author's conviction that the long-run solution to the problem is political in nature. Broad sociopolitical changes are needed to improve the efficiency of the system. Decentralization of economic decisions linked with effective forms of self-management would increase the identification of employees with their workplace and would assist in changing the people's attitude to common ownership of the means of production. Despite all the propaganda slogans in the socialist countries, the concept of common ownership has never been internalized by the people. The factories, in the eyes of the workers, are "theirs," not ours.

Although economic democracy in the workplace would certainly improve the attitude to work and to common property, it would not be sufficient to established an efficient economic system. Democracy in the workplace and in the localities must be supplemented with democracy on a national scale. As Brus and Kowalik point out: "The possible solution has to be sought in bringing in the element which is missing from all hitherto known varieties of existing socialism, including the Yugoslav version. This missing element is genuine democratic control over the responsibility for decisions taken on the macro scale."[28]

Needless to say, democracy at the macrolevel, like democracy in general, has a value in itself; but it is also important for economic efficiency in the socialist countries. The special role of democracy on a macroscale for economic efficiency lies in the fact that there is a limit to decentralization under socialism. The state cannot relinquish, even in the most decentralized variety of socialism, certain macroeconomic decisions without facing serious socioeconomic consequences. In order to guarantee a few fundamental desiderata of the economic system—such as (a) growth at the full employment level and some form of job security; (b) some relative stability of prices, especially consumer prices; and (c) a reasonable degree of equality in the distribution of income between strata and regions—the government must maintain control over such macroeconomic decisions as the size of the accumulation fund, the structure of a substantial part of investment, the distribution of income between major strata in society, and the overall level of prices for important goods.[29]

To go beyond this broad boundary of decentralization would create a certain amount of unemployment in both open and hidden forms, clear price inflation, and increase in wage differentials and income disparities between regions, and underutilization of capacity so that supply could be easily adapted to demand.

These assertions are not based merely on the logic of the system but on historical experience. The Yugoslav experiment, with all its important achievements in adapting the structure of supply to demand, in making better use of raw materials and equipment, and in improving the quality of goods, has failed as far as the main desiderata of macroeconomic stability are concerned. The Yugoslavs have a very high rate of inflation, outstripping all Western European countries, a substantial level of unemployment, and an increase in the disparities of income among the various republics (which is one of the main sources of political tension and separatist tendencies troubling Yugoslavia today).[30]

From the fact that the state must play an important role in economic life in a socialist country—a greater role than the most interventionist state in capitalist society—it follows that the economy cannot be entirely depoliticized as a result of economic reforms. What is necessary, then, is increased political democracy, a democratization at the center. Macrodecisions by nature are based on political considerations, which in turn are based on certain value criteria. There must be a political mechanism that will control the central planners' macrodecisions, a mechanism that will ensure that the decisions are to some extent a result of compromise between different social forces. This history of all socialist countries proves that the central authorities, if not checked by autonomous political institutions, are strongly inclined to sacrifice today's consumption to tomorrow's, investing too heavily and very often using a capital-output ratio that is too high, with all the negative consequences of these actions for consumers. In order to ensure a proper choice of investment rate, aggregate technique, and between short- and long-run levels of consumption, the central authorities must be democratically controlled. A more decentralized political system is required under these circumstances.

Although such fundamental sociopolitical changes now look more remote than ever, especially after the destruction of the Solidarity movement, these ideas are as topical as ever today, and they will be tomorrow. In the long run increased democracy is the only alternative for the socialist countries to overcome a deep socioeconomic crisis.

# Appendix

Table A

## Distribution of Full-Time Earnings of Males and Females in the State Sector in Hungary (September Data)

| | Industry | | | | | | Agriculture and forestry | | | | | |
|---|---|---|---|---|---|---|---|---|---|---|---|---|
| | 1966 | | 1968 | | 1974 | | 1966 | | 1968 | | 1974 | |
| | M | F | M | F | M | F | M | F | M | F | M | F |
| $P_5$ | .57 | .68 | .55 | .67 | .57 | .63 | .51 | — | .55 | — | .59 | .55 |
| $P_{10}$ | .67 | .74 | .66 | .72 | .65 | .71 | .60 | .67 | .62 | .66 | .68 | .66 |
| $P_{15}$ | .75 | .77 | .73 | .76 | .71 | .76 | .66 | .70 | .69 | .72 | .73 | .75 |
| $P_{25}$ | .82 | .84 | .80 | .83 | .80 | .84 | .78 | .79 | .82 | .81 | .82 | .83 |
| $P_{75}$ | 1.21 | 1.22 | 1.23 | 1.23 | 1.24 | 1.21 | 1.23 | 1.21 | 1.27 | 1.22 | 1.22 | 1.22 |
| $P_{85}$ | 1.39 | 1.33 | 1.39 | 1.32 | 1.41 | 1.34 | 1.38 | 1.39 | 1.36 | 1.40 | 1.36 | 1.39 |
| $P_{90}$ | 1.50 | 1.39 | — | 1.37 | 1.55 | 1.46 | 1.50 | 1.51 | 1.51 | 1.48 | 1.49 | 1.51 |
| $P_{95}$ | 1.71 | 1.47 | — | 1.57 | 1.80 | 1.64 | 1.70 | 1.63 | — | 1.67 | 1.70 | 1.73 |
| Median estimated in forints | | | | | | | | | | | | |
| (M) | 2,045 | 1,390 | 2,135 | 1,441 | 3,287 | 2,210 | 1,749 | 1,212 | 1,849 | 1,294 | 2,926 | 2,026 |
| $P_{95}/P_5$ | 3.0 | 2.16 | — | 2.34 | 3.16 | 2.60 | 3.33 | — | — | — | 2.88 | 3.14 |
| $Q_3 - Q_1*/M$ | .39 | .38 | .42 | .40 | .44 | .37 | .45 | .42 | .45 | .41 | .40 | .39 |
| $Q_3/Q_1$ | 1.48 | 1.46 | 1.52 | 1.48 | 1.55 | 1.44 | 1.58 | 1.53 | 1.55 | 1.50 | 1.48 | 1.47 |

Table A (continued)

| | Construction | | | | | | Transport and communications | | | | | |
|---|---|---|---|---|---|---|---|---|---|---|---|---|
| | 1966 | | 1968 | | 1974 | | 1966 | | 1968 | | 1974 | |
| | M | F | M | F | M | F | M | F | M | F | M | F |
| $P_5$ | .57 | .61 | .56 | .60 | .60 | .59 | .60 | .69 | .59 | .61 | .56 | .52 |
| $P_{10}$ | .66 | .76 | .69 | .66 | .68 | .67 | .67 | .73 | .67 | .70 | .66 | .67 |
| $P_{15}$ | .76 | .71 | .74 | .72 | .73 | .72 | .74 | .77 | .76 | .73 | .72 | .73 |
| $P_{25}$ | .83 | .79 | .81 | .80 | .81 | .80 | .84 | .83 | .83 | .81 | .81 | .83 |
| $P_{75}$ | 1.23 | 1.28 | 1.20 | 1.26 | 1.26 | 1.28 | 1.21 | 1.22 | 1.22 | 1.23 | 1.24 | 1.23 |
| $P_{85}$ | 1.41 | 1.41 | 1.36 | 1.37 | 1.43 | 1.46 | 1.32 | 1.32 | 1.35 | 1.32 | 1.39 | 1.37 |
| $P_{90}$ | 1.52 | 1.55 | — | 1.49 | 1.58 | 1.62 | 1.43 | 1.37 | 1.46 | 1.40 | 1.49 | 1.49 |
| $P_{95}$ | 1.76 | 1.79 | — | 1.71 | 1.86 | 1.87 | 1.57 | 1.49 | — | 1.59 | 1.68 | 1.66 |
| Median estimated in forints (M) | 1,958 | 1,373 | 2,122 | 1,425 | 3,423 | 2,359 | 1,867 | 1,427 | 1,945 | 1,472 | 2,951 | 2,179 |
| $P_{95}/P_5$ | 3.08 | 2.93 | — | 2.85 | 3.10 | 3.17 | 2.62 | 2.16 | — | 2.60 | 3.0 | 3.19 |
| $Q_3 - Q_1*/M$ | .40 | .49 | .39 | .46 | .45 | .48 | .37 | .39 | .39 | .42 | .43 | .40 |
| $Q_3/Q_1$ | 1.48 | 1.62 | 1.48 | 1.57 | 1.56 | 1.60 | 1.44 | 1.47 | 1.47 | 1.52 | 1.53 | 1.48 |

Table A (continued)

## Distribution of Full-Time Earnings of Males and Females in the State Sector in Hungary (September Data)

| | Trade | | | | | | Material production sector total | | | | | |
|---|---|---|---|---|---|---|---|---|---|---|---|---|
| | 1966 | | 1968 | | 1974 | | 1966 | | 1968 | | 1974 | |
| | M | F | M | F | M | F | M | F | M | F | M | F |
| $P_5$ | .53 | .59 | .51 | .56 | .53 | .58 | .56 | .62 | .55 | .61 | .57 | .59 |
| $P_{10}$ | .60 | .68 | .59 | .66 | .63 | .69 | .64 | .71 | .65 | .71 | .65 | .70 |
| $P_{15}$ | .67 | .74 | .67 | .72 | .69 | .73 | .72 | .76 | .74 | .74 | .71 | .75 |
| $P_{25}$ | .80 | .81 | .79 | .80 | .79 | .82 | .82 | .83 | .81 | .82 | .80 | .83 |
| $P_{75}$ | 1.24 | 1.27 | 1.23 | 1.27 | 1.26 | 1.26 | 1.23 | 1.24 | 1.22 | 1.24 | 1.24 | 1.23 |
| $P_{85}$ | 1.40 | 1.40 | 1.42 | 1.41 | 1.45 | 1.44 | 1.39 | 1.36 | 1.39 | 1.35 | 1.41 | 1.36 |
| $P_{90}$ | 1.51 | 1.53 | — | 1.57 | 1.61 | 1.57 | 1.51 | 1.42 | — | 1.42 | 1.55 | 1.50 |
| $P_{95}$ | 1.73 | 1.73 | — | 1.76 | 1.90 | 1.83 | 1.73 | 1.61 | — | 1.65 | 1.79 | 1.69 |
| Median estimated in forints | | | | | | | | | | | | |
| (M) | 1,913 | 1,399 | 2,023 | 1,463 | 3,064 | 2,259 | 1,945 | 1,377 | 2,050 | 1,435 | 3,180 | 2,212 |
| $P_{95}/P_5$ | 3.26 | 2.93 | — | 3.14 | 3.58 | 3.15 | 3.09 | 2.60 | — | 2.40 | 3.14 | 2.86 |
| $Q_3 - Q_1{}^*/M$ | .44 | .46 | .44 | .47 | .47 | .44 | .41 | .41 | .41 | .42 | .44 | .40 |
| $Q_3/Q_1$ | 1.55 | 1.57 | 1.56 | 1.59 | 1.59 | 1.54 | 1.50 | 1.50 | 1.50 | 1.52 | 1.55 | 1.48 |

Table A (continued)

| | Nonmaterial production sector | | | | | | State sector total | | | | | |
|---|---|---|---|---|---|---|---|---|---|---|---|---|
| | 1966 | | 1968 | | 1974 | | 1966 | | 1968 | | 1974 | |
| | M | F | M | F | M | F | M | F | M | F | M | F |
| $P_5$ | .48 | .57 | .51 | .56 | .54 | .51 | .55 | .60 | .54 | .59 | .57 | .54 |
| $P_{10}$ | .54 | .62 | .58 | .61 | .62 | .59 | .63 | .68 | .63 | .68 | .64 | .67 |
| $P_{15}$ | .60 | .66 | .65 | .66 | .68 | .67 | .71 | .74 | .73 | .73 | .71 | .72 |
| $P_{25}$ | .71 | .76 | .76 | .76 | .78 | .78 | .82 | .81 | .80 | .80 | .79 | .82 |
| $P_{75}$ | 1.21 | 1.31 | 1.30 | 1.30 | 1.29 | 1.30 | 1.24 | 1.26 | 1.23 | 1.26 | 1.25 | 1.25 |
| $P_{85}$ | 1.39 | 1.48 | — | 1.49 | 1.52 | 1.51 | 1.41 | 1.38 | 1.40 | 1.37 | 1.42 | 1.41 |
| $P_{90}$ | 1.54 | 1.63 | — | 1.62 | 1.69 | 1.66 | 1.52 | 1.44 | — | 1.50 | 1.56 | 1.55 |
| $P_{95}$ | 1.77 | 1.80 | — | 1.84 | 1.99 | 1.85 | 1.75 | 1.70 | — | 1.69 | 1.82 | 1.77 |
| Median estimated in forints (M) | 2,151 | 1,411 | 2,150 | 1,445 | 3,127 | 2,173 | 1,951 | 1,384 | 2,060 | 1,437 | 3,173 | 2,202 |
| $P_{95}/P_5$ | 3.69 | 3.15 | — | 3.28 | 3.68 | 3.62 | 3.18 | 2.83 | — | 2.86 | 3.19 | 3.27 |
| $Q_3 - Q_1{}^*/M$ | .49 | .54 | .54 | .54 | .51 | .52 | .42 | .44 | .42 | .45 | .45 | .43 |
| $Q_3/Q_1$ | 1.69 | 1.71 | 1.71 | 1.71 | 1.66 | 1.66 | 1.52 | 1.55 | 1.52 | 1.56 | 1.57 | 1.52 |

*Source:* See Table 1.

Table B

## Average Monthly Wages and Salaries in Major Sectors of the Socialized Economy (State sector total = 100)

| Sectors | 1960 | 1961 | 1962 | 1963 | 1964 | 1965 | 1966 | 1967 | 1968 | 1969 | 1970 | 1971 | 1972 | 1973 | 1974 | 1975 | 1976 | 1977 | 1978 |
|---|---|---|---|---|---|---|---|---|---|---|---|---|---|---|---|---|---|---|---|
| Industry | 105.7 | 105.0 | 105.0 | 104.2 | 103.1 | 103.0 | 102.4 | 102.0 | 100.9 | 100.0 | 99.4 | 98.7 | 98.5 | 100.6 | 100.9 | 101.1 | 100.5 | 101.0 | 101.0 |
| Construction | 106.9 | 106.5 | 107.2 | 109.1 | 106.6 | 107.2 | 107.6 | 110.5 | 109.5 | 109.2 | 109.4 | 107.8 | 107.4 | 108.2 | 109.2 | 110.1 | 110.2 | 109.8 | 109.2 |
| Agriculture and forestry | 92.5 | 92.9 | 90.0 | 91.3 | 91.8 | 91.9 | 92.1 | 93.4 | 94.5 | 97.7 | 99.7 | 98.2 | 97.5 | 95.2 | 97.1 | 96.3 | 94.0 | 94.3 | 93.4 |
| Transport and communications | | 97.8 | 97.5 | 97.7 | 96.7 | 101.4 | 101.6 | 100.4 | 100.9 | 102.2 | 104.8 | 104.7 | 104.9 | 104.3 | 105.5 | 105.3 | 103.9 | 102.7 | 103.0 |
| Trade | | 92.7 | 91.5 | 91.3 | 90.0 | 90.4 | 91.7 | 94.1 | 94.2 | 94.2 | 93.3 | 92.1 | 91.5 | 89.7 | 89.4 | 89.0 | 88.1 | 87.6 | 87.3 |
| Nonproductive sector | 97.5 | 99.0 | 99.7 | 98.3 | 98.5 | 98.8 | 99.3 | 100.2 | 98.1 | 98.1 | 97.9 | 101.7 | 102.2 | 99.0 | 96.7 | 96.4 | 94.9 | — | — |
| Urban cooperatives | 96.2 | 93.0 | 93.6 | 93.6 | 93.3 | 93.4 | 91.4 | 94.2 | 92.6 | 93.5 | 95.7 | 95.4 | 93.9 | 90.6 | 89.9 | 89.0 | 87.5 | — | — |
| Socialist sector, total | 99.7 | 99.5 | 99.6 | 99.6 | 99.7 | 99.5 | 99.3 | 99.5 | 99.3 | 99.3 | 99.5 | 99.3 | 99.0 | 98.9 | 98.8 | 98.6 | — | — | — |
| Ratio of highest to lowest paid sector | 115.6 | 116.4 | 119.1 | 121.2 | 117.9 | 116.9 | 117.7 | 117.3 | 118.2 | 117.0 | 118.8 | 117.0 | 117.4 | 120.6 | 122.1 | 123.7 | 125.1 | — | — |

Sources: A lakosság jövedelme es fogyasztása 1960–1975, (Budapest: KSH, 1976), 10; F.K.A. 1976; ibid., 1978 (1980), table 15A, 64, and table 10A, 122.

Table C

## Percentage Distribution at Current Prices by Major Source of Income on a per Capita Basis

| Year | Income derived from work (earned income) | Income derived from social benefit in money | in kind | Social benefit total | Income from other sources |
|------|------|------|------|------|------|
| 1960 | 80.4 | 7.0 | 11.4 | 18.4 | 1.2 |
| 1961 | 79.6 | 7.4 | 11.7 | 19.1 | 1.3 |
| 1962 | 79.0 | 7.7 | 12.0 | 19.7 | 1.3 |
| 1963 | 78.4 | 7.9 | 12.3 | 20.2 | 1.4 |
| 1964 | 78.1 | 8.0 | 12.2 | 20.2 | 1.7 |
| 1965 | 77.1 | 8.6 | 12.4 | 21.0 | 1.9 |
| 1966 | 76.4 | 9.4 | 12.3 | 21.7 | 1.9 |
| 1967 | 76.6 | 9.6 | 12.1 | 21.7 | 1.7 |
| 1968 | 76.0 | 9.9 | 12.1 | 22.0 | 2.0 |
| 1969 | 75.6 | 10.0 | 12.2 | 22.2 | 2.2 |
| 1970 | 74.5 | 10.4 | 12.4 | 22.8 | 2.7 |
| 1971 | 73.7 | 10.9 | 12.6 | 23.5 | 2.8 |
| 1972 | 72.8 | 11.7 | 12.7 | 24.4 | 2.8 |
| 1973 | 72.2 | 12.5 | 12.8 | 25.3 | 2.5 |
| 1974 | 71.4 | 13.3 | 12.7 | 26.0 | 2.6 |
| 1975 | 70.6 | 14.4 | 12.9 | 27.3 | 2.1 |
| 1976 | 69.3 | 15.6 | 13.1 | 28.7 | 2.0 |
| 1977 | 70.6 | 16.6 | 12.0 | 28.6 | 0.8 |
| 1978 | 69.8 | 16.6 | 12.7 | 29.3 | 0.9 |
| 1979 | 68.4 | 17.9 | 12.7 | 30.6 | 1.0 |
| 1980 | 67.0 | 19.0 | 13.0 | 32.0 | 1.0 |
| 1981 | 66.9 | 18.7 | 13.6 | 32.3 | 0.8 |
| 1982 | 66.5 | 19.2 | 13.7 | 32.3 | 0.6 |
| 1983 | 65.5 | 19.1 | 14.2 | 33.3 | 1.2 |

*Sources: S.E 1972* (Budapest: KSH, 1973), 377, table 4A; ibid., *1974* (1976), 359, table 3; ibid., *1976* (1977), 308, table 3A; ibid., *1980* (1981), 356, table 3A; ibid., *1983* (1984) table 19(1), 246; *Statistical Yearbook 1974* (Budapest: Central Statistical Office, 1976), 359, table 3.

Table D

# Distribution of per Capita Household Income* by Social Stratum in Hungary

| | Manual workers | Peasants | Double-income group | Nonphysical employees | Self-employed | Active household together | Pensioners | All households |
|---|---|---|---|---|---|---|---|---|
| | | | | | 1967 | | | |
| $P_2$ | — | — | — | — | — | — | — | — |
| $P_5$ | — | — | 0.53 | 0.56 | — | — | — | 0.56 |
| $P_{10}$ | 0.59 | 0.58 | 0.62 | 0.63 | — | 0.58 | — | 0.64 |
| $P_{15}$ | 0.66 | 0.62 | 0.68 | 0.69 | 0.63 | 0.65 | — | 0.75 |
| $P_{25}$ | 0.77 | 0.74 | 0.79 | 0.79 | 0.75 | 0.76 | — | 1.30 |
| $P_{75}$ | 1.28 | 1.30 | 1.23 | 1.25 | 1.36 | 1.29 | 1.30 | 1.30 |
| $P_{85}$ | 1.47 | 1.49 | 1.39 | 1.42 | 1.56 | 1.47 | 1.50 | 1.48 |
| $P_{90}$ | 1.61 | 1.64 | 1.50 | 1.57 | 1.74 | 1.61 | 1.64 | 1.63 |
| $P_{95}$ | 1.83 | 1.86 | 1.70 | 1.83 | 2.10 | 1.84 | 1.91 | 1.87 |
| $P_{98}$ | — | — | — | — | — | — | — | — |
| Median estimated in forints | 1,017 | 1,061 | 1,122 | 1,332 | 1,030 | 1,101 | 756 | 1,068 |
| $P_{98}:P_2$ | — | — | — | — | — | — | — | — |
| $P_{95}:P_5$ | — | — | 3.21 | 3.27 | — | — | — | — |
| $P_{90}:P_{10}$ | 2.73 | 2.83 | 2.42 | 2.49 | — | 2.78 | — | 2.91 |
| $P_{85}:P_{15}$ | 2.23 | 2.40 | 2.04 | 2.06 | 2.48 | 2.26 | — | 2.31 |
| $\dfrac{Q_3 - Q_1}{M}$ ** | 0.52 | 0.56 | 0.44 | 0.46 | 0.61 | 0.52 | — | 0.54 |
| $Q_3/Q_1$ | 1.67 | 1.75 | 1.55 | 1.58 | 1.82 | 1.69 | — | 1.72 |
| Number of brackets | 22 | 22 | 22 | 22 | 22 | 22 | 22 | 22 |

Table D (continued)

1972

| | Manual workers | Peasants | Double-income group | Nonphysical employees | Self-employed | Active household together | Pensioners | All households |
|---|---|---|---|---|---|---|---|---|
| P₂ | — | — | — | — | — | — | — | — |
| P₅ | 0.49 | 0.47 | 0.54 | 0.56 | 0.45 | 0.49 | — | 0.45 |
| P₁₀ | 0.60 | 0.56 | 0.63 | 0.64 | 0.56 | 0.60 | — | 0.56 |
| P₁₅ | 0.67 | 0.64 | 0.70 | 0.70 | 0.61 | 0.66 | — | 0.64 |
| P₂₅ | 0.77 | 0.75 | 0.80 | 0.79 | 0.75 | 0.77 | 0.73 | 0.75 |
| P₇₅ | 1.27 | 1.31 | 1.24 | 1.28 | 1.28 | 1.28 | 1.35 | 1.30 |
| P₈₅ | 1.44 | 1.52 | 1.39 | 1.49 | 1.53 | 1.48 | 1.61 | 1.49 |
| P₉₀ | 1.57 | 1.68 | 1.51 | — | — | 1.63 | 1.80 | 1.66 |
| P₉₅ | 1.80 | — | 1.73 | — | — | 1.87 | 2.16 | 1.90 |
| P₉₈ | — | — | — | — | — | — | — | — |
| Median estimated in forints | 1,380 | 1,479 | 1,607 | 1,811 | 1,756 | 1,525 | 964 | 1,475 |
| P₉₈:P₂ | — | — | — | — | — | — | — | — |
| P₉₅:P₅ | 3.67 | — | 3.20 | — | — | 3.82 | — | 4.22 |
| P₉₀:P₁₀ | 2.62 | 3.0 | 2.40 | — | — | 2.72 | — | 2.96 |
| P₈₅:P₁₅ | 2.15 | 2.38 | 1.99 | 2.13 | 2.51 | 2.24 | — | 2.33 |
| $\frac{Q_3 - Q_1}{M}$ ** | 0.49 | 0.56 | 0.44 | 0.49 | 0.53 | 0.51 | 0.63 | 0.55 |
| Q₃/Q₁ | 1.64 | 1.75 | 1.55 | 1.62 | 1.70 | 1.67 | 1.86 | 1.73 |
| Number of brackets | 22 | 22 | 22 | 22 | 22 | 22 | 22 | 22 |

Table D (continued)

## Distribution of per Capita Household Income* by Social Stratum in Hungary

|  | 1977 | | | | |
|  | Manual workers | Nonmanual workers | Self-employed | Total active households | All households |
| --- | --- | --- | --- | --- | --- |
| $P_2$ | 0.41 | 0.52 | 6.00 | 0.41 | 0.39 |
| $P_5$ | 0.53 | 0.61 | 0.46 | 0.53 | 0.51 |
| $P_{10}$ | 0.63 | 0.67 | 0.58 | 0.63 | 0.60 |
| $P_{15}$ | 0.70 | 0.72 | 0.68 | 0.69 | 0.67 |
| $P_{25}$ | 0.79 | 0.80 | 0.78 | 0.79 | 0.78 |
| $P_{75}$ | 1.25 | 1.28 | 1.32 | 1.27 | 1.27 |
| $P_{85}$ | 1.42 | 1.48 | 1.63 | 1.46 | 1.47 |
| $P_{90}$ | 1.56 | 1.63 | 1.83 | 1.60 | 1.61 |

| | | | | | |
|---|---|---|---|---|---|
| $P_{95}$ | 1.75 | 1.88 | 2.11 | 1.84 | 1.84 |
| $P_{98}$ | 2.02 | 2.27 | — | 2.20 | 2.20 |
| Median estimated in forints | 2,105 | 2,530 | 2,343 | 2,231 | 2,181 |
| $P_{98}:P_2$ | 4.93 | 4.37 | — | 5.36 | 5.64 |
| $P_{95}:P_5$ | 3.30 | 3.08 | 4.59 | 3.47 | 3.61 |
| $P_{90}:P_{10}$ | 2.48 | 2.43 | 3.16 | 2.54 | 2.68 |
| $P_{85}:P_{15}$ | 2.03 | 2.06 | 2.40 | 2.12 | 2.19 |
| $\dfrac{Q_3 - Q_1}{M}$ ** | 0.46 | 0.48 | 0.54 | 0.48 | 0.49 |
| $Q_3/Q_1$ | 1.58 | 1.60 | 1.69 | 1.61 | 1.63 |
| Number of brackets | 22 | 22 | 22 | 22 | 22 |

*Source: A.C 1972,* (Budapest: KSH, 1975), 54; ibid., *1977* (1980), 68.

*Including social benefits in cash but not in kind.

**$Q_3$—upper quartile; $Q_1$—lower quartile; M—median.

Table E

**Social Benefits in Kind per Capita for Households of Different Social Strata (Workers = 100)**

| | 1967 | | | | | | 1972 | | | | |
|---|---|---|---|---|---|---|---|---|---|---|---|
| | Health | Education | Food subsidies | Other benefits | Together | | Health | Education | Food subsidies | Other benefits | Together |
| Peasants | 81.0 | 90.0 | 14.4 | 41.4 | 71.8 | | 81.7 | 98.0 | 25.8 | 57.0 | 81.1 |
| Double-income groups | 70.4 | 91.7 | 48.3 | 43.2 | 71.5 | | 77.6 | 94.0 | 83.4 | 61.1 | 81.9 |
| Nonmanual workers | 109.9 | 143.2 | 134.0 | 195.0 | 140.5 | | 105.9 | 140.9 | 156.6 | 203.9 | 138.8 |
| Self-employed | 71.4 | 105.3 | 30.7 | 96.1 | 85.7 | | 92.4 | 93.2 | 40.5 | 100.2 | 91.0 |
| Pensioners | 225.1 | 27.5 | — | 97.9 | 109.5 | | 163.9 | 24.1 | — | 149.6 | 95.4 |
| Total | 104.7 | 98.5 | 71.9 | 98.7 | 98.7 | | 102.6 | 99.7 | 87.7 | 116.5 | 102.8 |

*Source: A.C 1972* (Budapest: KSH, 1975), 87.

Table F

# Per Capita Income of Members of the Socialized Sector (Annual Net Income per Person) in Poland

|  | 1967 | | | 1968 | | | 1969 | | | 1970 | | | 1971 | | |
|---|---|---|---|---|---|---|---|---|---|---|---|---|---|---|---|
|  | T | M | N | T | M | N | T | M | N | T | M | N | T | M | N |
| $P_5$ | 0.52 | — | 0.51 | 0.51 | — | 0.51 | 0.51 | 0.52 | 0.54 | 0.50 | 0.52 | 0.54 | — | — | 0.51 |
| $P_{10}$ | 0.58 | 0.60 | 0.60 | 0.59 | 0.59 | 0.59 | 0.60 | 0.59 | 0.61 | 0.60 | 0.59 | 0.62 | 0.58 | 0.60 | 0.59 |
| $P_{15}$ | 0.65 | 0.65 | 0.66 | 0.66 | 0.65 | 0.65 | 0.66 | 0.66 | 0.67 | 0.66 | 0.66 | 0.68 | 0.65 | 0.66 | 0.67 |
| $P_{25}$ | 0.75 | 0.75 | 0.77 | 0.78 | 0.75 | 0.75 | 0.77 | 0.76 | 0.77 | 0.76 | 0.76 | 0.77 | 0.76 | 0.76 | 0.77 |
| $P_{75}$ | 1.32 | 1.33 | 1.33 | 1.35 | 1.33 | 1.30 | 1.34 | 1.31 | 1.28 | 1.30 | 1.33 | 1.31 | 1.31 | 1.33 | 1.30 |
| $P_{85}$ | 1.57 | 1.59 | — | 1.55 | 1.60 | — | 1.52 | 1.57 | — | 1.51 | 1.54 | — | 1.53 | 1.54 | — |
| $P_{90}$ | 1.70 | 1.78 | — | — | 1.74 | — | — | 1.71 | — | 1.67 | 1.72 | — | — | 1.71 | — |
| $P_{95}$ | — | — | — | — | — | — | — | — | — | — | — | — | — | — | — |
| Median estimated in Zlotys (M) | 14,000 | 12,571 | 16,518 | 14,744 | 13,354 | 17,584 | 15,531 | 14,029 | 18,312 | 16,083 | 14,398 | 18,823 | 18,737 | 17,065 | 21,230 |
| $P_{95}/P_5$ | — | — | — | — | — | — | — | — | — | — | — | — | — | — | — |
| $P_{90}/P_{10}$ | 2.93 | 2.97 | — | — | 2.95 | — | — | 2.90 | — | 2.78 | 2.92 | — | — | 2.85 | — |
| $Q_3{-}Q_1/M$ | 0.57 | 0.58 | 0.56 | 0.57 | 0.58 | 0.55 | 0.57 | 0.55 | 0.51 | 0.54 | 0.57 | 0.54 | 0.55 | 0.57 | 0.53 |
| $Q_3/Q_1$ | 1.76 | 1.77 | 1.73 | 1.73 | 1.77 | 1.73 | 1.74 | 1.72 | 1.66 | 1.71 | 1.75 | 1.70 | 1.72 | 1.75 | 1.69 |

Table F (continued)

|  | 1973 | 1974 | 1975 | 1976 | 1978 | 1980 | | | 1982 | | |
|---|---|---|---|---|---|---|---|---|---|---|---|
|  | T | T | T | T | T | T | M | N | T | M | N |
| $P_5$ | 0.48 | — | 0.50 | 0.49 | 0.49 | 0.48 | 0.50 | 0.49 | — | — | 0.60 |
| $P_{10}$ | 0.57 | 0.58 | 0.59 | 0.58 | 0.58 | 0.57 | 0.58 | 0.58 | 0.64 | 0.66 | 0.68 |
| $P_{15}$ | 0.63 | 0.65 | 0.65 | 0.65 | 0.64 | 0.64 | 0.65 | 0.66 | 0.69 | 0.70 | 0.73 |
| $P_{25}$ | 0.75 | 0.75 | 0.76 | 0.75 | 0.76 | 0.75 | 0.76 | 0.75 | 0.79 | 0.78 | 0.81 |
| $P_{75}$ | 1.32 | 1.31 | 1.31 | 1.29 | 1.35 | 1.33 | 1.31 | 1.31 | 1.27 | 1.28 | 1.26 |
| $P_{85}$ | 1.52 | 1.53 | 1.53 | — | — | — | 1.53 | — | 1.44 | 1.44 | — |
| $P_{90}$ | 1.70 | — | 1.73 | — | — | — | 1.65 | — | 1.55 | 1.57 | — |
| $P_{95}$ | — | — | 1.93 | — | — | — | — | — | — | — | — |
| Median estimated in Zlotys(M) | 20,347 | 22,807 | 25,397 | 27,697 | 32,251 | 39,745 | 36,226 | 45,001 | 79,619 | 74,062 | 85,847 |
| $P_{95}/P_5$ | — | — | 3.86 | — | — | — | — | — | — | — | — |
| $P_{90}/P_{10}$ | 2.98 | — | 2.93 | — | — | — | 2.84 | — | 2.42 | 2.38 | — |
| $Q_3-Q_1/M$ | 0.57 | 0.56 | 0.55 | 0.54 | 0.59 | 0.58 | 0.55 | 0.55 | 0.48 | 0.50 | 0.45 |
| $Q_3/Q_1$ | 1.76 | 1.75 | 1.72 | 1.72 | 1.77 | 1.77 | 1.72 | 1.75 | 1.60 | 1.64 | 1.56 |

Source: R.S., Budżety gospodarstw domowych; Statystyka Polski, No. 35, 57, 81, 84, 99, 128. (Warsaw: GUS); Reprezentacyjne badania warunków bytu ludności [Sample analyses of the well being of the population] (Warsaw: GUS, 1970), part 3.

Note: M-Manual Workers; N-Nonmanual employees, T-Total).

# Notes

CHAPTER I

1. An extreme case of reversing the growing tendency of the investment rate (I/Y) is the Polish economy. The collapse of the Gierek regime strategy of accelerating growth by means of foreign credit from the West forced the government in the second half of the '70s to reduce the share of investment in the national income in a wild and incoherent manner, creating further imbalances in the economy. A good description of this period is in W. Kuczynski, *Po wielkim skoku* [After the great leap] published unofficially in 1979 in Warsaw by the independent publishing house Nowa; see also Z. Fallenbuchl, "The Polish Economy in the 70's," *East European Economies Post-Helsinki* (Washington: U.S. Congress Joint Economic Committee, 1977).

2. A comprehensive analysis of economic reforms in Eastern Europe is in W. Brus, *The Economy of Eastern Europe after the Second World War* (Oxford: Oxford University Press, 1982). The English version represents vol. 3 of the *Economic History of Eastern Europe* which will be published in 1985 by Oxford University Press.

3. Gy. Peter, "A gazdaságosság és jövedelmezőség jelentősége a tervgazdálkodásban" [The importance of economic efficiency and profitability in a planned economy], *Kozgazdasagi Szemle*, 1956, 695-711.

4. "Tezy rady ekonomicznej w sprawie niektórych kierunków zmian modelu gospodarczego"[Thesis of the Economic Council concerning the direction of changes of the economic model], *Dyskusja o polskim modelu gospodarczym* [A Discussion of a Polish Economic Model] (Warsaw: KiW, 1957), 261-78. An interesting review of the "Thesis" in the Western literature is in G. R. Feiwel, *The Economics of a Socialist Enterprise* (New York: Praeger, 1965), 17-25. There is a great deal of literature on discussions of the economic model of Poland, including: *Dyskusja o polskim modelu gospodarczym* [A discussion of a Polish economic model] (Warsaw, 1957); *Ekonomiśći dyskutuja o prawie wartośći* [Economists discuss the problems of the law of value)] (Warsaw: KiW, 1956); W. Brus, *Prawo wartosci a problematyka bodźców ekonomicznych*

[The law of value and problems of economic incentiveness] (Warsaw: KiW, 1956); O. Lange, "Political Economy of Socialism," "Role of Planning in Socialist Economy," "Basic Problems of Socialist Construction"—all three in *Problems of Political Economy of Socialism*, O. Lange ed. (New Delhi: People's Publishing House, 1962).

5. See W. Brus, *Ogólne problemy funcjonowania gospodarki socjalistycznej* (Warsaw: PWN, 1964); English version, *The Market in a Socialist Economy* (Boston: Routledge and Kegan Paul, 1972); Ota Šik, *Plan and Market Under Socialism* (White Plains, N.Y.: International Arts and Sciences Press, 1967); E. Liberman, "Once Again on the Plan, Profits, and Bonuses," *The Liberman Discussion: A New Phase in Soviet Economic Thought*, vol. 1, Myron E. Sharpe ed. (White Plains, N.Y.: International Arts and Sciences Press, 1965).

6. The intellectual pioneering role of Polish economic science in the '50s, in a country with less mature conditions for practical implementation of reforms, is a very interesting sociological phenomenon.

7. See Brus, *The Market in a Socialist Economy*; O. Lange, "How I see the Polish economic model," *Papers in Economics and Sociology* (Warsaw: PWN, 1970).

8. O. Lange's economic model of 1956-57 differs substantially from his previous decentralized model, formulated in *On the Economic Theory of Socialism* (Minneapolis: University of Minnesota Press, 1964). He grants the central planner much more power and prerogatives in at least two important areas: (1) The central planner decides the investment structure for most of the investment funds, whereas in his previous model the Central Planning Board left the structure of investment to entrepreneurs guided only by the interest rate established by the center. In other words, the socialist directors decide where and how to invest. (2) Prices of most goods must be determined or controlled by the state and conveyed to the enterprises as parameters to guarantee the independence of prices from the particular interest of the enterprise, whereas the parametric nature of prices in his previous model is ensured, in one form or another, by the free market or by the trial-and-error method used by the center to establish prices.

9. The "New Economic Mechanism" in Hungary from the outset in 1968 proposed a gradual reduction in the relative amount of state-controlled prices, at the same time increasing not only free market prices but also introducing ceiling prices for some goods in the socialized sector. From this point of view the Hungarian model probably gives more scope to nonstate-controlled prices than the decentralized model of W. Brus and O. Lange.

10. V. Novozhilov calls such an economic model indirect centralization. See *Ekonomika i matematicheskie metody* [Economics and mathematical methods], vol. 1, no. 5, Moscow, 1965.

11. The fathers of a decentralized model with a regulated market mechanism were skeptical that the central planner would be able to guide the enterprises' current activities with only economic instruments—without using orders to some degree. Administrative orders would be inevitable because: (i) there is a

NOTES TO PAGES 7-10     167

danger of monopolistic tendencies, especially in the socialist countries. Some enterprises with monopolistic positions would try to maximize their profit against the interests of the public. (ii) Time is always a factor; in those cases where quick structural changes are a necessity, direct orders would be more effective. (iii) A weak buyer's market and high rates of growth create shortages of raw materials. The role of the market declines and leads to orders, rationing, etc. In other words, the possibility of the market playing an important role is linked with the general pattern of the economy. High rates of growth lead to tight planning, and this in turn leads to a much greater role of administrative orders.

12. A detailed description of the economic reforms in Hungary is in Bela Belassa, "The Economic Reform in Hungary," *Economics*, vol. 37, no. 145, February 1970, 1-23; *Reform of the Economic Mechanism in Hungary, Nine Studies*, Istvan Friss ed. (Budapest: Kiado, 1969).

13. P. Wiles, *Economic Institutions Compared* (Oxford: Blackwell, 1977), 445.

14. P. Sweezy, "The Transition to Socialism," *Monthly Review*, no. 1, May 1971, 1-17; M. Ellman, *Soviet Planning Today* (London: Cambridge University Press, 1971); F. Parkin, *Class Inequality and Political Order* (London: Paladin, 1975); D. Milenkovitch, *Plan and Market in Yugoslav Economic Thought* (New Haven: Yale University Press, 1971); D. Lane, *The End of Inequality? Stratification Under State Socialism* (Harmondsworth: Penguin, 1971).

15. W. Brus, *The Economics and Politics of Socialism* (London: Routledge and Kegan Paul, 1973).

16. I. Friss, *Economic Laws, Planning, Control* (Budapest: Kiado 1971); O. Gado ed., *Reform of the Economic Mechanism in Hungary: Developments 1968-1971* (Budapest: Kiado, 1972).

17. W. Brus, *The Economics and Politics of Socialism*, 37-41; "Income Distribution and Economic Reforms in Poland," *Il Politico*, vol. 39, no. 1 (Padua: University of Pavia, 1974); A. M. Vacic, "Distribution According to Work and Commodity Production," *Acta Oeconomica*, vol. 18 (3-4), no. 1, 1977, 227-45.

18. M. Markus and A. Hegedus, "The Role of Values in the Long-Range Planning of Distribution and Consumption," *Hungarian Sociological Studies, Sociological Review*, Monograph no. 17, 1972.

19. It must be stressed, however, that government policies in the field of distribution are not, for whatever reasons, always successful. Sometimes the results achieved by government policies can be completely different from the desired objective. We have therefore not only the spontaneous working of the market mechanism but also, so to speak, the spontaneous working of the planned mechanism. This lack of success of government policies in the field of distribution of earnings can be a result of a multitude of government actions in different fields of socioeconomic life that contradict and nullify its objective, as far as the differentiation policy is concerned; or forces are at play over which the government has no control or insufficient control, forces which countervail

the action of government policies (e.g., shifts in the supply of labor, demographic changes in the population and labor force, changes in the social composition of the labor force, etc.). From this it follows that we should not *a priori* assume that government policies and its instruments in the field of distribution of earnings always work in accordance with the deliberate aims of the government.

20. Official data about earnings in the socialized sector both in Poland and Hungary include the following elements:

1) Wage-rate payments for time and piecework (usually per hour) of manual workers and basic salary rates (usually per month) of nonmanual workers.

2) Supplementary payments, e.g., for seniority, health hazards, overtime work, working on holidays, special payments for highly qualified personnel, equivalence of pay in kind, and some money social benefits in the form of holidays, etc.

3) Bonuses, premiums, and rewards of different kinds for meeting goals and overfulfillment or special achievement. This category also includes payment for overfulfillment of piecework norms.

From these elements of earnings it is obvious that wage rates are only a part of manual workers' earnings, and basic salary rates are only a part of the earnings of nonmanual employees.

21. Harvey Leibenstein, in his essay "Allocative Efficiency vs. X-efficiency," *American Economic Review*, vol. 56, June 1966, 392–415, distinguishes efficiency linked with optimal conditions for allocating resources to given techniques to satisfy competing ends from efficiency resulting from using the most input-saving technique available. This kind of efficiency he called X-efficiency. The accent here is on reducing cost by more intensive and better work, saving raw materials, and proper care of equipment by employees. Not more resources but the best use of those you have is the most important way to reduce cost and to cut waste. Liebenstein believes that it is not differences in skill and education but differences in willpower to work well among individual workers and managers that produce major reductions in cost. The losses that result from a lack of X-efficiency are much more important than losses from allocative inefficiency.

22. In 1970 the following principle of wage differentiation was established. The Center established the minimum and maximum wage rate for manual workers (ranging from 4 to 16 forints per hour). The differentiation within the limits of 4 : 1 is based on two characteristics of work: the level of skill and the working conditions, including the physical effort required by the job. Four levels of skill and four degrees of working conditions were defined. Decisions about other components of differentiation, including the grades in each category, were decentralized and left to the discretion of the firm or ministries. For nonmanual employees the basis of salary differentiation was the level of qualifications and the number of years in the job, rank in the structure, the number of subordinates, and in some cases the size of the enterprise. Professional skill and rank were separated, so that expertise could be highly rewarded without the worker holding a high managerial position.

23. In the Yugoslav model, understood as a theoretical construct on a high level of abstraction, the question of how the interplay of the market mechanism and the center influences the differentiation of earnings is not relevant. The market forces in this model determine both the vertical and the horizontal differentials. But for the actual Yugoslav economy from 1965 to 1975, this question was in fact relevant. The state in Yugoslavia, although to a lesser degree than in Hungary, intervened in the distributional pattern of wages, especially in the vertical differential pattern.

24. S. I. Shkurko, *Soverhenstvovanie norm i systema zarobotnoi platy*, [The improvement of production norms and the wage system] (Moscow, 1975), 100–2.

25. It should be stressed that significant increases in wages are a precondition for increasing differentials because without such an increase, differentials can be widened only at the expense of low-paid employees. Small wage increases in the '60s and '70s in most socialist countries obviously limited chances to widen wage differentials.

26. See Henry Phelps Brown, *The Inequality of Pay* (Berkeley and Los Angeles: University of California Press, 1977), 322–32.

27. See more detail in G. Grossman, "The Second Economy of the USSR," *Problems of Communism*, vol. 26, September-October 1977, 25–40.

28. See P. Sweezy, "On the Transition from Capitalism to Socialism," *Monthly Review*, vol. 15, no. 11, March 1964, 569–90; "Market and Plan, Plan and Market," *American Economic Review*, vol. 67, no. 2, February 1977, 67–68; H. Ticktin, "Socialism, the Market and the State: The Class Structure of the U.S.S.R. and the Soviet Elite," *Critique*, no. 3, 1977, and no. 9, 1980.

29. See "Problems of Profitability and Income Distribution," *New Hungarian Quarterly*, vol. 12, 1971, 41.

30. For more details, see O. Gado, *The Economic Mechanism in Hungary, How It Works, in 1976* (Budapest: Kiado, 1976).

31. See a discussion about new changes in the economic mechanism of Hungary in J. Katona, "A Discussion about the Directives of the XII Congress of the Hunagrian Communist Pary," *Partelet*, no. 11, 1979; T. Nagy, "The Hungarian Economic Reform: Current Issues and the Future," *Trends in World Economy*, no. 33, I. Dobozi and H. Matejka eds. (Budapest, 1981), 151–63.

32. K. Marx and F. Engels, *Werke*, vol. 23 (Berlin: Deitz Verlag, 1974), 213.

33. K. Marx, "The Civil War in France," in K. Marx and F. Engels, *Selected Works* (Moscow: Progress Publishers, 1970), 28.

34. F. Engels, *Anti-Dühring* (Moscow: Progress Publishers, 1954), 278–79

35. See A. Bergson, *The Structure of Soviet Wages* (Cambridge, Mass.: Harvard University Press, 1944), 16.

36. S. Lakos, "Questions of Social Equality," *The New Hungarian Quarterly* (Printemps, 1975).

37. F. Pryor, *Property and Industrial Organization in Communist and Capitalist Nations* (Bloomington: Indiana University Press, 1973); *Public Expen-*

*ditures in Communist and Capitalist Nations* (Homewood, Ill.: Irwin, 1968).

38. A. Nove, *The Economies of Feasible Socialism* (London: George Allen & Unwin, 1983), 83.

39. N. E. Rabkina and N. M. Rimashevskaia, *Osnovy differentsiatsii zarabotnoi platy i dokhodov naseleniia* [The basis for differentiating earnings and incomes of the population] (Moscow: Ekonomika 1972), 15. Their point of view is shared by A. Ia. Boiarskii, *Matematiko-ekonomicheskie ocherki* [Mathematical-Economic Essays] (Moscow: Gosizdat, 1962), 111; W. D. Belkin, *Tseny edinogo urovnia i ekonomicheskie izmereniia na ikh osnove* [Prices of a single level and economic measurement on their basis] (Moscow: Ekonomizdat, 1963), 50–51.

40. V. F. Maier, *Dokhody naseleniia i rost blagosostoianiia naroda* [Incomes of the population and the increase of the well-being of the people] (Moscow: Mysl, 1968), 36; E. I. Kapustin, *Kachestvo truda i zarabotnaia plata* [Quality of Labor and Earnings] (Moscow: Mysl, 1964), 78.

41. See V. Kovyzhenko, "Problems of Reducing Complex Labor to Simple Labor in Marxist Political Economy," *Problems of Economics*, no. 4, August 1973, 147–57; I. Anan'eva, "Differentiation of Wages According to the Complexity of Labor," *Problems of Economics*, no. 12, April 1974, 60–77; A. Dainovskii, "Reduction of Labor and Expenditures on Personnel Training," *Problems of Economics*, no. 10, February 1974, 60.

42. See I. I. Kuzminov, V. S. Dunaev, and V. V. Tsiakonov eds., *Ekonomicheskii zakon raspredeleniia po trudu* [The economic law of distribution according to labor] (Moscow, 1975), 18.

43. See B. M. Levin, *Sotsial'no-ekonomicheskie potrebnosti: zakonomernosti formirovaniia i razvitiia* [Socioeconomic needs: principles of formation and development] (Moscow), 1974), 165.

44. Z. Fainburg, "The Current Stage of the Scientific and Technical Revolution and Social Planning," *Nauchno-technicheskaia revolutsiia i sotsial'nyi progress* [The scientific-technical revolution and social progress] (Moscow 1972), 196.

45. See M. Yanowitch, *Social and Economic Inequality in the Soviet Union: Six Studies* (Armonk: M. E. Sharpe Inc., 1977), 11–14.

46. The "objective law" was questioned by a group of labor economists who claim that the differentials established in the '30s were excessive for the conditions of the '50s and '60s. See R. A. Batkaev and V. I. Markov, *Differentsiatsiia zarabotnoi platy v promyshlennosti SSSR* [The differentiation of earnings in Soviet industry] (Moscow, 1964), 32.

47. See A. Chilosi, "The Ideological Roots of Soviet and Eastern European Distribution Policies: Socialist and Communist Income Distribution," seminar paper, St. Anthony's College, Oxford; Carl Riskin, "Maoism and Motivation: Work Incentives in China," *China's Uninterrupted Revolution*, V. Nee and J. Peck eds. (New York: Pantheon, 1975).

48. Marx's scattered remarks about abolishing money as a unit of economic calculation of goods and resources in a socialist society and introducing instead a new measure based on a labor unit were taken very seriously by the Bolsheviks

in the period of war communism. Even in 1918 the Supreme Council of the National Economy (VSNKH) had ordered the Research Institute of the Finance Commissariat (Ministry) to present its views about a new moneyless system. After lengthy discussions in the beginning of 1921, a special committee was created in the Finance Commissariat, led by the distinguished economist S. Strumilin, to work out immediately a new unit for economic calculation. This committee proposed two accounting units: (1) one to measure the amount of simple labor spent on goods, called *trudovaia edinitsa* [labor unit], abbreviated *tred*. A simple labor unit (*tred*) was considered a normal day or the hours work of an average laborer without qualifications fulfilling the work norm 100%. (2) One unit was to measure utility. Strumilin proposed measuring utility by the daily food ration necessary to replenish the energy of an adult not working. This bundle of goods, measured in terms of calories, he labeled *dovolstvie* (supplies), abbreviated *dov*. Each member of society would have a booklet recording the amount of credit of consumer goods measured in *dov's* each citizen is entitled to in accordance with how many working units (*tred*) had been accumulated. A more detailed description is in S. Strumilin, *Problemy ekonomiki truda* [The economic problems of labor] (Moscow, 1925).

At the end of 1921 the Soviet government had entirely abolished the concept of "labor money" and restored money as a part of the new Economic Policy (NEP).

Strumilin's proposals, as well as other similar proposals at this time, had numerous weaknesses, but the major failures were:

a) the inability to reduce skilled to simple labor in a meaningful way;

b) the inability to recognize which work hours are socially necessary and which are not;

c) the inability to move beyond the concept of measuring utility in terms of energy.

49. In socialist countries, especially in the USSR, it is assumed that the grade system reflects different dimensions of the quality of labor. The tariff system in the narrow sense consists of four elements: (1) a set of basic rates differentiated for various branches and industries and payable to the least skilled workers; (2) a set of skill scales determines how much more is paid to a skilled worker than an unskilled one in different branches and sectors; (3) additional pay for working in difficult conditions (arduous, unpleasant work, etc.); and (4) extra pay for geographical location expressed in the form of a coefficient. Differentials among various enterprises of the same branch are not considered normal under a centralized model because, according to the Soviet view, this would violate the principle of equal pay for equal work, which is considered the essence of the socialist principle of distribution.

50. Some economists in socialist countries think that the efficiency requirements of the state can be formulated as one synthetic index, namely, maximization of the rate of growth of national output; others deny that in a complex society one economic objective can be the aim of the socialist state. For more details, see Lange, *On Economic Theory*.

51. Although both socialist and capitalist economic systems need income

differentials, it does not follow that they need to be the same in both systems or even in different countries of the same system. The differences in training costs, the degree of restriction of entry to different jobs imposed by trade unions or other institutions, prejudices of the education system in job selection, differences in tastes and cultural tradition, etc., have a serious influence on wage differentials. It is difficult not to agree with Alastair McAuley: "What is appropriate for Britain or the U.S.A. may well not suit the U.S.S.R.; what is right in the thirties may be inadequate today." See *Economic Welfare in the Soviet Union* (London: Allen and Unwin, 1979), 179.

52. See K. Davis and W. E. Moore, "Some Principles of Stratification," *American Sociological Review*, vol. 10, no. 1-6, 1945, 242-49.

53. See more detail in G. A. Huaco, "The Functional Theory of Stratification," *Inquiry*, no. 9, 1966, 215-40; S. Lukes, "Socialism and Equality," *The Socialist Idea*, L. Kolakowski and S. Hampshire eds. (Reading: University of Reading, 1974); W. Wesolowski, "Some Notes on the Functional Theory of Stratification," *Polish Sociological Bulletin*, 3-4, 1962, 23-38. Some sociologists do not see why the social requirement of division of labor necessitates income disparities and social stratification. According to Ralf Darhrendorf (see "On the Origin of Social Inequality," P. Laslett and W. G. Runciman eds., *Philosophy, Politics and Society* [Oxford: Blackwell, 1962]) and the Polish sociologist Wesolowski (in "Some Notes"), social stratification can take place without income inequality. At the root of stratification is not the need to induce people via pay differentials to acquire some skills but the hierarchical structure of organization and the system of command and authority. Stratification is inevitable because of differential authority or power. Those who give the commands, even if their income is not higher than those who obey commands, still form a distinct social group.

54. For example, in the Soviet Union in 1969 the average earnings for workers in the coal mines were 210 rubles per month, whereas the average earnings for the engineering technical personnel (including all managers) in light industry were only 138 rubles monthly. Moreover, the average earnings of coal miners were higher than the average earnings of the engineering-technical personnel in most industries and branches. See V. E. Komarov, *Ekonomicheskie problemy podgotovki i ispolzovaniia kadrov spetsialistov* [The economic problems of preparation and utilization of expert cadres] (Moscow, 1972), 190. The picture in other socialist countries in this matter is not very different.

55. These views have been most strongly expressed by the architects of the reform in Hungary in the first year of implementing the reforms, especially by R. Nyers. A variant of this "socialist" functional theory of distribution is expressed by a Bulgarian economist, Ch. Kiuranov, "Aspects of Distribution of Personal Earnings and Earnings Stratification in Bulgaria," Z. Fallenbuchl ed., *Economic Development in the Soviet Union and Eastern Europe*, vol. 1 (New York: Praeger, 1974). A switch to intensive methods of growth in the socialist countries must increase the dispersion of earnings because the role of science and of educated people in the process of production is growing. They must therefore be better rewarded. However, according to Kiuranov, this in-

crease in differentials is temporary.

56. Anan'eva, "Differentiation of Wages."

57. See an interesting presentation by A. M. Okun, *Equality and Efficiency: The Big Trade-off* (Washington, D.C.; Brookings, 1975).

58. See more detail in T. Kasprzyk, *Bodźce ekonomiczne w przedsiebiorstwie przemysłowym* [Material incentives in an industrial enterprise] (Warsaw: PWN 1963), 539; S. Borkowska, "Ocena efektywności systemu plac wewnątrz WOG" [Assessment of the effectiveness of wages in big economic organizations], *Płace w przemsłowych wielkich organizacjach gospodarczych* [Wages in big industrial organizations] (Warsaw: PWE, 1978); E. E. Lawler, *Pay and Organizational Effectiveness: A Psychological View* (New York, 1971), 117–26; R. Weil, "Methods of Wage Payment," *Wage Determination, Organization for Economic Cooperation and Development* (Paris, 1974), 168–69.

59. See *Politics, Economics and Welfare*, (New York: Harper, 1953), 150.

60. Dahl and Lindblom, *Politics, Economics.*

61. See more detail in Pryor, *Public Expenditures.*

62. In the socialist countries, as in the capitalist ones, very often educated people with professions earn at the beginning of their careers no more than a skilled manual worker. As time goes by, however, educated professionals will gain higher pay. In the socialist countries we still observe a strong pressure to get into the universities, to join the noble professions, even if some of them do not guarantee higher earning prospects than skilled manual labor.

63. See K. Szikra Falus, "Wage Differentials in Hungary," *Acta Oeconomica*, vol. 25, no. 1–2, 1980, 163–72.

64. In 1973 about 40% of all manual workers in Polish industry were on a piecework system of payment, whereas in the early '50s this figure was nearly 70% (see L. Jacukowicz, *Proporcje plac w polsce* [Wage proportions in Poland] Warsaw: PWE, 1974). The same declining tendency is evident in the Western countries. However, the proportion of manual workers on piecework in industry is much lower in the Western than in the Eastern countries. See H. G. Lydall, *The Structure of Earnings* (Oxford: Oxford University Press, 1968).

65. All other socialist countries have a direct personal income tax for employees in the socialized sector. However, this income tax is not very progressive and represents a small part of the total earnings according to J. Adams's calculations (*Wage Control and Inflation in the Soviet Bloc Countries* [New York: Praeger, 1979], table 22, 38), and in the USSR the income tax in 1975 represented only 10.4% of the total wage fund. In Poland the tax rate for the highest wage bracket did not exceed 15% in 1968 (see *Dziennik Ustaw* [Decree Monitor], 1968, no 5, item 29, 30).

66. Some economists (e.g., Izabella Bolkowiak, "Podatki, Podatki" [Taxes, taxes], *Życie Gospodarcze*, 1982, no. 39) propose taxing all incomes exceeding, for example, the average wage, irrespective of sources. The tax rate would not be too steep in the lower brackets, and a 50% rate would be the limit for the highest income bracket.

67. J. Kornai, *Economies of Shortage* (Amsterdam: North Holland 1980), chap. 13.

68. Official Solidarity spokesmen have demanded establishing by law that the highest wage cannot be more than 3.5 times the average wage, and the minimum wage cannot be less than half of the average wage. Hence only a 7 : 1 spread of wages would be permitted—which is much less than before 1980 when, as we will see, the spread of extreme wages sometimes exceeded 30 : 1. It is interesting to note that the Party Congress in July of 1981 in principle accepted the maximum ceiling on wage dispersion proposed by Solidarity.

69. Although it would be an exaggeration to assume that governments in other socialist countries will be guided entirely in their incomes policy by their perception of the egalitarianism of the Polish workers, certain signals of sensitivity to this issue have become apparent. For example, in Hungary it is no accident that there were in 1981–82 many statements by party officials in the newspapers and party organs that the trade unions should better defend worker interest and play a bigger role as partners of the party.

70. See D. Milenkovitch, *Plan and Market in Yugoslav Economic Thought* (New Haven: Yale University Press, 1971).

71. See S. Estrin, "Income Dispersion in a Self-managed Economy," *Economica*, vol. 48, May 1981, 181–94; D. Milenkovitch, "The Case of Yugoslavia," *American Economic Review: Papers and Proceedings*, vol. 67, no. 2, February 1977, 60–67.

72. See. H. Flakierski, "Polish Economic Reforms," *The Soviet Union and Eastern Europe in the 1980's: Multidisciplinary Perspectives*, S. McInnes, W. McGrath, P. J. Potichnyj eds. (Oakville, Ontario: Mosaic Press, 1978).

73. According to *1981 World Bank Atlas*, 18, per capita income in 1980 in Poland was $3,900 and in Hungary it was $4,180; see also J. B. Kravis, A. Heston, and R. Summers, *World Product and Income: International Comparison of Real Product*, Phase III (Baltimore: John Hopkins University Press), 276; comparisons of per capita national incomes for the CMEA countries have been done by I. Beliaev, *sblizenie ekonomicheskogo razvitiia sotsialisticheskhikh stran* [declining differences in economic development in the socialist countries] (Moscow, 1975).

74. In Poland and Hungary in 1977, the ratio of urban to rural population was respectively 57 : 43 and 52 : 48. Although a larger proportion of the population lives in villages in Hungary than in Poland, the relative amount of the labor force employed in agriculture is smaller in Hungary than in Poland. This reflects both better natural endowment and more modern agriculture in Hungary than in Poland. See *Kraje RWPG 1960–1975* [CMEA countries 1960–1975] (Warsaw: Gus, 1976), table 1 (184), 147, and table 7 (32), 29; *Polska 1918–1978* [Poland 1918–1978] (Warsaw: Gus 1978); *Statistical Yearbook of Hungary, 1980* (Budapest: KSH, 1981), 55.

75. The importance of these and other factors as requirements for international comparisons are well explained by S. Kuznets in "Quantitative Aspects of the Economic Growth of Nations: the Distribution of Income by Size," *Economic Development and Cultural Change*, vol. 11, part 2 (Cambridge,

Mass.: Harvard University Press, 1971).

76. See more in detail, S. Widerszpil, "Przestarzalość i aktualność problematyki klasy robotniczej" [The obsolescence and topicality of the working-class problematic], *Studia nauk politycznych*, vol. 1 (Warsaw, 1968).

77. Household income per capita as a recipient unit obviously has some shortcomings in the sense that it fails to take into consideration differences in consumption by persons of different ages and any economies of scale of the household. A better unit for the measurement of inequality, especially when groups of different demographic composition are compared, would be income per consumption unit. But Hungarian statistics do not provide systematic data over time for income distribution per standardized consumer unit.

78. Mixed households of workers and peasants are classified in the official Polish statistics as households with a double source of income, namely, incomes from work in the socialized and nonsocialized sector and incomes from farming privately owned farms.

79. The national product concept in the socialist countries is based on an accepted interpretation of the Marxian (or classical) tradition of distinguishing between "productive" and "nonproductive" activities. Only the former are considered as generating a real product. "Productive" activities take place in the sphere of material production (i.e., industry, construction, agriculture, transport, communications, and trade). Contrary to Western practice, in socialist countries economic activities in the "nonproductive" sphere (i.e., public administration and justice, education, science, culture, health, sport, finance and insurance, defense, and political, social, and religious activities) are not regarded as contributing to the national product. They are considered "nonproductive" services, and their "value" (or cost) is not included in the national product. However, it is necessary to take into account the value of material goods used in the course of providing these "nonproductive" services. Consequently it is the practice of most socialist countries to include the value of these material goods in one of two subcategories of the national product according to their durability:

1) Collective consumption includes, for example, the value of such items as food for hospitals, facilities for running administrative offices (i.e., furniture, ink, paper, gas), facilities for schools, food and clothing for the army, etc.

2) Nonproductive investment includes residential as well as public buildings, schools, hospitals, theaters, military installations, administrative buildings, etc.

80. For more detail about this method, see J. M. Michal, "An Alternative Approach Measuring Income Inequality in Eastern Europe," Z. Fallenbuchl, *Economic Development*; "Size Distribution of Earnings and Household Incomes in Small Socialist Countries," *Review of Income and Wealth*, December 1973.

81. This is recommended by E. Vielrose, *Rozklad dochodów wedlug wielkości* (Warsaw: PWE, 1960).

82. The quotient is one of the major indicators of inequality used in Hungary. The quotient is the ratio of the average wages above the arithmetical mean to

the average wages below the mean. In a less precise manner we can calculate the quotient just by dividing the top five decile groups by the bottom five decile groups. This method of measuring inequality has been worked out and explained in detail by O. Elteto and E. Frigyes, "New Income Inequality Measures as Efficient Tools for Causal Analysis and Planning," *Econometrica*, vol. 36, no. 2, 1968.

83. For a discussion of the weak and strong points of different measures of inequality, see A. B. Atkinson, "On the Measurement of Inequality," *Wealth, Income and Inequality*, A. B. Atkinson ed. (Penguin Education, 1973); M. H. Allingham, "The Measurement of Inequality," *Journal of Economic Theory*, vol. 5, 1972; J. M. Michal, "Size Distribution of Household Incomes and Earnings in Developed Socialist Countries: with a Proposed Marginal-Utility-Weighted Gini Coefficient," paper presented at the International Economic Association Conference, Noordwijk-aan-Zee, Netherlands, April 1977.

CHAPTER II

1. As can be seen from Table 1, there is actually a third subperiod of 1982–83, when relative dispersion of earnings started to rise again. However, we are not dealing in detail with this subperiod, because we have very incomplete data. The frequency distribution for 1982 was available only for the socialized sector in total. We have no data for this year for other tables dealing with distribution of earnings.

2. The overall distribution expressed by the Lorenz Curve for the total state sector and industry illustrates the findings in Table 1. The Lorenz Curve of the distribution of earnings in industry and the state sector as a whole in 1966 lies wholly within the Lorenz Curve of the distribution in 1974.

3. Data about distribution by sex are not included in Table 1 due to space limitations. Data on men's and women's distribution are in Appendix Table A.

4. According to all available data, relative earnings of women in the socialist countries are not dramatically different from Western societies. However, in most socialist countries the ratio of female to male earnings is higher than in the United States or England but not very different from Sweden, France, Austria, West Germany, etc., where this ratio is approximately 0.65–0.70. A higher ratio of female to male earnings in the socialist countries than in many capitalist ones is a result of: (a) greater access to traditionally male occupations (engineers, doctors, lawyers, etc.); (b) extremely high participation by women in the labor force, especially in the prime working years; (c) greater continuity of employment. An interesting analysis of this problem is in L. E. Sutter and H. P. Miller, "Income Differences between Men and Career Women," John Huber ed., *Changing Woman in a Changing Society* (Chicago:

University of Chicago Press, 1973), 200-1; John R. Moroney, "Do Women Earn Less under Capitalism?" *Economic Journal*, vol. 89, no. 3, September 1979, 601-13; J. G. Chapman, "Equal Pay for Equal Work," D. Atkinson, A. Dallin, and G. W. Lapidus eds., *Women in Russia* (Stanford: Stanford University Press, 1977).

5. Z. Ferge calculated that only 70% of the lower wages paid to women can be attributed to inferior schooling and access to top positions; the remaining 30% should be attributed to discrimination and prejudice (see *A Society in the Making* [Penguin, 1979], 184-85).

6. In secondary education diplomas the differences between the sexes are not substantial, but still in 1973 about 25% more males got diplomas than females among 18-year-olds and over.

7. In 1973 women represented only 12.1% of all lawyers, 13.1% of all engineers, and 38% of all economists.

8. F. Levcik, "Comments on Distribution of Incomes in Centrally Planned Economies," Z. Fallenbuchl, *Economic Development*.

9. J. Michal, "Size and Distribution of Earnings and Income in Czechoslovakia, Hungary and Yugoslavia," paper presented at the American Economic Association (Toronto, December 1972).

10. Although there are no data on how wages and salaries are dispersed among different segments of the nonmaterial production sphere, data have recently been published by the Central Statistical Office about measures of inequality expressed by the quotient of particular segments of the nonmaterial sectors of the socialized economy. They are:

|  | 1974 | 1976 | 1978 | 1980 |
|---|---|---|---|---|
| Personal and economic services | 1.94 | 1.94 | 1.88 | 1.81 |
| Health, culture, education, and social welfare services | 2.00 | 2.09 | 2.05 | 2.01 |
| Communal, state administration, and other services | 1.98 | 2.05 | 2.05 | 1.99 |
| Socialized sector total | 1.90 | 1.89 | 1.85 | 1.82 |

*Sources: F. K. A.* 1978 *(Budapest: KSH, 1980), 15; ibid.,* 1980 *(1981), 20.*

11. See K. Szikra Falus, "A berkülönbsegek nehany kerdese" [Some problems of wage differentation], *Tarsadalmi Szemle*, no. 3, 1980, 49, 51, 53.

12. See M. Yanowitch, *Social and Economic Inequality*, 31.

13. See J. Adam, *Wage and Taxation Policy in Czechoslovakia 1948-1970* (Berlin: Duncker and Humbolt, 1974), 88-91.

14. Ibid., 85-88.

15. The year 1980 is a very specific year from the point of view of our analyses. It is, so to speak, a watershed between two epochs: the end of the old Gierek regime and the ascendence of the Solidarity mass movement. In the last three to four months of 1980, important decisions were made that profoundly affected the relative dispersion of earnings and incomes. However, the full impact of the egalitarian demands of Solidarity in the fields of wages and incomes was evident only in 1981-82 and later. This is why in 1980 we observe

only a moderate decline in relative dispersion of earnings and incomes.

16. These findings are corroborated by L. Beskid, "Stopień rozpiętośći plac realnych netto w Polsce w okresie 1956-1972" [The dispersion of net real wages in Poland 1956-72], *Ekonomiczne i spoleczne problemy spozycia* [Economic and social problems of consumption] (Polish Academy of Sciences, 1976); L. Beskid and T. Czoloszyński, *Problemy nierównomierności rozkladu plac realnych netto w Polsce w okresie 1956-1970* [Problems of unequal distribution of net real wages in Poland 1956-70] (Warsaw: Polish Academy of Sciences, 1972).

The increases in relative dispersion for 1972-78 expressed by the decile ratio ($D_9/D_1$) also show a modest increase in relative dispersion of wages and salaries, which was reversed in the Solidarity period with a sharp decline in this ratio. The decile ratio for manual and nonmanual employees has changed as follows:

| Year | Manual | Nonmanual |
|------|--------|-----------|
| 1970 | 2.73 | 2.97 |
| 1972 | 2.68 | 2.95 |
| 1976 | 2.84 | 3.13 |
| 1978 | 2.87 | 3.14 |
| 1980 | 2.74 | 2.97 |
| 1982 | 2.17 | 2.47 |

*Source:* R. S. 1981 *(Warsaw: GUS), table 10 (188), 169; ibid.,* 1983, *table 10 (210), 146.*

17. Although in the construction sector relative dispersion has increased only in the middle of the distribution over time, this sector has always had the highest relative dispersion of all productive sectors. In 1973 the highest 2% ($P_{98}$) of earners received nearly 8 times more than the lowest 2% ($P_2$).

18. In 1953 average monthly wages in the construction sector (the highest-paid sector) were nearly double the lowest-paid sector (health). In 1960 the ratio of the highest-paid sector (science) to the lowest (forestry) was only 1 : 1.72. In consecutive years the rates of the highest- to the lowest-paid sector were:

| 1970 | Science/forestry = 1.68 |
| 1976 | Construction/health = 1.48 |
| 1978 | Science/health = 1.47 |
| 1979 | Construction/trade = 1.38 |
| 1980 | Construction/trade = 1.36 |

19. We will deal with this problem in more detail in the last part of this book.

20. It is worth stressing that the degree of concentration measured by the coefficient of decile differentiation is nearly the same for all sectors of the

socialized economy. See *R. S. 1981* (Warsaw, GUS), table 10 (188), 169. A good example of similarities in concentration of wages would be the coal-mining sector and the food industry. In spite of the fact that the average wages in 1980 were approximately 2.5 times higher in the coal-mining industry than in the food-processing industry, in both sectors 55% of all employees had differences in wages not larger than 1.8 times. The fact that 55% of the employees receive very similar wages is considered by some economists as a disincentive for better work (see W. Krencik, "Zróznicowanie plac" [Differentiation of wages], *Życie Gospodarcze*, no. 5, 1982.

21. L. Beskid, "Sprawiedliwy czy egalitarny" [Just or egalitarian], *Polityka*, no. 5, 1982.

22. Nearly 21% of all employees in the health sector received below 900 zl. per month; the figure for education is 18.4%. Such earnings comprise no more than 40% of the median in 1973.

23. One indirect approximate indicator of the discrepancy between earnings of ranking professionals and unskilled or semiskilled manual workers is the median earnings of employees with university education and primary education. In 1973 the median for employees in the socialized sector with university education was on the average about 6% higher than for those with primary education. (The medians were calculated on the basis of data in *Tendencje rozwoju społecznego* [Tendencies of social development] [Warsaw: GUS, 1979].

24. See W. D. Connor, *Socialism, Politics and Equality* (New York: Columbia University Press, 1979).

25. See L. M. Słomczynski and K. Szafnicki, "Zróznicowanie dochodów z pracy" [Dispersion of work-related incomes], W. Wesolowski ed., *Zróznicowanie spoleczne* [Social stratification] (Warsaw: Polish Academy of Sciences, 1970).

26. See T. Przyciszewski, "Wydatki i preferencje mieszkaniowe ludnośći na tle polityki gospodarczej panstwa" [Expenditures and housing preferences of the population in conjunction with the economic policy of the State], *Publikacje Instytutu Budownictwa Mieszkaniowego—IBM* [Publications of the Institute of housing construction], no. 40 (Warsaw, 1963), 119; W. Czerzerda, "Warunki i życzenia mieszkaniowe róznych grup ludnosci" [Conditions and housing demands of different groups of the population], *IBM*, no. 44 (Warsaw, 1964), 35.

27. This unfavorable picture is confirmed by some data from the Central Statistical Office (see *Tendencje rozwoju*, table 8, 268). According to this source, over 70% of all households where the heads of the households are engineers have all modern facilities, whereas for unskilled manual workers' households the figure is only 26.3%.

28. Intersystem comparisons of discrepancies in manual and nonmanual earnings are difficult to make precisely because of differences in the definitions of manual and nonmanual employees. However, the differences in earnings of these groups in the two systems are too substantial to be a result of different statistical classifications alone. The decline in discrepancy of earnings between

manual and nonmanual employees is a tendency observed as well in the Western world after World War II. The relative decline in earnings of professional and clerical workers is well illustrated in the Western literature. See A. B. Atkinson, *The Economics of Inequality* (Oxford: Clarendon Press, 1975), table 5.1, 76. However, this process has gone much farther in the socialist countries than in the capitalist ones, and the relative position of nonmanual employees is still much higher in the Western countries than in the socialist ones. Nowhere in the Western countries has the ratio of nonmanual to manual earnings reached such a low level. This ratio is usually around 2 : 1 in most Western countries. See A. B. Atkinson, *The Economics of Inequality*, and R. J. Nicholson, "The Distribution of Personal Income," *Wealth, Income and Inequality*, A. B. Atkinson ed. (Penguin, 1973). As far as the prewar period in Poland and Hungary is concerned, the ratio of nonmanual to manual earnings was much higher than after the war. M. Kalecki's estimates indicate a ratio of 2.2 : 1 for the prewar year of 1937 for Poland (see "Porównanie dochodu robotników i pracowników umyslowych z okresem przedwojennym" [Comparisons of blue- and white-collar workers' incomes with the prewar period], *Kultura i społeczeństwo*, no. 1, 1964, table 2, 35–40. In prewar Hungary we observe a tendency like that in Poland. (See Z. Ferge, *A Society in the Making*, table 5/4, 172.)

29. See F. Parkin, *Class Inequality and Political Order* (New York: Praeger, 1971), 147; David Lane, *The Socialist Industrial State; Towards a Political Sociology of State Socialism* (London: Allen and Unwin, 1976), 176–90.

30. H. Najduchowska's study is in J. Szczepański ed., *Przemysl i społeczeństwo w Polsce Ludowej* [Industry and society in socialist Poland] (Warsaw, 1970), 96–97.

31. This point of view is shared by P. Machonin, "Social Stratification in Contemporary Czechoslovakia," *American Journal of Sociology,* vol. 75, 1970, 725–41.

32. In the Marxian tradition the problem of overcoming socioeconomic differences between manual and nonmanual workers is part of the broader issue of overcoming the social division of labor between physical and mental work as a precondition to overcoming separate professional interests and fulfilling the dream of making work interesting and creative, a dream of disalienated labor. But Marx was aware this will take place only in the higher stage of communism, in an advanced communist society. See K. Marx, *Economic and Philosophical Manuscripts*, translated by T. B. Bottomore, Erich Fromm, *Marx' Concept of Man* (New York: Ungar, 1971).

33. This is one of the lowest ratios in this respect in Europe. However, it must be stressed that in 1978, only 3% of the labor force in the socialized sector received a minimum wage, whereas this percentage is much higher in the Western countries.

34. In all known distribution patterns of earnings (incomes) in the East and West, the median is smaller than the mean (see tables 6 and 7); the distribution is skewed to the right. Hence more than half of the labor force received earnings below the average level.

35. See the panel discussion in the weekly *Polityka*, "Ofiarność i zachlanność" [Sacrifice and greed], no. 25, 1979.

36. Ibid., see A. Tymowski's part in the panel.

37. The importance of favoritism of a special kind has increased in the last years in Poland due to severe shortages and market disorganization. A special network for exchanging favors to get goods and services has become widespread. Money very often is irrelevant; what matters is whether you can provide goods and services in exchange for other goods and services. This is a special kind of barter that undermines normal exchanges and demoralizes the public.

38. The difference between the price of a car on the free market and the official government price is often equal to two average annual wages.

39. For more details see A. Tymowski, "Ofiarność i zachlanność"; "Reguly krojenia chleba" [Principles for dividing the loaf], *Polityka*, no. 43, 1979.

40. See E. Skalski, "Naturalia i beneficja" [Privileges in kind and benefits], *Polityka*, no. 51–52, 1979; K. Daszkiewicz, "Co sie komu należy" [What some people are entitled to get], *Nowe drogi*, no. 10, 1979.

41. See L. Zienkowski, "Nasze dochody i co o nich myślimy" [Our incomes and what do we think about them], *Polityka*, no. 51–52, 1979.

42. I was informed during a visit to Budapest by some Ministry of Finance officials that the main sources of moonlighting in Hungary are:

1. *In agriculture*: Fifty percent of all workers have small plots as an additional source of income. According to estimates made by the Ministry of Finance, incomes from all small plots, including those of the peasantry, represent about 10% of national income, and the value of their produce represents about 16% of personal consumption.

2. *Building industry*: A substantial number of flats in Hungary are being built by families themselves. Very often two or three families build a house together. Considering that most the work is done by the members of the families themselves, the value of the house is higher than the total cost of materials. The difference is obviously extra income, which is captured by the statistics of the national income but is not captured by the distributional statistics for earnings of persons and strata. Income from moonlighting in the building industry represents, according to estimates, 2.5% of national income.

3. *Services*: Repairs of radios, televisions, and cars, tips in restaurants and hotels, extra fees charged by doctors and nurses for special services, etc.

Although in Hungary some moonlighting is institutionalized by granting special permission to perform extra work, which allows the authorities to have some control over this process, the majority of such income is not recorded, hence it does not enter the picture of actual earnings of particular income groups.

43. It is paradoxical that some high-ranking officials in Hungary find moonlighting very beneficial for the work ethic, for good craftsmanship. Moonlighting for them is a sort of school for good work, the experience and knowledge from which will spill over into workers' behavior in normal work at socialist enterprises. This is obviously a very bizarre strategy to improve work discipline and diligence. It is well known that slack work on the job in

"normal time" is a way of saving energy for the "real" job—moonlighting. Some workers, as one economist has shrewdly observed, steal not only goods from enterprises but something more valuable—time.

44. For Hungary compare the changes in average wages over time for different sectors in Appendix table B and the medians in table 1.

45. See table 6 and table 9 for Poland; for Hungary, table 4 and *A lakosság Jövedelme és fogyasztása 1960–75* [Incomes of the population and their consumption in 1960–75] (Budapest: KSH, 1976), 12.


CHAPTER III


1. In all Eastern European countries budget analysis refers to household and not to families. A multihousehold is defined as a group of two or more living in the same dwelling (or room) and combining part or all their earnings and other income in order to meet the needs of the household. A single household refers to any person who maintains himself alone. Although most households are family households, composed of wife, husband, and their children, there are households composed of family *sensu stricto* plus members of the so-called extended family (cousins, grandparents, etc., or people not related to the family at all). There are also households where the people do not comprise a family or an extended family but just a group of people living together under the same roof and joining their incomes to maintain themselves.

2. See *Social stratification in Hungary* (Budapest: 1967); Hungarian Statistical Office, *A lakosság 1968–1969* (Budapest: KSH, 1970).

3. The average size of household for different occupations in 1972 varies as follows: total nonmanual 3.20; total manual outside agriculture 3.55; skilled workers 3.53; unskilled workers 3.55; semiskilled workers 3.59; managers, senior administrators, professionals 3.28; the average of all types together 3.46 (see *A. C. 1972* (Budapest: KSH, 1975). It is interesting that 45% all households in 1962 were mixed; earners belonged to more than one occupational group. However, only 12% of all households have simultaneously both manual and nonmanual earners. See *Social Stratification in Hungary*, 118. These proportions have probably not changed very much since 1962, so that they still influence income distribution.

4. There are other differentiating factors, e.g., sex, age, type of settlement, school degree, etc., but they are not dealt with here.

5. See *A keresetek szorodása és szerepe, a munkás—alkalmazotti háztartások jövedelmében* [The share of earnings in the household income of employees] (Budapest: KSH, 1971).

6. See O. Eltetö and By. Láng, "Income Level and Income Stratification in Hungary," *Acta Oeconomica*, vol. 7, no. 3–4, 1971.

7. However, if the ratio of the highest 5% to the lowest 5% is taken, the difference was 7 to 1 in 1967 and 10 to 1 in 1962.

8. A more rapid increase in social benefits than earnings will positively influence the relative dispersion of household per capita income only if we assume that social benefits will not negatively affect one of the covariances at the righthand side of the equation (see the equation on p. 82). If, for example, the covariance of (Y/W) with (K/N) increased the relative dispersion of activity rates by the same magnitude as the variance (Y/W) influenced the decline in variance (Y/N), the relative dispersion of household per capita income would be unchanged. Unfortunately, we do not know in quantitative terms how these covariances influence each other. We can only say on the basis of logic that a more equal distribution of social benefits will affect the relative dispersion of activity rates, on balance, rather positively—the relative dispersion of activity rates (K/N) will be reduced. More kindergartens, child-care allowances, schooling, etc., for the less affluent families as a result of a more equitable distribution of social benefits will likely increase the activity rates of the less affluent more than the more affluent. The possibilities for increasing activity rates are much larger in less affluent families, which are usually large and have lower activity rates than more affluent families. As we will see, affluent households, in most cases smaller in size, have already achieved very high activity rates, and no major reserves exist for increasing them.

9. See *A lakosság 1960–1979* (Budapest, KSH, 1981).

10. *A lakosság 1968–1969.*

11. The peasants and double-income groups have gained the most, as have top managerial strata. The "double-income group," according to Hungarian statistics, is one in which the head of the household is a manual worker and there are other manual workers in the household employed both in agriculture and in other sectors.

12. However, if we compare the disparities between per capita household income of the top managerial strata belonging to the top decile with those per capita household incomes of unskilled workers belonging to the lowest decile, then the difference is nearly 10 : 1.

13. For the United States see *U.S. Bureau of the Census. Current Population Report, Consumer Income* (Series P-60, No. 117, December 1978, 22; for the U.K., R. J. Nicholson, "The Distribution of Personal Income," 99–110; for Canada, I. Adams, W. Cameron, B. Hill, and P. Penz, *The Real Poverty Report* (Edmonton: Hartig, 1971).

14. See F. Paukert, "Income Distribution at Different Levels of Development: A Survey of Evidence," *International Labour Review* (vol. 108, no. 2–3, August-September 1973); S. Kuznetz, "Economic Growth and Income Inequality," *American Economic Review* (vol. 45, 1955), 1–28.

15. See A. Schmidt, "A személyi jövedelemlosztás a szocializmusban" [Distribution of personal incomes under socialism], *Közgazdasági és jogi* (Budapest: Kiado, 1964), 88.

16. Although by 1965 members of cooperatives were eligible to receive family allowances, benefits were smaller than for families in the socialized sector.

17. Family allowances represent the second largest item (after pensions) in

total expenditures on social benefits in cash. They constituted around 15% of all social benefits in cash in 1980 (*A lakosság 1960–1975* 18; *S. E. 1980* [1981], 359).

18. According to the publication of the official statistical office, *A. C. 1977* (1980), 190, income per consumption unit is obtained by converting all members of the household into equivalent adult units. (For example, a child up to 3 years of age is 0.4 and between 4 and 6 years of age 0.5 of an adult unit; a pensioner is 0.8 of an adult; a child above age 13 is 1.0 adult unit, etc.) These equivalents of adult units are in turn combined with an economies-of-scale parameter. An 0.4 unit is added in Hungary to the sum of the equivalent units of the households. A one-person household would be $1.0 + 0.4 = 1.4$ consumer units. A household of two adults and a child of two would accordingly be 2.8 consumer units $(1.0 + 1.0 + 0.4) + 0.4 = 2.8$. Although equivalent adult units and parameters of economies of scale are based on budget study samples, they are to some degree arbitrary and not very flexible over time.

19. See Z. Ferge, *A Society in the Making*, 219–20.

20. See *Kutatási koncepcio, az életszinvonal-politika tudományos megalapozásához 1977–1985* [A research concept for establishing an objective policy for standard of living in 1977–85] (Budapest: KSH, 1977), 8.

21. See Z. Ferge, "Main trends in Hungarian social policy," *New Hungarian Quarterly*, vol. 22, no. 86, summer 1982, table 1, 137–49; G. Abonyi, *A társadalombiztositási törvény és gyakorlata* [The Social Security Act and its practice] (Budapest: Kiado, 1979).

22. See Abonyi, ibid.

23. Hungarian law already permits fathers to receive a grant for staying home if the mother is ill.

24. In 1958 pension rights were granted to members of cooperatives, but their retirement age was made five years higher. The new Social Security Act of 1975 equalized retirement ages in the socialized and cooperative sectors, reducing the retirement age of members of cooperatives by one year between 1975 and 1980.

25. The lengthening of the employment period required to be eligible for a full pension is rather out of step with efforts by the authorities to reduce poverty among pensioners because it increases, *ceteris paribus*, the number of pensioners with low old-age pensions.

26. In Hungary as in the Soviet Union and East Germany, pensioners are encouraged to continue to work. In Hungary, for example, manual workers receive an additional 7% of the original pension for each year of work, whereas nonmanual employees get only 3%. The preferential treatment of pensioners working in manual occupations reflects more intense shortages for manual than nonmanual labor, and probably a proworker ideological bias as well.

27. See *Statistical Yearbook 1970* (Budapest: Central Statistical Office, 1971), table 17; *A lakosság 1960–1975*, 10–11; *S.E 1980* (Budapest: KSH, 1981), table 2A, 387, and table 18A, 140.

28. What is more, between 1962 and 1972 we observe a relative deterioration of the old pensioners' position in this respect. The following figures

illustrate this: in 1962 about 85% of pensioner households and 72% of active households received monthly per capita income below 1,000 forints, whereas in 1972 those figures were respectively 36 and 14%. In 1972 active households reduced their weight in the low per capita income brackets to one-fifth, and the pensioners to only a half of the previous weight. See *Jövedelemelosztás Magyarországon* [Distribution of earnings in Hungary] (Budapest: KSH, 1967), and *A.C 1972* (1975), 55.

29. *A.C 1977* (1980), 69.

30. Only in 1972 were some adjustments made in pensions. But a 2% per annum increase in pensions would not reduce the differences between the old and new pensions. The fact that not everyone at retirement age received full pensions and that pensions were not fully indexed made the relative distribution of pensions more unequal than earnings.

31. Z. Ferge, *A Society* 235-36.

32. See *Demográfiai Évkönyv 1974* (Budapest: KSH, 1975), 202, 279.

33. See *A lakossági jövedelmek szinvonala és szóródása 1967* [The level of incomes of the population and their dispersion in 1967] (Budapest: KSH, 1972), table VIII, 3a, 229. No later data about housing subsidies were published. The subsequent issues of household statistics included rent subsidies under the heading "Other social benefits in kind."

34. For example, in 1969 nonmanual employees received over six times more higher education than workers. See Elteto and Lang, "Income Level"; in 1977 the top 10% of households received four times more university education, six times more rent and food subsidies, and three and a half times more cultural facilities than the lowest 10%. As far as the elite is concerned (enigmatically called "Leaders, Intellectuals"), in 1977 their children received eight times more university education than the children of unskilled workers (see *A.C 1977* [1980], 162).

35. See more detail in Z. Ferge, *A Society*, 263-73.

36. Only 2.6% of the childless households and 6.7% of households with one child have a per capita income below 1,000 forints a month.

37. Although there is no official established poverty line in Hungary, it is enough to say that according to the Hungarian Central Office, in 1972 to maintain one child at a normal level required 1,230 forints per month. At the same time, the monthly family allowance for two children was no more than 300 forints.

38. It is true that not only are people in the socialist countries interested in their relative position, but absolute differences in income are also carefully observed by average people. This attitude to differentials was confirmed during a visit to Budapest. Any relative increase in dispersion of incomes sharply accelerates absolute differences and makes them more visible, especially when incomes of all groups are growing. Why are people and policy-makers sensitive to absolute differences? We have no clear answer. Professor P. Wiles has suggested to me that this could be linked to the stage of development, which affects the marginal utility of money in a different way in the wealthy and nonwealthy countries. In a country like Hungary, the marginal utility of money

has not diminished very much.

39. This is confirmed by statistical data. See *S.E 1978* (Budapest: KSH, 1979), table 30, 380; ibid., *1980* (1981), table 2A, 28. These data indicate that the overall activity ratio in the period 1960–80 increased mainly due to the increase in the female activity ratio. At the same time, the average size of the households declined from 3.1 in 1960 to 2.8 in 1980. This was mainly the result of a sharp increase (percentagewise) in the number of households without children and a dramatic decline in the proportion of households with more than three children. In 1960 households with three or more children represented 12.9% of all households; in 1980, only 6.4%.

40. During a visit to Budapest in 1978, I had the opportunity to discuss this problem with my Hungarian colleagues in the Central Statistic Office. They strongly support the point of view that the activity ratio has increased in large households faster than in smaller ones. Data for Poland for 1963–69 also show that the activity ratio of large households increased faster than that of smaller households. See T. Komorniczek, *Dynamika i rozpietość dochodów realnych* [The dynamics and dispersion of real incomes] (Warsaw: PWN, 1971).

41. See Note 8.

CHAPTER IV

1. See *Budżety rodzin pracowników zatrudnionych w gospodarce uspołecznionej poza rolnictwem i leśnictwem 1963–1965, Seria Statystyka Polski—Materialy Statystyczne* (Warsaw: GUS, 1967), part 14, (136); A. Krawczynska, "Czynniki demograficzne róznicujçe dochody gospodarstw domowych" [Demographic factors differentiating incomes of households], *Ekonomiczne i spoleczne problemy spożycia* [Economic and social aspects of consumption] (Warsaw: Ossolineum, Polish Academy of Sciences, 1976).

2. See Z. Sufin, "Badanie i planowanie warunków, życia" [Research and planning on material well-being], *Ekonomiczne i spoleczne.*

3. See O. Elteto and Gy. Lang, *Income Level*; L. Beskid, *Konsumpcja w rodzinach pracowniczych* [Consumption in households of employees] (Warsaw: PWE, 1977), chapter 2; T. Cioloszynski, "Place a dochody" [Wages and Incomes] (mimeo) (Warsaw: Polish Academy of Sciences, 1976).

4. In Hungary we observed a similar phenomenon. Although Hungarian peasants equalized their earnings with and even surpassed the nonagricultural sector, this achievement was partially a result of more intensive work, both on individual plots and in collective fields. The average annual number of working days for the cooperatives has markedly increased, whereas the workweek in industry and other nonagricultural sectors was reduced in the 1970s. See more detail in Zh. Orolin, *Economic Studies in Hungary's Agriculture*, I. Bennet and J. Gyenis eds. (Budapest: Kiado, 1977).

5. According to J. S. Zegar, "Mity i fakty" [Myths and facts], *Życie*

*Gospodarcze*, no. 29, 1982, the peasants' per capita income in comparison with employees' per capita income was:

|      |              |
|------|--------------|
| 1979 | 92.4%        |
| 1980 | 90.2         |
| 1981 | 102.2        |
| 1982 | 91.9 estimate |

The sharp improvement in the relative position of the peasantry in 1981 is linked with: (a) an official increase in agricultural prices by nearly 70%, while at the same time the cost of production goods for agriculture increased by only 28%; (b) an increase in incomes by approximately 125% for goods sold on the free market. This source of income was a result not only of higher prices on the free market but also an increase in the share of food sold on the free market. In 1982 the official increase in agricultural prices paid by the state was smaller than in '81; together with enormous increases in the prices paid by peasants for agricultural investments and producer goods, these prices have pushed the relative position of the peasantry back to the level of 1979.

6. Another indicator of differences in standard of living between town and village is the degree of saturation of durable goods and sanitation facilities in the household. According to official statistical data, *Maly rocznik statystyczny 1982* (Warsaw: GUS, 1982), table 21(86), 88, in 1980 saturation with durable goods and facilities per 100 households of employees and peasants respectively was:

| Running water     | 87 (36)  |
|-------------------|----------|
| W.C               | 73 (21)  |
| Bath taps         | 70 (26)  |
| Central heating   | 57 (17)  |
| T.V.              | 104 (82) |
| Cars              | 20 (12)  |
| Refrigerators     | 34 (59)  |
| Washing machines  | 103 (92) |

7. In real terms the value of social benefits in 1981–82 declined. This manifested itself in an acute shortage of medication, drugs, and hospital equipment, a sharp decline in the number of children sent to summer camps and vacation, and a decline in enrollments in colleges and universities. See more detail in M. Pohorille, "Inflacja a sprawiedliwość społeczna" [Inflation and social justice], *Polityka*, no. 25, 1982.

8. The Economic Institute of the Planning Commission and the Institute of Work and Social Welfare have worked for many years to define a basic minimum consumption standard for a working urban household and households of pensioners. According to their calculations, in 1975 the minimum consumption standard per person in a household of six members was 1,400 zl, and about 2,000 zl per month in 1980, which was approximately 40% of the average wage in the socialized sector.

9. See L. Ostrowski, "Dochody rolników" [Incomes of the peasantry], *Życie Gospodarcze*, no. 14, 1982.

10. See A. Basta, "Podzwonne dla demograficznych strachów" [The death knell of demographic fears], *Perspektywy*, no. 5, 1980.

11. A note of qualification is appropriate here about the reasons for infant mortality. The level of per capita household income is, in our opinion, the most important factor that influences infant mortality because it affects all aspects of life, including proper diet and nutrition and household hygiene, all of which have a strong impact on infant mortality. However, there are factors affecting infant mortality that to a large degree are independent of the level of per capita income, namely, the availability of doctors and hospitals and their quality in different areas. Rural areas are still underprivileged vis-á-vis urban areas in this respect. Thus on both accounts—levels of per capita income and saturation with doctors, hospitals, and sanitation facilities—we would expect a higher infant mortality rate in rural than in urban areas. Statistical data confirm that rural areas have a higher infant mortality rate than towns; however, the differences are not dramatic and have a tendency to decline. In 1970 the infant mortality rate in Poland was 31.6 for urban areas and 34.8 for rural areas (per thousand infants born). In 1978 these figures were respectively 22.2 and 22.9 per thousand. See *R.S 1979*, table 20(67, 41; *Tendencje rozwoju*, table 100, 137.

12. See *Tendencje rozwoju*, table 44, 92.

13. For more detail, see an interview with the Solidarity representatives: Helena Góralska and Irena Wojcicka, "Dodatek drożyzniany" [Cost of living allowances], *Solidarność*, no. 13, 1981.

14. Over 2.2 million out of a total of nearly 5 million pensioners (elderly and disabled people) were eligible for pension increases—over 15% of the Polish population. This proportion will have a tendency to grow because the retirement age has been reduced in general, and the early retirement of over half a million people from idle factories was encouraged in order to ease the hidden unemployment that has emerged with vast underutilization of capacity.

15. In 1978 the minimum old-age pension was only 1,300 zl per month, whereas the minimum wage was 1,600 zl per month.

16. See Irena Dryl, "Stary czlowiek i kryzys" [The elderly and the crisis], *Życie Gospodarcze*, no. 20, 1982.

17. It was agreed that all pensions granted before August 1, 1981, should be considered pensions of the old portfolio and subject to change. All pensions granted before 1981 would be recalculated in accordance with the wage an individual would earn if she or he retired in 1981. One of the unresolved problems in this controversy between Solidarity and the government was the privileged "political" pensions for the top echelons of the administrative and party structure. As a result of 1982 measures, by and large the old portfolio of pensions has disappeared in this year. However, due to a lack of means the state decided in 1982 that year-by-year indexation of pensions would start only in 1986. As a result a "new" old portfolio of pensions has emerged since 1982. In 1985 the government prepared a new proposal for liquidating the "new" old

portfolio of pensions before year-by-year indexation starts. Although the proposals are still being discussed and criticized (see H. Góralska and A. Wik-
torow, "Nie podważajmy celu ustawy" [We should not undermine the objective of the decree], *Życie Gospodarcze*, No. 8, 1985), it seems obvious that the
government's latest proposals are much less favorable for pensioners than the
proposed reform of 1981, which bore the strong inprint of Solidarity demands.

18. This conclusion is also apt for the welfare states of the Western world.
In England the last Labour government of Mr. Callaghan, despite its commitment to improve the welfare system, was prevented from doing so by declining
productivity and output, and many aspects of the welfare system were neglected.

19. In the highest per capita income bracket, 85% of women are in the
active labor force, whereas for the least affluent group, the figure is only 16%.

20. See Komorniczek, *Dynamika i rozpiętość*, table 18, 110.

21. Unfortunately we have no data on how activity ratios changed in the
Solidarity period and its aftermath. We can only infer that the reduction of the
retirement age and some drop in employment will probably reduce the overall
activity ratio.

22. See Komorniczek, *Dynamika i rozpiętość*, table 21, 122.

23. See T. Dmoch, "Wplyw spożecznych funduszów spożycia na rozklady
dochodów ludnośći" [The influence of social benefits on the dispersion of
incomes of the population], *Tendencje rozwoju*; M. Pohorille, *Spożycie zbiorowe i swiadczenia społeczne* [Public consumption and social benefits] (Warsaw: PWE, 1975), chap. 4.

24. See Komorniczek, *Dynamika i rozpiętość*, table 9, 74.

25. According to data from the Central Statistical Office (*Tendencje rozwoju*, 254–57), the ratio of the top to the lowest decile of per capita income due
to social benefits is reduced for employees' households from 6.4 to 5.0 times
and for peasant households from 10.0 to 7.2 times.

26. See Z. Zaluski, *Polski problem No. 1* [The No. 1 Polish problem]
(Warsaw, 1972), 230–31; J. Balcerek, "Rola społecznych funduszów spożycia" [The role of social consumption], *Polityka gospodarcza a polityka
społeczna* [Economic and social policy] (Warsaw, 1971), 111.

27. Pohorille (*Spożycie zbiorowe*, 155) is a proponent of this point of view
in Poland.

28. In his book *Minimum Socialne* [Social minimum] (Warsaw: PWE,
1973) A. Tymowski favors an egalitarian way of distributing social benefits.

29. See Appendix Table C; A. Racz, "Incomes of the Population and Their
Proportions in Hungary," *Acta Oeconomica*, vol. 119 (2), 1977, table 3, 206;
M. Rogowiec and B. Tylec, *Kierunki przemian konsumpcji w latach 1963–1973
w wybranych krajach RWPG* [Directions of changes in consumption in 1963–
73 in some CMEA countries] (Warsaw: Biblioteka Instytutu Handlu Wew-
nentcznego, 1977); H. Kocianowa, "Differentiation of Incomes and Consumption in Socialist Countries, with Czechoslovakia and the GDR as Examples,"
*Eastern European Economics* (translation from Russian), Fall 1979, vol. 18,
no. 1, 3–27.

CHAPTER V

1. See N. E. Rabkina and N. M. Rimashevskaia, "Distributive Relations and Social Development," *Problems of Economics*, vol. 22, no. 3, July 1979, 40–48; H. Kocianova, "Differentiation of Incomes." In the Western literature the best known source explaining differences in income disparities among countries or between different periods in the same country is S. Kuznets, *Economic Growth*, 1–28. According to his concept there is an inverse relationship between the stage of development and income disparities. The higher the stage of development of a country, the lower the disparities in income distribution. From Kuznets's principle it would be expected that as time goes by and a country becomes more developed, its income disparities would decline. This developmental principle does not hold very well for all socialist countries. The example of Poland and Hungary is a good case in point; we do not observe in those countries a decline in income disparities as time passes and they become economically more mature. On the other hand, such a correlation can be observed in Russia. A broader review of different concepts explaining income disparities among countries is in M. D. Ward, *The Political Economy of Distribution, Equality versus Inequality* (New York: Elsevier-North Holland, 1978), chaps. 3–5.
2. See Falus, "Wage Differentials."
3. See Falus, "Some Aspects."
4. In 1974 the inheritance tax was made more progressive in Hungary. Some new property taxes were introduced and the old ones tightened up. High taxes on second residences and privately owned luxury houses were levied. The purpose of this taxation was to discourage ostentatious wealth and compensate for tax evasion on incomes derived from property, especially from real estate speculation stemming mainly from housing shortages.
5. The relaxed pace of work in most socialist countries is considered by some Western economists a systemic feature: a guaranteed job in the existing factories and a small amount of effort for a small amount of goods at given prices. Hence people accept low wages and shoddy goods for stability of jobs and prices. See D. Granick, *Enterprise Guidance in Eastern Europe: A Comparison of Four Socialist Economies* (Princeton: Princeton University Press, 1975). The famous Polish economist O. Lange used to tell his friends and associates that existing socialism is a paradoxical system. On the one hand socialism is the most liberal regime that has ever existed as far as tolerance of a relaxed pace of work is concerned; on the other hand, in the political sphere socialism is highly demanding and intolerant.
6. For more detail see R. Uvalić "Functions of the Market and Plan in the Socialist Economy," R. Stojanovic ed., *Yugoslav Economists on Problems of Socialist Economy* (White Plains, N.Y.: International Arts and Sciences Press, 1964); B. Vusković, "Social Inequality in Yugoslavia," *New Left Review*, no. 95, January-February 1976, 26–45.
7. See more detail in S. R. Sacks, "Entry of New Competitors in Yugoslav

Market Socialism,'' Research Series of the Institute of International Studies, University of California, Berkeley, no. 19, 1973; S. Estrin, ''Industrial Structure in a Market Socialist Economy,'' University of Southampton Discussion Paper (mimeo, no. 7717, 1978).

8. Kornai, *Economics*.

9. The economic reforms implemented in Hungary in 1968 made the budget constraint, according to Kornai, less soft, shortages diminished, and the state was less paternalistic than before. But despite progress in this field, the Hungarian economy still works predominantly under a soft budget constraint.

10. J. Kornai, ''The Dilemmas of a Socialist Economy: The Hungarian Experience,'' *Cambridge Journal of Economics*, no. 4, 1980, 150.

11. W. Brus and T. Kowalik, ''Socialism and Development: Joan Robinson and Beyond,'' a paper written during W. Brus's and T. Kowalik's fellowships (Columbia University, New York, and the Wilson Center, Washington, D.C., respectively) as a part of a joint project, published under a slightly changed title (''Socialism and Development''), *Cambridge Journal of Economics*, no. 3–4, 1983, 243–55.

12. In our discussion and analysis of the Solidarity program we used mainly the following documents: (a) The Gdansk Accords in August 31, 1980. Accord on the 21 points of the Gdansk agreement. An English version of the Gdansk Accords is in Appendix 2 of Neal Ascheson, *The Polish August* (Penguin Books, 1981). (b) The official program of the Independent Self Governing Trade Union Solidarity, adopted by the First National Congress of Delegations, Gdansk, October 7, 1981 (first translated by the U.S. Foreign Broadcast Information Service, November 4, 1981). Published in Polish in *Solidarność*, No. 29, 1981. (c) Program (Sięc) of Poland's Network of Leading Factories. (d) Documents from the Solidarity Center for Social and Welfare Research published in *Solidarność* no. 13 and 35, 1981. (e) DIP (Doswiadczenie i przyszłość) [Experience and the Future], ''Jak z tego wyjść'' (What are the solutions) (Warsaw, May 3, 1980); translated in *Poland Today* (Armonk, N.Y.: M. E. Sharpe, 1981).

13. In a nutshell, the Solidarity movement has put forward the following postulates and demands:

1) An increase in the basic monthly wage of each employee by 2,000 zl as compensation for price measures. This lump-sum increase, labeled Wałęsa's bonus (Wałęsówki), by its very nature, if implemented, would immediately reduce relative disparities.

2) The establishment in cooperation with Solidarity of a social minimum indicator and on this basis working out rules to compensate for cost-of-living increases.

3) A ceiling on the highest wages; the highest wages should not be more than 7 times the minimum wage and 3.5 times the average wage. Solidarity has also proposed a progressive income tax if per capita household income exceeds the average national wage.

4) For the same job, function, and skills, payment should be equalized throughout the country, sectors, and branches. A minimum national wage

should be implemented which should be half the average wage, but not smaller than the social minimum.

5) Piecework payments should be abolished wherever possible.

6) There should be a substantial increase in welfare funds, especially family allowances, pensions, and annuities, etc. These funds must be protected from inflationary erosion by indexing. Under the pressure from Solidarity the government agreed to increase all family allowances, but the increases had to be preferential for families with lower income per capita. Solidarity representatives demanded that family allowances also be differentiated according to the age of the child. The union adhered to a general policy that compensation for price increases must protect the real earnings of the least prosperous workers and their families. Compensation must be equal in magnitude for all employees. In 1982 Solidarity called for the implementation of a social minimum as a guideline for an income policy. The union believed that an increase in social benefits is the best tool to protect the poor and overcome poverty.

7) Annual pensions should increase systematically and should be linked to changes in the lowest wages. The government should raise pensions to the level of the social minimum and gradually equalize the old portfolio of pensions with the new one. In establishing the level of pensions, increases in the cost of living should be taken into consideration.

8) The state should grant maternity leave for three years. For the first year after birth pay should be 100% of normal earnings. In the second year it should be 50% of earnings, but not less than 2,000 zl per month. The demand for a three-year maternity leave should be met gradually in the first half of 1981.

9) The state should upgrade health services by providing more material funds and by improving doctors' and nurses' pay relative to other categories of employees in the socialized sector.

10) The state should eliminate most special privileges, and those which remain must be announced to the public.

11) Any layoffs of workers in any form, even if warranted by the efficiency of the enterprise, would be opposed.

14. Despite Maoist rhetoric, no one in China has ever asked to limit the highest wages to 3.5 times the average wage plus a tax on per capita household income whenever it exceeds the average national wage.

15. See more detail in Anna Tatarkiewicz, "Pytanie o cel" [A question about aims], *Literatura*, no. 6, 1981; Z. Suffin, "Egalitaryzm i sprawiedliwość społeczna" [Egalitarianism and social justice], *Polityka*, no. 7, 1981.

16. S. Nowak, "Values and Attitudes of the Polish People," *Scientific American*, vol. 245, no. 1, July 1981, 45-53. Another work by this author in the same field is "Social Attitudes of Warsaw Students," *Polish Sociological Bulletin*, no. 1-2, 1962, 91-104. Research in the field of public opinion polls done by other teams of sociologists corroborated Nowak's findings. See, for example, a survey done on the basis of a sample of 3,000 workers by L. Gilejko, *Klasa robotnicza w społeczeństwie socjalistycznym* [The Workers in Socialist Society], A. Wajda ed. (Warsaw, 1979), 210-29.

17. S. Nowak, "Values and Attitudes."

18. A public opinion poll conducted by the Polish Academy of Science (IFiS PAN) in 1980 and in the middle of 1981 indicates that a substantial part of society does not accept the existing relative dispersion of earnings and per capita household income. Those dispersions were considered excessive. Although there were differences of opinion among different social strata as to how far earnings should be equalized, there was a consensus that a ceiling should be put on high wages and that the lowest wages should grow faster than high ones. The majority of those questioned agreed that the dispersion of wages should be reduced, so to speak, on the margin, liquidating the very high and very low wages. People do realize that for 80–90% of all employees, wages are very little differentiated, and changes can therefore be made only at the margin.

19. See A. Pravda, "Poland 1980: From Premature Consumerism to Labor Solidarity," *Soviet Studies*, vol. 34, no. 2, April 1981, 167–99.

20. See more detail in T. Kowalik, "Planning and Freedom: a Polish Dilemma 1944–1981," colloquium paper of the Woodrow Wilson International Center for Scholars (Washington, D.C., October 26, 1981).

21. "Tactics and Strategy of the Network Action," *NTO* (monthly of NSZZ Solidarność, Mazowsze) (Warsaw, July 1981), 68–70; Network of Solidarity Organizations in Leading Factories, "Position on Economic Reforms of the Country," published in English in *Solidarność, Gdansk* (special, no. 29, September 5, 1981).

22. O. Lange, "Jak sobie wyobrazam"; W. Brus, *The Market*.

23. T. Kowalik, "The Economics of Solidarity," a working paper written at the Wilson International Center for Scholars (Washington, D.C., 1983).

24. The Solidarity Program assigns this task not to the central authority but to territorial bodies that will use a national fund created to shift resources to needy regions.

25. In a broader context this point is made by H. Brand, "Solidarity's Economic Program," *Dissent*, spring 1982, 162–66.

26. L. Kolakowski, "The Myth of Human Self-Identity," *The Socialist Idea*, L. Kolakowski and S. Hampshire eds. (London: Quartet, 1977).

27. In Poland the years 1979–82 are better characterized as ones of deep depression rather than stagnation. It is enough to say that national output in 1982 was smaller than in 1978 by 26%. Such a decline is almost unprecedented in any socialist or even capitalist country. The catastrophic decline can be compared only to the drop in output in the United States during the Great Depression. Although the decline in national output was arrested in 1983 and the economy started to grow at a respectable rate of 5–6%, the level of national output in 1984 was still smaller than in 1978 by approximately 14% and on a per capita basis by 19% (see *R.S. 1984*; *Komunikat GUS o wynikach 1984r, z lutego 1985, Publikowane dokumenty Centralnego Planu Rocznego na 1985* [Communiqué of the Central Statistical Office about 1984 economic results, February 1985, published documents of the Central Annual Plan for 1985]. The long-term prediction prepared by the Institute of Econometrics and Statistics at the University of Łódź forecasts for 1985 a national output growth rate of 4.2% and for the entire period of 1986–90 an average annual growth rate of about

3.8% (see W. Juszczak and W. Welfe, "Prognoza rozwoju gospodarczego Polski do roku 1990" [Prognosis for the economic development of Poland to 1990], "*Życie gospodarcze*, (no. 14, 1985). These figures would indicate that national output in 1990 would be only approximately 10% higher than in the precrisis year of 1978.

28. See Kowalik, *Socialism and Development*.

29. W. Brus, in the framework of his model of a planned economy with a built-in market mechanism, formulates the following minimum pre-conditions for decision making by the Center. (1) Macroeconomic decisions concerned with long-term development must be made by the Center. The government must decide: (a) the size of the accumulation and consumption fund, (b) the structure of a substantial part of the investment fund, and (c) the distribution of income among the main strata of society. (2) The rules of behavior or the objective function of the subsystems must be established from a national point of view (what to maximize or minimize). The state, while laying down the objective functions of the subsystems using macrocriteria, must prescribe at least in general terms the rules that link the economic result of the enterprises to the incomes of its employees. This is necessary to ensure that the wage fund is compatible with the supply of consumer goods and with the established social structure of incomes. (3) The government must maintain some control over the parameters of the objective functions and cost functions of the enterprises. The prices of manufactured goods and services and of the factors of production constitute the parameters of the objective function. For the sake of efficient guidance of the subsystems, prices must maintain their parametric quality. (For more detail, see W. Brus, "Commodity Fetishism and Socialism," *The Economics*.

30. Data about the increased inequality of incomes among strata and regions are in M. Ellman, *Planning Problems in the USSR* (Cambridge: Cambridge University Press, 1973), tables F.1 and F.2, 142–43; Volimir Rajković, "Appraisal of the Implementation of the Economic Reform and Current Problems," *Ekonomist Zagreb*, no. 6, 1969.